The Catholic Ethic and the Spirit of Community

JOHN E. TROPMAN

GEORGETOWN UNIVERSITY PRESS/WASHINGTON, D.C.

Georgetown University Press, Washington, D.C.
© 2002 by Georgetown University Press. All rights reserved.
Printed in the United States of America.

10 9 8 7 6 5 4 3 2 1   2002

This volume is printed on acid-free offset book paper.

Library of Congress Cataloging-in-Publication Data

Tropman, John E.
  The Catholic ethic and the spirit of community / John E. Tropman.
    p. cm.
  Includes bibliographical references and index.
  ISBN 0-87840-890-8 (pbk. : alk. paper)
    1. Christian ethics—Catholic authors. 2. Community—Religious aspects—
Catholic Church. I. Title.

  BJ1249 .T76 2002
  241'.042—dc21   2001040796

To my wife,
Penelope Savino Tropman,

for theoretical support of,
and practical demonstration of,
the Catholic ethic

WELFARE MATTERS . . . BUT FAMILY DOES TOO
Catholic Bishops Challenge Pieces of Welfare Bill; Fear a Rise
in Abortions

> Headline from Robert Pear, "Catholic Bishops Challenge
> Pieces of Welfare Bill," *New York Times,* March 19, 1995, A1.

COMMUNITY MEANS HELPING OTHERS
A Sociologist Dissects the Mean Streets of New York

Dr. Jackall's eye was trained mostly on the police, whose ethos of
self-sacrifice in service of the common good derives primarily from the
department's Irish-Catholic heritage. Almost all of the officers, he
found, shared the more ennobling aspects of this ethos.

> From a review of *Wild Cowboys: Urban*
> *Marauders and the Forces of Order* (Cambridge, Mass.:
> Harvard University Press, 1997) by Peter Monaghan,
> *Chronicle of Higher Education,* October 10, 1997, A17.

THE ENVIRONMENT COUNTS AS PART OF COMMUNITY
Catholics to Help Clean Up Clinton River

Talk about holy water. The Roman Catholic Archdiocese of Detroit
has decided that cleansing the Clinton River and its tributaries will be a
major public service project. . . . "It's in our faith tradition to be good
stewards of the earth," Dan Piepszowski, leader of the archdiocese's
service department said. . . .

> Emilia Askari, "Catholics to help clean up the Clinton River,"
> *Detroit Free Press,* March 11, 1998, 1A.

HELPING DISADVANTAGED PEOPLE ACHIEVE

Our original purpose was twofold. Where education was an unfulfilled need, we wanted to make it available. For poor youth (to) whom life offered few choices we would give our service freely so that they could afford higher learning and thereby advance their station and their capacity for service in society.

Policy Statement in Higher Education,
Indiana Province Congregation of the Holy Cross.

A THOUGHTFUL PERSPECTIVE

1) First, the Catholic understanding of society in general and the state in particular proposes a middle ground approach between the extremes of individualism and collectivism.

2) Second, the principle of subsidiarity . . . to transfer to the larger and higher order collectivity functions which can be performed and provided for best by lesser and subordinate bodies. . . . The state thus exists as a help (*subsidium*) for individuals. . . .

3) Third, the Catholic tradition has insisted that the principles of justice must govern economic life in society. The tradition has recognized three different types of justice—commutative, distributive, and legal or social. Commutative justice governs the relationship between one individual and another. Distributive justice governs the relationship between the community as a whole or the state and individuals. . . . Social justice or legal justice governs the relationship of the individual to the common good. . . . [S]ocial justice recognizes the contribution all must make to the common good, but especially emphasizes the right of the marginalized to participate in every way in the life of society.

4) Fourth, Catholic social teaching in more recent times has developed a theory of human rights including so-called economic rights . . . grounded in the dignity of the human person. . . .

5) The understanding of private property in the Catholic tradition has always included an important social dimension. . . . In early Christianity the social aspect of the goods of creation was strongly emphasized. The very existence of private property was often understood as result-

ing primarily from the fall or the presence of sin in the world, and not resulting from a demand of human nature as such.

6) Sixth, Catholic social teaching has recently insisted on a preferential option for the poor.

From "Ethical Principles of Catholic Social Teaching behind the United States Bishops' Letter," by Charles Curran. *Journal of Business Ethics* 7 (1988): 413–16. Used by permission of Kluwer Academic/Plenum Publishers.

THE CATHOLIC CONTENT OF PRESIDENT KIM'S NOBEL PRIZE

Forgive a certain parochial tone here, but in virtually all the news accounts of South Korean President Kim Dae Jung's Nobel Peace Prize, there was scant attention paid to the significant role his Catholic faith has played in his formation.

President Kim is the first Korean to receive a Nobel Prize and was cited for his tireless efforts for peace and reconciliation on the Korean peninsula, the last frontier of the Cold War.

Cardinal Stephen Kim Sou-hwan, retired archbishop of Seoul, who first nominated Kim as a candidate for the Nobel Peace Prize in 1992, said, "The award is an honor not only for President Kim but also for the entire Korean people. President Kim's efforts for democracy and human rights were finally recognized internationally."

Shortly after the Norwegian Nobel Committee announced Kim as this year's laureate, he said that he would share the peace honor with victims of South Korea's past authoritarian regimes, and his supporters at home and abroad. "I will continue to make efforts for democracy and peace on the Korean peninsula and throughout Asia and the world," he said.

Kim faced many trials, including attempts on his life and years of imprisonment and exile under past military regimes. In those tumultuous years when South Korea was under the authoritarian grip of President Park Chung Hee, Kim successively became a dissident, an exile, a death-row prisoner and, again, an exile. Through it all, he was a determined human rights campaigner and a champion of democracy.

The darkest moments came in 1973 when the exiled Kim was kidnapped from a Tokyo hotel by agents of the South Korean government and was about to be dumped, bound and blindfolded, into the sea when agents from the United States intervened to save him.

Kim ties his current passion for peace and reconciliation to a spiritual experience he said he had at that time. As his political enemies prepared to drown him, God intervened, he said. "I used to pray twice a day," he said, "but at that crucial moment I didn't and was only thinking about how I could save myself. At that moment, Jesus Christ stood beside me. I firmly held his sleeves, honestly begging for my life. A few seconds later, red beams of light flashed through my blindfold, and I heard a boom, boom! Then there was the sound of planes approaching and somebody calling my name."

His life was spared.

"All my hard trials experienced in the past—imprisonment, frequent detention, torture and forced exiles—happened in the process of God's redemptive work," he said in 1993, "and in that sense, I think, I have also participated in God's salvation project."

Such a strong religious outlook is not unusual for Koreans, according to scholars of Korea's contemporary religious history. Andrew E. Kim, writing for Korea Overseas Information Service, notes that Korea's long history of political vulnerability to Chinese and Japanese control, Japanese colonialism, and then the Korean War has provided fertile ground for Christianity and its theology of salvation-in-history.

The Catholic Church in South Korea during the past four decades has been a rallying point in Korean society for human rights causes. Christianity, first introduced to Korea in the late 1700s, has grown faster in South Korea than in almost any other country. Though estimates of the Christian population vary, reliable data-gatherers say it increased from 4 million in 1974 to 22 million—nearly half the population—in 1997. About 3 million of those are Roman Catholics.

An intriguing aspect of Korea's introduction to Christianity is that it came through laymen rather than missionary priests. Around 1770, Chong Tu-won learned about Christianity through Catholic literature encountered on a visit to China. He brought it back to Korea, where scholars with a strong interest in Western civilization studied it.

Although Korean Catholics are often described as conservative, the label hardly fits President Kim. "I firmly belief that God exists and lives in a variety of forms, also in Buddhism, Confucianism and other religions," he said.

From "The Catholic Content of President Kim's Nobel Prize." *National Catholic Reporter,* October 27, 2000. Used by permission.

Contents

Tables and Figures

Chapter 12

Chapter 13

Appendix D

Foreword

John Tropman's *The Catholic Ethic and the Spirit of Community* is a wonderfully comprehensive treatment of Protestant and Catholic orientations to the notion of "helping" and social welfare. This book contrasts the Protestant esteem for individualism, work, and wealth with the Catholic social traditions of communal responsibility, social justice, and respect for the poor. It is a work of theology, history, sociology, and public policy.

When I read the manuscript, I was somewhat daunted, as I am neither theologian, historian, sociologist, nor policy analyst. I punted: I read it as a practitioner of helping. My vocation is social work, and I've traveled through direct service and administrative jobs in sectarian, government, and private foundation settings. Every day, social workers and policymakers struggle with what we do with poor people, how we treat them, and what we do about the "condition" of poverty. Usually, we are unconscious of the religious and cultural influences that shape our views and decisions. John Tropman's historical odyssey creates a template of Protestant and Catholic archetypes for better understanding the root values that drive our decisions.

Not that we fit neatly into one or another camp based on religious affiliation—nor that religion per se is a dominant reference point. The United States is an amalgam of religious peoples, however, with a culture, government, and judicial system that are imbued with Judeo-Christian values and artifacts, despite our claim of separation between church and state. In fact, it is a Protestant culture.

John's elevation of a Catholic ethic in many ways holds a mirror to the beliefs we take for granted or act on without thought. For example, the erratic course of American poverty policy—what John describes as (borrowing from Brucs Jannson at the University of Southerr. California) a "reluctant welfare state"—is seen more clearly in the Protestant ethic of individual responsibility, work as a virtue, and the notion of "deserving" and "undeserving" poor. It is interesting to note that the most recent welfare reform was titled "The Personal Responsibility and Opportunity Act."

This book does not claim that Catholics think one way and Protestants another. In fact, John spends considerable time discussing the melding of ethics and identifying dominant and subdominant influences that all groups share. What is important to those of us who make decisions every day that affect other people is to understand what moves us. This book provides a valuable insight into our worldviews that are rooted in theology, history, and sociology and, in turn, are reflected in our public policy.

James V. Denova
Senior Program Officer
Claude Worthington Benedum Foundation
Pittsburgh, Pennsylvania

Preface

As we move into the twenty-first century, interest in religion and religious culture is expanding on almost every front. Religious schools—Catholic, Lutheran, or Jewish—are growing in the United States at a rapid rate. Religion seems to be at the core of conflicts in the Mideast and the Balkans. The Taliban destroy Buddhist statues in the name of Islam. Everyone seems to have her or his ear to God's lips.

What is unclear in all this activity is what, actually, is going on? In *The Catholic Ethic in American Society* (Tropman 1996, 178–79), I introduced the idea of religion as a multilevel concept as follows:

Protestant Practice	Catholic Practice
Protestant policy/documents/rules	Catholic policy/documents/rules
Protestant churches and sects	Catholic churches and sects
The Protestant Ethic	The Catholic Ethic
Alpha Attitude/Culture	Omega Attitude/Culture

In this list, what we conventionally think of as "religion" occupies the first three tiers: practices, policies, and organizations. Conflict can occur between any pair, and the more encoded a person or a community (in which practice, policy, and organization become a single, undifferentiated belief/action system) is, the more conflict is likely. It does not stop there, however. The first three tiers are built up and sustained by a deeper, more underlying set of values. I have called them "ethics," or complex, multifaceted bundles of values that embody certain orientations toward the world. Individuals may not be aware they have a "Protestant ethic" or a "Catholic ethic." Individuals from one religion may have some of the ethic of the "other" one. If one were to be a "cultural" Protestant or a "cultural" Catholic, one would "hang out" at this level. Yet it goes deeper. Below these two religious ethics is a cultural disposition that generates and infuses everything above it. Simply put, I encapsulate Alpha and Omega cultures as individualistic and collective, at their core. They represent fundamental worldviews that construct the reality around them.

Science discovers reality; culture creates it. Cultural reality is suffused with meaning to its bearers. Cows become sacred cows, slivers of wood become portions of the True Cross, reliquaries are infused with totemic power; the list goes on and on. Because culture creates reality, it constantly must be re-created. Because cultures can die and their meaning become diffused, the realities they create must be resurrected, if you will. Rituals and ceremonies of all types are part of this process of re-creation and resurrection. In an era of change—indeed, hyperchange, of webyear speed (a webyear is three months)—older cultural systems are under massive attack. They are at once grieving cultural death and angry. They are experiencing "cultural lag" whereby the structure of the world moves faster then the belief systems that interpret it. Cultures therefore are seeking to re-create the "way we were."

In my view, we must go deeper into an analysis of religion as culture, to try to understand that as important as practices, policies, and organizations (conventional "religion") are, we cannot deeply understand the conflicts in our world until we go to the level of ethics and cultures.

In this book I hope to shed further light on one of the ethics—the Catholic ethic. The series of quotes and comments at the beginning of the book offer an illustrative perspective on the Catholic ethic at work.

Acknowledgments

Every work has people who influenced it. I would like to mention some of them here and express my thanks.

My wife Penny, as the dedication evinces, was in many ways the spark that set the whole idea in motion. She continues to regard rewards as more randomly yours than rightfully yours (and in this respect thinks like Edwards Deming). She kept asking, "Why do some have more than others?" and "How can the well off feel so, well, *entitled* to their well-offness, on the one hand, and so dismissive and disparaging of those who have less, on the other?"

Educational experiences shape us. My undergraduate school, Oberlin College, has a motto—learning and labor—that was for me an example of the fusion complexities of results and effort.

The University of Chicago also was influential. The studies done there on the urban place—who were also, most always, the urban poor—did much to acquaint me with the worlds of "the gold coast and the slum." Data from University of Chicago's National Opinion Research Center's General Social Survey appear in chapter 11.

The University of Michigan is a rich place. I want to thank the colleagues, students, and staff members who contributed in so many different and positive ways to the completion of this volume. Professors Henry Meyer and Bill Birdsall were especially helpful. Jim Davidson of Purdue University has been a constant source of stimulation.

Of course, I also must mention those who have contributed the appendices. Gregory Baum's "Theological Reflections on the Catholic Ethic" is superb. Tom Harvey's essay on the practical elements of charity provides a Catholic ethic perspective. I thank Catholic Charities USA for permission to reprint material from the Cadre Study. And Gerhard Schwab's analysis of the social encyclicals of the Catholic Church is unbelievably helpful. Beyond their contributions here, each has contributed intellectually and emotionally to *The Catholic Ethic and the Spirit of Community*.

Over the years, many people have been involved in this project. Becky Bahlibi contributed her superb typing and manuscript management. Terry Gallagher added improvements too numerous to mention with his superb editing. He is the friend of the felicitous phrase and the terror of turgid text. (He would hate this!)

Two students from the joint doctoral program in social work and social science provided immeasurable help: Katie Richards-Schuster and Becky Stotzer. Each read the manuscripts and assisted in developing sources, ideas, and perspectives. Their help made this effort an exciting intellectual journey. Each contributed something special as well. Katie brought her sociologist's eye to the project. Becky brought a psychologist's eye and an editor's perspective. She was especially helpful, as well, in the final, complex process of putting this all together.

Terry Torkko did an outstanding job of editing the text. Greg Casccione worked with the text from the perspective of a Catholic intellectual and made improvements to every page. Greg also provided encouragement and support.

Thanks go as well to the Lilly Endowment, whose generous support of the Catholic ethic project at the University of Michigan was a material aid to this project.

The Catholic Ethic:
Whys and Wherefores

This book is about the Catholic ethic and the spirit of community. As readers may recognize, my title inverts the one given by Max Weber to his famous study of modern society, *The Protestant Ethic and the Spirit of Capitalism* ([1906] 1956).[1]

Enter Max Weber

Weber sought to show that the Protestantism of the Reformation had a "deep structure." He called it the Protestant ethic, and he argued that it influenced the development of the form of economic and social organization we call capitalism. Weber's assertions are not incontestably true. Even today, however, the power and vitality of his insights have become so much part of the sociological and popular lore that, in an odd sense, they may well be true.

Weber wrote his book about 100 years ago. Amazingly, over almost a century, no one introduced the idea of another ethic. Although there was a book called *The Lutheran Ethic* (Kersten 1970), my 1986 article "The 'Catholic Ethic' versus the 'Protestant Ethic'" was the first specifically to introduce the concept of a Catholic ethic. Michael Novak used the concept in his book *The Catholic Ethic and the Spirit of Capitalism* (1993). My 1996 book, *The Catholic Ethic in American Society,* provided a general explication of the concept. Since that publication, many readers have urged me to do a more detailed assessment. I agree. People asked me if there are any data, even of a preliminary sort, that could shed further light on Catholic/Protestant differences. I have included some of that material here, mainly from public opinion surveys in the United States.

The Catholic Ethic

In this volume I continue a discussion of the Catholic ethic idea. The Catholic ethic is based more on what Weber called *Wertrationalitat*—in which ends are rooted in a more collective sense of oneness—than *Zweckrationalitat,* in which ends are determined more through individualistic rationality. The Catholic ethic is based in the form of economic and social organization generally called "community" as opposed to "society." This is like Tonnies' distinction between *Gemeinshaft* and *Gesellshaft* (Tönnies [1887] 1957).

A "community" implies strong connections with others, a sense of "we are all in the same boat," and norms of helping, supporting, and cooperating with others. I suggest that this should mean that the Catholic ethic is a community-oriented, helping ethic. It is supportive of "charity" (as in Catholic Charities), although I prefer the word "helping" instead because "charity" has acquired a somewhat negative undertone, implying subordination of the receiver to the giver. If the Protestant Ethic is an "achievement" ethic, the Catholic ethic is a "helping" ethic.

What, one might ask, is an "ethic"? From my perspective, an ethic is a package of ideas, values, norms, attitudes, and beliefs that characterize a people, a region of people, a hemisphere of people. Thus, we might talk about eastern and western ethics; male and female ethics; or American, South American, Russian, and Japanese ethics. *Ethic*, as used here, is a sociological rather than philosophical term. It refers to thoughts about conduct, rationalizations for conduct, justifications for conduct, ideas about situations, and guides for actions that characterize a people or group of people. *Ethic* as used here does not refer to questions about right and wrong in a judgmental sense, only about right and wrong in an analytic sense. For example, "The Z ethic thinks thus and so is right and thus and so is wrong." We are not evaluating those postulates with regard to their merits on any ground, although we may have our own personal views. Instead, as social analysts, we are observing the disposition; looking at the conditions under which the disposition arises, continues, and may or may not continue; and seeking to outline the implications of such a disposition.

Social Structures, Social Values, Cultures, and Subcultures

In looking at and trying to understand the world around us, two perspectives have been popular. One is the "social structuralist" perspective, which uses as the primary vehicle of cause and explanation the nature of the concrete reality in which we live. Marx used this perspective; he looked at the position one had in the division of labor. On a more individual level, B. F. Skinner, the Harvard behaviorist (Skinner 1971) was such a thinker as well. Skinner believed that our behavior was a product of reinforcing and extinguishing conditions, more or less in the here-and-now. Historically this tradition is Aristotelian and materialist in persuasion. In popular argot, it is the sword that counts, not the pen. The structuralist perspective looks at the "hard side" of reality—the places we work, the tools we use, the climate we experience—as life's great shapers. It's the softer side of sociology.

On the other hand are the Platonic, nominalist, and "pen" traditions. Max Weber fits here; he argued that a set of ideas (the Protestant ethic) caused/explains the development of capitalism. Again, on the individual level, Freud was such a thinker, believing that feelings in our heads directed actions. Once those feelings were righted or released, better behavior would follow. These perspectives are espoused by "social values" theorists. Social values thinkers argue that ideas, values, norms, beliefs, and attitudes are the driving forces for people, communities, and societies. For the purposes of this analysis I define a social value as an idea to which commitment has been attached. An "ethic" is a packaged pattern of social values. This is what Weber meant by "ethic"—and what I mean as well.

The term *ethic*, however, differs from the term *culture*. I use *culture* in the anthropological sense, to refer to the *combination* of common thoughts and actions—patterns, really—that characterize a group of individuals. This distinction is important. Social structure and social values are somewhat archetypal—neither affects individuals, communities, and societies in the straightforward way that thinkers have proposed (although Weber recognized this through his use of the concept of the Protestant ethic as an "ideal type"). Culture is created and enacted out of the tools of social structure and social values in the here-and-now. Patterns of culture are enactments that have identifiable, enduring qualities.

Perhaps a food example will assist. Consider ingredients (structure) and recipes (ideas). They can exist without anyone doing anything with them. Then someone decides to make the dish (enact the recipe). How the recipe turns out depends in part on how good it was in the first place; it also depends, however, on the nature of the exact ingredients available, the skill of the cook, the heat of the particular oven, and the like.

In this sense culture, like Durkheim's (1951) concept of *anomie*, is a collective term. An individual does not "have" culture, although she or he may have its individualized counterpart—a personality. Culture is a group property; it involves the characteristically common combination of thoughts and actions of a particular group.

Thus, the Catholic ethic is an abstraction of sorts, a pancultural, panhistorical collection of ideas, values, beliefs, attitudes, norms, and so forth. It is for me what the Protestant ethic was for Weber—an *ideal type* or quintessential representation.

Catholic culture, on the other hand, is always a here-and-now or then-and-there concept. It is almost always "hyphenated" (medieval Catholic culture, American Catholic culture, Irish Catholic culture, French Catholic culture, Hispanic Catholic culture, Black Catholic culture, and so on).

Even within Catholic cultures there are subcultures. Not all Irish Catholics have the same "culture"; there are regional variations. Thus, even the concept of culture ignores variation that is patterned and exists over time. Nonetheless, in spite of cultures and subcultures, there is a river than runs through them—the Catholic ethic.

Capitalism and Community: Words Matter

Weber used the term *capitalism* because, I think, it was his term for what he was trying to explain about why some areas of Germany were prosperous and thriving while others were not. The choice of that term as it worked its way into his title has provided much cause for debate, however—perhaps as much as the Protestant ethic idea itself. After all, what *is* capitalism? Was what Weber saw really capitalism, or was it mercantilism, or whatever? Similarly, modifications of the term have come into play. Thinkers uses the term *social capitalism* to try to soften the seemingly harsh word *capitalism*. Lester Thurow has three capitalisms in his book *Head to Head* (1992). He uses *individualistic capitalism* to describe American-style capitalism, or at least the capitalism in which the winner takes all. He uses *communal capitalism* to refer to a capitalism in which winner takes most but has a responsibility to the society in which he or she lives. This type of capitalism is characteristic of Europe, Thurow says; his usage is similar to others' use of the term *social capitalism*. Thurow also uses the term *producer capitalism*, in which the society takes most—characteristic of medieval Europe (the cathedral builders) and postwar Japan.

What Weber meant by capitalism might just as well have been conveyed by another word—say achievement, or individualism. One can speculate about a book called *The Protestant Ethic and the Spirit of Achievement*, or *The Protestant Ethic and the Spirit of Individualism*, or (like Tönnies) *Community and Society*. I think that last title would have been the better one. The spirit of society encompasses the entrepreneurial, urban, individualistic, acquisitive package that Weber called capitalism. For this book, I have used the word *community*, playing off the title Max Weber should have used.

Wholes and Parts

What we call things makes a difference. The process of naming them reflects reality, but it may create a reality as well.

One last important point has to do with questions about the whole versus the parts. Many problems with the Protestant ethic as a concept stem from the fact that, as one scholar with whom I have discussed these matters says, "There are really several Protestant ethics—one for each denomination." The diversity and pluralism within Protestantism indeed raise a problem. I point to some of that multiplicity myself a bit later on, in reviewing data on religious orientation and various measures of helping. Apart from denominational differences, there are racial differences among Protestants (African American Protestants versus white Protestants) and class (high-status Protestants versus middle- and lower-status Protestants, or high church versus low church). One might ask, then, if it even makes sense to talk about a "Protestant ethic."

On the other hand, almost in direct opposition to the plurality of Protestantism is the commonalty of Catholicism. Many people think that "Catholics" are one thing, speak with one voice, think exactly alike (often at the same time of day), and have, in effect, no variation. A Catholic ethic makes no sense here either, one might argue, because "the Church" articulates Catholic thought and speaks for Catholics on all matters of importance—and many of no importance.

In one case, then, a concept is challenged because of the diversity it contains. In scientific terms, there is *too much variation* to make it a good predictor. In the other case, the concept is challenged because the uniformity means there is *no variation.*

Both positions are too extreme, in my view. Although there are a lot of denominational, racial, and class differences within the Protestant fold, there is a core approach to the world that can be identified and considered. The Protestant ethic is a good name for it. On the other hand, there are a lot of differences and distinctions within Catholicism that often go unnoticed. One example is the liberal/conservative split (Cross 1958; Greeley 1991a, 1991b). Others involve ethnic differences (W. C. Miller 1976) and a distinction between the parishioner (the believer) and the parish (the institutional church). Conceptually, the Catholic ethic is a good name for a set of core understandings that have their roots in early Christianity—2,000-year-old beliefs and practices that have had various interpretations and applications over time. Such differences appear everywhere. Humor, as always, is a good place to look. There is an old story about a question being asked of a rabbi, a priest, and a minister. The rabbi begins with, "The tradition requires . . . "; the priest begins his reply with, "The church says . . . "; and the minister begins, "Well, I think. . . . " The differences in approach suggested by this story capture exactly the kind of difference that the Catholic ethic and the Protestant ethic (and, perhaps, the Jewish ethic—but that is another piece of research) are meant to stimulate.

Caveats

At the end of most works of scholarship, authors insert a caveat—a caution to readers that for various reasons (the nature of the sample, problems with the data, etc.) the conclusions offered should await further research and exploration. I do the same, but I put it at the beginning rather than the end. There are several kinds of problems with which the reader will want to make an acquaintance.

One problem is epistemological. Can one "prove" that an ethic exists? If so, what would such proof comprise? The Protestant ethic hypothesis has been around for 100 years and is still debated. I also think that, at this initial point, it is not possible to "prove" that the Catholic ethic exists. Instead, I hope to suggest that it is a reasonable, plausible, and obvious idea, although it has not been fully described before.

A second, related problem has to do with results or impacts. Can I show conclusively that the Catholic ethic has certain specific impacts? Not really. Impacts are differential and various. That is partly because the Catholic ethic must interact with several specific "structures" in specific locales. This is one result of the principle of subsidiarity (arguing that problems should be handled at the lowest possible level.) The Catholic ethic acts as an influence, rather than a cause.

Third, there is the "either/or" issue. Is one *only* a "Protestant" or a "Catholic," or could there be some kind of mixture? It's an odd question, but I have an answer that lies in the conflict theory of values, which I develop in *American Values and Social Welfare* (Tropman 1989). In that work, I argue that values come in pairs—such as achievement and equality, competition and cooperation, equity and adequacy, and so on. These values balance each other, and each of us has some of each value pair within us, although one or the other of the pair may be the dominant value for us. This is not a question of right or wrong, good or bad; it is only a question of values mix. No single value can serve us in all circumstances. As Lipset points out in *The First New Nation* (1963), one way to look at the history of the United States is to see it as a contest between values of achievement on one hand and equality on the other.

It seems intuitively clear, at least to many Americans, that one could combine values of achievement and equality, even if it might be a struggle. It seems less clear—perhaps even counterintuitive—that one could combine a Catholic ethic and a Protestant ethic.

There are several ways one might respond to this consideration. One is to point out that although the ethics are "religious" in one sense, they are secular or "civil" in some of their iterations and applications; hence, cultural combinations would be possible in specific contexts.

Another approach would be to suggest, as I do here, that the religions themselves are "crystallizations" of responses to needs and perspectives. Hence, there are *underlying* perspectives, worldviews, orientations *from which* religions emerge, and *to which* they respond. As such, the orientations called the Catholic ethic and the Protestant ethic reflect (this point may seem a bit hard to accept) more basic perspectives on the world and in the more basic form are *not* mutually exclusive. Although at the moment one cannot "have" more than one religion at a time, there is no reason why one cannot have *perspectives* of more than one. The aforementioned distinctions between collective and individualistic orientations might be an example of a basic values package. So too are distinctions between "community" orientation and "society" orientation. Durkheim's observation that there are two kinds of solidarity—mechanical and organic—also refers to basic antinomies (Durkheim 1960a). These concepts are a basis for Hawley's (1950) distinction between categorical connections (a kind of mechanical solidarity in which connection is based on sameness, like an association of realtors) and corporate connections (a kind of organic solidarity in which connection is based on individualism and interdependence, like an orchestra).

The presence of both ethics within cultures and personalities, then, suggests the need for two other conceptual sets. One involves dominance and subdominance, a conceptual frame that suggests that although most of us may have both sets of values within us, one set is dominant and the other is subdominant. For example, someone may be very committed to achievement, yet still believe in equality. The weights may be different, however. The reverse also can be true. Because someone is committed to equality does not mean that she or he has no commitment to achievement.[2]

Dominance and subdominance raise the issues of foreground and background. Subdominant commitments may be more in the background of our cultures and our selves. They may be called out only on certain occasions. For example, I might be achievement oriented in the classroom and equality oriented among my children. The point is that what is manifest does not mean that nothing latent exists.

A final caveat has to do with readers' reactions to the concept of the Catholic ethic, especially as it is portrayed as a helping ethic and a community-based ethic. These things *seem* good; in the main, they are good. They have a dark side, however. The Protestant ethic as well— with its emphasis on individualism, self-help, and achievement—also seems good, and it *is* good. This ethic also has its dark side, however.

Neither ethic is "better" than the other. Even if a reader has a preference for one, that does not make it better (any more than my preference for butter brickle ice cream makes it better than other ice cream flavors).

What Interests Me about the Catholic Ethic?

Readers of *The Catholic Ethic in American Society* (1996) have asked me why I undertook this exploration. As much as I am aware of my reasons, I share some of them here. Like the reasons for most interests, they are an amalgam of personal and intellectual.

As a Catholic, I have always "sensed" a difference in Protestant and Catholic communities as I have experienced them. Perhaps that sense of difference is something that lay dormant until I read Max Weber.

For me, *The Protestant Ethic and the Spirit of Capitalism* (Weber [1906] 1956) has always been attractive. Even though there is still controversy about it, it "felt right" when I first read it; it feels right still. That does not mean, however, that it is all that needs to be said on the subject of religious values and economic behavior. Perhaps the best way to look at Weber was to think alongside him. Much energy has been spent in trying to figure out whether Weber was "right" or "wrong." This focus diverted (and diverts) scholars from asking about the *ways* he might be right—and what those ways might suggest with respect to other types of religious impact.

Another reason has to do with my interest in the way we Americans (and, by contrast, other societies) think about people in need, those with less, those *in poverty*—and, similarly, the way we Americans (and, by contrast, other societies) think about helping "them" (Oates 1969). The word often used for helping poor people is "charity"; as I have mentioned, however, it has acquired a somewhat negative, unsavory nuance. In general, as I argue in *Do Americans Hate the Poor?* (Tropman 1998), Americans have negative attitudes toward disadvantaged people. Admittedly, our national record is mixed. Much good happens, but there is a suspicion of poor people and a sense always present that somehow, in some way, poverty is poor people's *fault*. This idea of fault comes through again and again. There is a further underlying notion that if it is your fault that you are poor, you do not deserve help. This idea of the "deserving poor" indicates that poverty is a moral as well as economic category. Why this attitude should exist is a question that has always interested me, especially because we live in a relatively affluent society. Indeed, it seems that the more affluent we become, the more poor people bother us. Philadelphia, for example, developed a voucher system for providing handouts to poor people, so that beggars would not spend cash gifts on unnecessary items such as alcohol and tobacco. One headline discussing this system referred to providing aid to the "needy, not the greedy." Why anyone would associate "greed" with a beggar mystifies me, especially because we have many of examples of truly greedy people around. Lots of them work in savings and loans, however, or as chief executives of Fortune 500 firms.

I also believe that, in spite of many commonalities, the Catholic and Protestant religious ethics have different ideas about poverty, its causes, and cures. Kersbergen (1995) captures this idea well, although he uses language that refers to individual Catholics and Protestants, rather than ethics:

> Catholics have fundamentally different views of poverty than Protestants. Whereas the latter regard being poor as a state to be avoided because it is taken as proving damnation, the former consider poverty as an opportunity to do good, and the act itself of doing good is "infused" by the duties of neighborly love. The poor themselves, however, even occupy a special place in the Gospel, for Jesus' message was that poverty facilitates salvation. Charity assumed its importance in this context of achieving forgiveness of committed sins through the accumulation of good works to the benefit of those privileged to suffer (the poor). These are the central components of the spirit of social capitalism and this spirit addresses the rich and poor alike (Kersbergen 1995, 198).

There also are sociological reasons for this exploration. As a sociologist, I am an "ideological" sociologist—one who interests himself or herself in the force of ideas in history. This perspective is Platonic and nominalist; it focuses on the pen rather than the "sword" and emphasizes thought over action. This preference in no way implies diminution of other perspectives, especially those that emphasize or stress Aristotelian, materialist, "swordish," and action-oriented points of departure. Each has its place; each contributes to understanding and need not compete; each supplements but does not supplant. The idea of "inventing," "discovering," "precipitating," or "recognizing" a new idea is irresistible, even if this new idea actually is a reconfiguration of an old idea. I hope readers find it as much fun as I do.

Thus, I ask the reader to continue to journey with me in exploring the Catholic ethic concept. Part of my excitement for this kind of conceptual work also comes from my own personal orientation—social science. Someone once said that all the world is divided into lumpers and splitters. (It must have been a lumper!) I am a lumper. I seek first the general commonalties and lines of demarcation; then I refine them. Others work in the opposite way, building to generalizations from specific points. I seek forests, whereas others prefer trees. I do not, however, *create* forests. Moreover, the fact that some specific forests may be mixed, with some evergreens and some leafy trees, does not mean that one cannot usefully use that difference as a point of separation.

In short, I enjoy developing and painting the big picture. I recognize, however, that there are lots of small scenes within the mural, and I want to assure readers who might wonder that the generalist and particularistic perspectives are both valid.

PART I

The Catholic Ethic and the Spirit of Community

The idea behind Weber's *The Protestant Ethic and the Spirit of Capitalism* ([1906] 1956), essentially, was that the ideas and values that formed the core of the Protestant ethic drove, pushed, permitted, or caused the development of capitalism. It is not necessary to think that there was intention for this relationship to be so. Causes of things do not always think or start out to be causes of things, and the paths of relationships sometimes are indirect and difficult to discover. Even today there is uncertainty about whether the Protestant ethic *really* caused capitalism, whether the reverse was the case, or whether they were simply two social phenomena that occurred simultaneously and became linked. I am not trying to answer that question here. Instead, I am using the happy occasion of covariation as a springboard to another set of questions. I posit: IF there is a Protestant ethic, THEN it seems reasonable to talk about a Catholic ethic; IF that Protestant ethic had some relationship to the spirit of capitalism, THEN the Catholic ethic might have relationships to the spirit of something too—in this case, the spirit of community. I explore this idea in chapter 1.

As I suggest, however, once the idea of a Catholic ethic is articulated, it seems pretty obvious. When "obvious" things have not been obvious then that *lacuna*, too, requires exploration. Chapter 2 attends to that task.

CHAPTER 1

The Catholic Ethic and the Protestant Ethic

That there should be a "Catholic ethic" seems, the moment one says it, abundantly clear. Really, why *not*? The whole idea seems rather reasonable, given the Protestant ethic concept. In point of fact, however, the Catholic ethic concept has only begun to come into currency. Given the popularity of the Protestant ethic concept, let's review the main elements of the conceptual frame of the Protestant ethic as a way to begin.

The Protestant Ethic

In contemporary American society, the concept of the Protestant ethic is powerfully pervasive, not only in technical discussions about the historical development of capitalism (Weber [1906] 1956) but in popular discussions about work, sacrifice, achievement, and so on (Ganster 1981; Tropman 1986). In sociology, the concept of the Protestant ethic has exercised a robust influence and continues to stimulate scholarly attention (Marshall 1982). It has generated all sorts of spin-offs; there even is a Protestant-ethic scale that measures attitudes regarding the Protestant ethic (Wollack 1971; Greenberg 1977; Ganster 1981).

Generally the concept of the Protestant ethic refers to a set of beliefs that support work—particularly, hard work—and give it a sort of transcendental and omnibus meaning and purpose. The Protestant ethic supports material and financial acquisition as opposed to sufficiency. In the Protestant ethic tradition, a person can never have too much money. Even people who are doing well should continue to persevere and acquire more. (The bar keeps going up!) The Protestant ethic tends to regard money as a symbol of and validation of success and achievement and thus transforms money from a tool to meet material needs into a symbol of fundamental character. In other words, having lots of money tends to mean that you are a good person; having little or no money tends to indicate that you might be lazy and not trying. *Ipso facto,* having money is good. The Protestant ethic implies an eroding scale of achievement in which the values and virtues of past accomplishment tend to recede and ever new, ever higher goals loom in the future. Because of "salvation panic" (you never really *know* about your celestial fate), a bit of reassurance in reserve cannot hurt.[1]

There are many positive elements in the Protestant ethic. Weber identified the individualistic and entrepreneurial elements of the ethic that drive individual and collective achievement. The opportunity for individual expression, the ability to make individual choices, and the accountability that such choices creates are very positive values that are an important underpinning of the American democratic model.

The personal experience of "grace" as an indicator of "salvation" (or being, or having been, "saved") makes change—the anticipation of it, the experience of it, the support of it, the encouragement of it—a part of daily life. The Protestant ethic is an ethic that not only supports but embodies the concept of transformational change.

There are some downsides, however. By extension, not having money is bad because the Protestant ethic tends to support people who have "made it," and there is a tendency to lack sympathy for those in financial distress. Indeed, the celestial calculus that "each soul rests upon its own bottom" becomes translated into the earthly "each tub on its own bottom" perspective. An individual's dignity depends not on the individual's being a "child of God" but on whether that "child" has made good (i.e., achieved financial success).

The Catholic Ethic

The Catholic ethic, unlike the Protestant ethic, is not a phrase that one hears often; indeed, until recently, many people may never have heard it. Once formulated and stated, however, it seems obvious, especially given the large number of Catholics in the United States (and worldwide) and the presence of a vigorous institutional church. The concept has developed into a coherent theory only relatively recently (Tropman 1986, 1996; Novak 1993).

An early use of the Catholic ethic concept occurred in the writings of Fanfani (1936). He writes about Catholic "ethics" as opposed to a capitalist "ethic." Wilbur, in his introduction to an edition of Fanfani's work, uses the phrase as well (Wilbur 1983, vii, quoted in Fanfani 1984). Mack, Murphy, and Yellin (1956, 295) also comment, "The Catholic Ethic propounded a culturally established emphasis on other-worldliness. . . ."[2] Andrew Greeley (1981) also employed the phrase. Greeley, however, introduced it as an illustrative fashion and as a literary device to explore an argument he was making with respect to the Protestant ethic, rather than as a social construct or sociological variable.

As I use the term, the Catholic ethic is a community-centered pattern of values. The community of individuals is at least as important as—and perhaps more important than—any one individual. The Catholic ethic emphasizes connectivity, loyalty, and involvement. It will offer you direct assistance, may not push you as much, and, in some cases, may remember if someone or some group has offended your community, even in times past. It is people oriented, so it supports work because people do it, not because of the results it produces. Money is fine, but having it does not make you a good, or better, person any more than not having it raises moral questions about you as in the Protestant ethic.[3] Metaphorically, the Catholic ethic is based on the idea that "a rising tide lifts all boats."

The positives of such an ethic are connectivity, a more "clan" mentality suggesting that, as you are one of "us" you are okay, a high degree of unconditional acceptance and the ready availability of help. These can provide reassurance and solace. One does not have to prove herself or himself on a regular basis. The question, "What have you done for me lately?" is simply not asked.

Catholic culture has many other answers than the appearance of grace to the problem of "salvation panic." Not only the sacrament of reconciliation (or confession) but the acquisition of salvation credit through good works (indulgences) can reduce the level of anxiety. These occur within the system, however. Hence, the Catholic ethic is more of a *transactional* than a *transformational* ethic. *It supports change* in *the system, rather than change* of *the system.*

Overview of the Two Ethics

These two ethics represent "archtypical" traditions. As Nussbaum says, "Traditions embody many years of many people's effort and thought; and it is likely that no deeply held view will have failed to get something right" (Nussbaum 1989, 36).

Religions might crystallize deeper values (Tropman 1996). As a way of comparing these two ethics, some "nonreligious" differences might be worth considering. I have selected five dimensions of difference that I believe embody the differences between the two worldviews and already have been developed, for other purposes, by other scholars.[4] The following chart lists them.

Protestant Ethic	Catholic Ethic
1. solo self	1. ensemble self
2. optimizing	2. satisficing
3. competitive	3. cooperative
4. self help	4. community help
5. public-regarding institutions	5. private-regarding institutions

In exploring these dimensions, I set them up in opposition to each other. Such distinctions are "ideal typical" in character.

Solo Self "versus" Ensemble Self

Sampson (1985) presents a detailed review and discussion of the concepts of solo self and ensemble self. He argues that the idea of individualism is conceptualized in different ways by indigenous psychology. His conclusion is that there is a very important difference between the solo self and the ensemble self that has to do with the way an indigenous culture defines the self/nonself boundary (1) and where the culture locates the fundamental source of power (2): "According to indigenous psychology in the United States, for example, there exists a region intrinsic to the person and a region of 'other'" (Sampson 1985, 15).

Such a culture locates control within the person as well and assumes that "mature persons are governed internally rather than externally." Sampson adds: "Such cultures tend to be characterized by a suspicion about and at times even an antipathy toward social institutions" (Sampson 1985, 16).

Internalized individualized control however is not the only way that control issues may be approached. Field control is possible: "These psychologies describe the location of power and control in a field of forces which includes, but goes well beyond, the person" (Sampson 1985, 16).

Such a distinction can be regarded as a fulcrum of difference between the Protestant ethic and the Catholic ethic. The Protestant ethic is characterized by solo-self orientations—what we tend to call "individualism." On the other hand, the Catholic ethic might be more appropriately regarded as based in the ensemble self. The person sits within a field of forces, including the family, the community, and the church—a field that actually helps her or him define herself or himself.

Optimizing "versus" Satisficing

A second distinction between the Catholic ethic and the Protestant ethic may center on the distinction made by March and Simon (1958, 141–42) between optimizing and satisficing in the seeking of solutions for day-to-day problems in organizations. In their example, March and Simon talk about the difference between finding the sharpest needle in the haystack and finding one sharp enough to use. The Protestant ethic tends to set up "optimal" standards. One is "saved" or one is not. There is an "either/or-ness" about the approach to an individual's status. One is "okay" or not. One is "poor" or not. In decision making, a satisfactory solution may well be the practical way to go. If one is talking about moral categories, however, degrees cease to matter. In this sense, the Protestant ethic is optimizing. In Weber's ([1906] 1956) terms, fate is predestined, and a person is saved or not saved. It is as simple as that. The Catholic ethic, on the other hand, using these terms of reference might be regarded as a "satisficing" ethic. (*Satisficing* means "good enough," as opposed to optimization.) With respect to salvation, at least, degrees matter. An individual moves toward salvation and occasionally moves back. It is a process rather than a state, and the human condition is considered in a similar fashion.[5]

Competition "versus" Cooperation

The Catholic and Protestant ethics appear to differ with regard to their approaches to the fundamental relationships between human beings. The Protestant ethic regards competition as central. According to the Protestant ethic, there apparently are not enough resources (corporeal or heavenly) to go around. The relationship in nature is "red in tooth and claw," and a human's life is destined to be—in the famous phrase of Thomas Hobbes—"nasty, brutish, and short." This perspective articulates well with an optimizing, solo-self point of view.[6] A limited-good orientation has a focus on the *accumulation and investment* of capital, not the *sharing and spending* of it.

The Catholic ethic, on the other hand, is more communal in its orientation, more involving of others. "What goes around comes around" might be a kind of motto. Cooperation is what makes the world go 'round—between priest and parishioner, between husband and wife, parents and children, heaven and earth, God and human. You are not alone on Jacob's ladder, even if you want to be.

Self-Help "versus" Community Help

Within the Protestant ethic framework, everyone is considered more or less responsible for himself or herself. Direct helping is something of a last resort. It not only uses resources that you might need; it actually may perpetuate the conditions that gave rise to the need in the first place. This general orientation has had a profound impact on the development of social policy in general and welfare programs in particular, in terms of speed and format. As Jansson (2001) points out, our society has been a reluctant welfare state.

Although the lack of sympathy that the Protestant ethic maintains for welfare activities is not frequently cited as a reason for America's relatively slow development of welfare state policies, Segalman (1968) says, "That a social welfare program (community helping program) should have developed at all under the Protestant Ethic is a matter of surprise . . . " (p. 128). (It developed, in part, as an expression of Catholic and Jewish communalism to the needs of their nineteenth-century immigrants and the individualism of the American host.)

The Protestant ethic, after all, emphasizes achievement, work, and getting ahead. It has supported the creation of a work ethic that is second to none, a society that is the envy of the world, and an economy that sustains not only itself but much of the world as well. There are some rarely discussed, but nonetheless potent, side effects to this ethic. What about people who do not get ahead? What of those who do not work? What of those who cannot provide for themselves? The Protestant ethic does not provide much individual or institutional solace to them. Indeed, we often blame poor and disenfranchised people—"blaming the victim," as Ryan (1971) puts it—for their plight. The capitalist system, which the rise of the Protestant ethic was supposed to support (*The Protestant Ethic and the Spirit of Capitalism* was Weber's title, remember) also supported competition and had little to offer those who were failures at, or victims of, the competitive process. The "hidden hand" of the market lifted some up and struck others down.[7] If you did not know enough to get out of the way, that was your problem. Those who pointed to these social costs, these social concerns, often were criticized and ridiculed. Social workers, one group that took on this role, often were called "bleeding hearts."

Help was present, but it was of a do-it-yourself variety. American's "pull yourself up by your own bootstraps" society provided free land in the West if you wanted to work it.

The quintessential Protestant ethic response to need may have been illustrated by the Nichlos plan developed in Oklahoma to handle hunger during the Depression. This idea proposed to scrape uneaten food from restaurant plates into five-gallon tins and pass it along to poor people who would prove their merit by chopping wood to be donated by farmers! The idea is so unbelievable that readers might like some detail. Here is Arthur Schlessinger Jr.'s account:

> Thus John B. Nichlos of the Oklahoma Gas Utilities Company wrote to his friend Patrick J. Hurley, the Secretary of War, about an idea he was trying out in Chickssha, Oklahoma. By the Nichlos plan, restaurants were asked to dump food left on plates into five gallon containers; the unemployed could qualify for these scraps by chopping wood donated by farmers. "We expect a little trouble now and then from those who are not worthy of the support of the citizens," Nichlos wrote philosophically, "but we must contend with such cases in order to take care of those who are worthy." Hurley was so impressed by the plan of feeding garbage to the homeless that he personally urged it on Colonel Woods (Schlessinger 1957, 179).

Once one has recovered from the "slops for the poor" idea, a question, of course, centers on the mindset that would generate such a plan, the culture that would even entertain it, and the transcendent sense of self that would lead a *rich* person to suggest such a thing. Only a culture that considered itself "two nations"—one rich and saved and one poor and unsaved—could come up with this kind of plan. The problem was that if one were morally unworthy, help was hard to give. Help usually meant *the dole*. Schlessinger goes on:

> Anything was better than the dole, a word invested with every ominous significance. . . . It was better, Calvin Coolidge said philosophically, "to let those who have made the losses bear them than to try to shift them to someone else." "Unemployment insurance," said Henry Ford, "would only insure that we always have unemployment." If this country ever voted a dole, said Silas Strawn, now head of the United States Chamber of Commerce, "we've hit the toboggan as a nation" (Schlessinger 1957, 179).

With respect to helping, the Protestant ethic is a stressed ethic. It wants to help, but it is worried that taking from godly people who have achieved and giving to those (possibly) "ungodly" who have not somehow is wrong, problematic, and destructive of motivation. Perhaps in no area are the stresses within the Protestant ethic more difficult than in this one area. Whom should we help, to what amount, and for how long?

Within the Catholic ethic tradition, helping is a natural part of the lived life. After all, there is no sharp distinction between people who need help and those who give it (although this may have been less true in the medieval period.) "There but for the grace of God go I" is a phrase that one hears fairly often in this belief system. The act of helping helps the helper (rather than harming the helper) and helps the helped person (rather than harming him or her). It is good for both. Because the act of helping helps the helper, however, it also does not matter who the helped person actually is, or whether she or he deserves it.

Public-Regarding Institutions "versus" Private-Regarding Institutions

The Protestant ethic tradition and the Catholic ethic tradition have institutions and organizations that help carry out the work of their cultures and are part of those cultures. What is different is that the respective traditions regard the purpose of institutions very differently. Within the Catholic ethic, the church is responsible for providing your access to salvation. There are things you have to do, of course, but you do them through your local church. The purpose of the church organization, then, is to provide individual parishioners with personalized help and salvation goods (opportunities for grace) and directions on the narrow road to the gates of heaven, where St. Peter is waiting.

The Protestant church has a different function. Here salvation is the responsibility of the individual person, achieved independently and individually. (Actually, you really do not "achieve" salvation—to the extent that you embrace predestination. You discover it.) The church may help, of course, but responsibility still is with the person. The role of the church, then, is not to provide salvation goods but to create community—in a word, to do the things that the individual cannot herself or himself do. The church service is less an encounter with the sacramental sacred, as it is for Catholics, and more a time for communal worship, prayer, and fellowship.

These two orientations have been described by Edward Banfield and James Q. Wilson as "private regarding" and "public regarding." In *City Politics* (1963), Banfield and Wilson were looking at different orientations toward governments. Some people regard government's function as providing personal help. These are private-regarding views. The function of the city councilperson, in this view, is to help you when you have a ticket, when your kid has been picked up by the cops, when you need a job. Governments provide personal goods. It is very similar—though Banfield and Wilson do not make this point—to the view of the parish and the parish priest within the Catholic ethic.

Another view of government, in which the government provides social goods, is a perspective in which the government does only those things that the individual cannot do for herself or himself. Hence, the government provides parks, community pools, recycling centers, trash pickup, water and sewer services, and so on. In this perspective, you do not go to the government for personal help. Self-help is the rule; you are as responsible for your own "career" as for your own salvation. This public-regarding attitude puts a whole different face on the functions and purposes of institutions and organizations. It is consistent with the Protestant ethic.

Community Helping

I have stressed the idea of "helping" within the context of community. What *is* the community helping values package? For me, it has five elements. Not all may be present all the time, but a preponderance is needed to make a community helping culture:

- Sympathy toward people in need, with special concern for the poor
- Willingness to provide concrete aid
- A desire to make the aid programmatic, as an addition to personal
- Support for the role of government in helping
- A sense of some collective responsibility for social conditions

First, there is a sympathetic and even positive view regarding people who need help, especially disadvantaged people. A focus on the conditions of poverty rather than its causes is characteristic of community helping concern. This does not mean that causes are irrelevant—only that the question of whose fault things are is not the first question asked. Mother Teresa of Calcutta embodied the Catholic ethic, par excellence.

A second element is the willingness to provide aid to disadvantaged people in concrete, practical forms such as cash, food, and so on. Good wishes are important, prayers no doubt vital, but the hungry person needs food; the naked person, clothes; the homeless person, shelter.

A third aspect of community helping concern is a desire to make assistance programmatic rather than only personal. Whatever one may do on an individual basis should be buttressed with and exist within a structural framework of aid. Social welfare concern manifests itself through encouragement and support of larger-scale programs to aid people in need. This aspect stresses the organization of assistance, in addition to its personalistic modes.

Although such programs may be private and public, a fourth aspect of community helping concern is that typically there is political support to establish and support aid programs. Thus, the role of government typically is expanded when social welfare concern is high. Political means, however, also may include private actions such as union organizing. Even there, however, political legitimacy through "labor-friendly legislation" often is generated to undergird and support organizing efforts.

Fifth, community helping concern is manifest in a general sense of collective responsibility for social conditions rather than a personal or individual responsibility. Such collective responsibility obtains with respect to efforts at remediation, but it also is present with respect to causation. Although community helping concern will not by any means set aside individual responsibility completely, there still is the sense that a variety of forces other than one's own efforts (or lack thereof) account for one's position in life. Such forces may include luck, family connections, providence or talents, and so on. This view naturally decreases the blame that poor people have to endure for their poverty; it also questions the wisdom and special talents that well-to-do people may claim as the cause of—and hence justification for—their wealth.

These five basic points create an axis around which community helping concern rotates. Naturally, questions will be raised about one point or another. Individual readers certainly will have quarrels with a specific point or two. I hope this distillation captures the essence of what is most commonly meant by community helping (or community welfare) concern. I hope it provides a point of reference for discussing belief systems that support community helping concern, as opposed to belief systems that are neutral toward or oppose community helping efforts.[8]

The Catholic Ethic and Community Helping

The Catholic ethic, as I seek to establish, takes a positive stance on these dimensions. In a variety of ways, it is "pro"-community helping. For example, the Catholic ethic contains a well-established and vital tradition of helping orientation that extends back through the medieval period to the very founding of the Catholic Church itself. This orientation no doubt relates to the fact that certainly in its early days, the Catholic Church was the church of disadvantaged and dispossessed people.

On a personal level, members of the community are willing to help each other out. Within the parish, personal help for personal and religious problems is always available.[9] Individual Catholics frequently are in the forefront of providing help to people who are most needy—as Dorothy Day of the Catholic Worker Movement exemplified; so did Katherine Drexel, who gave up her fortune for the education of American Indians and "Negroes" (African Americans).

Catholic social service organizations (Catholic Charities, St. Vincent De Paul, and others) are available to help Catholics and non-Catholics alike. Many parishes have—in addition to the "parish team" (one or more priests and others who help run the parish)—social workers and counselors who come into the parish and are available on a regular basis. Parishes also make collections and provide help to poor people, locally and internationally.

The Catholic ethic also supports organized governmental efforts to provide help—the so-called welfare state. Some of the influences running between Catholicism and the welfare state are reasonably direct.[10] Catholic Charities USA, the national organization of local charities, has supported governmental helping action since the turn of the twentieth century; in many instances, it has taken a leadership role.

Some of the influences are indirect—such as the attitude toward money and work and their place in an individual's life. Other influences are structural. The fact that the Catholic Church is a national and international organization with authoritative lines of power flowing from top to bottom gives it a certain weight and heft that may be missing in the Protestant tradition.

The Catholic ethic supports Catholic social thought and the formal organizations through which social thought is brought to bear on specific parishioners on one hand and, at a strictly organizational level, promulgated through and advocated by church officials directly to policy-makers at local, state, national, and international levels.

In general, the overall beliefs of Catholicism tend to support community helping in the following ways:

- There is and has been a focus on the disadvantaged and their plights as important.
- Concrete help is a part of this focus (from Jesus' activities curing the sick and helping the disadvantaged through St. Vincent De Paul to Catholic Charities USA; there are numerous examples).

- Although there is a sense of the importance of personal efforts, of course, programs, orders, and edicts directed from above to attend to disadvantaged people are accepted and followed.
- There has been more broad support for political means to reach these goals, including endorsements from the pulpit on Sunday.[11]
- Collective and communal responsibility and consideration has been an important element of Catholic history. Union support is one example; housing the homeless and feeding the hungry in churches is another. The list could go on, but the focus of communalism is present and active.

Conclusion

It is reasonable, after all, to think of the Protestant ethic and the Catholic ethic as two ethics, different sides of the same coin—one celebrating the individual and one celebrating the community. Although they have the labels Protestant and Catholic, these labels are current religious connections that have other manifestations in differing contexts. That is why there may be other belief systems that have similar foci that we do not call by these names. Moreover, as I discuss later in this book, each of us has some aspects of each ethic, although we would not necessarily think of ourselves as having two religions.

Caveats aside, there are significant differences in orientations—and these differences matter. I have sketched some of the preliminary differences here; the rest of this volume expands on these central contentions.

CHAPTER 2

The Hidden Ethic

Considering the fact that there are several powerful reasons for a Catholic ethic to exist, why has it not been articulated before? Why has the Protestant ethic remained alone—a sort of solo ethic? How did it corner the religious ethic market?

The answer must be that for some combinations of different but mutually supporting reasons, neither scholars nor Protestants nor Catholics apparently found it advantageous to examine religion-based differences generally or a Catholic ethic in particular. In the United States, at least, other venues were available for discussing differences; I focus on those in a moment. What of European scholars, however? After all, Max Weber was German, and Emile Durkheim was French. Why did they not take the bit and run with it?

Catholic Ethic Taken for Granted in Europe

One reason scholars of all religions might not have noticed a Catholic ethic in Europe is that it was so pervasive. The Protestant ethic concept responds, in a sense, to the "taken for granted" Catholic ethic. In Europe, Catholicism was so pervasive, so historical, that its influence could not be discerned.[1] Catholicism existed more than 1,500 years before the Reformation. Thus, when Weber looked at the European situation, it was the *differences*—which were (relatively) *new*, not what was already there—that formed the key element of his analysis. Hence, Weber ([1906] 1956) had no reason to emphasize Catholicism; the differences of Protestantism were key. For Durkheim (1951), the two religions were important variables, but neither Protestantism nor Catholicism achieved the level of an "ethic." Thus, one reason that no Catholic ethic was articulated was because it did not occur to anyone in Europe, given their background and milieu. It was, perhaps, like water to a fish.

Protestant Ethic Taken for Granted in the United States

Whereas the omnipresence of Catholicism in Europe may have led to its "invisibility," its absence in the United States may have had the same effect. In the United States, Protestantism was the founding doctrine. Although the concept of the "Protestant ethic" did not develop until much later (around the turn of the twentieth century), it must have seemed only to accurately reflect that which "everybody in the United States knew anyway"—namely, that Protestantism was a dominant, pervasive force in America. Even to Americans raised in the twentieth century, with Protestantism and Catholicism as the operative duality, it seems as if there must always have been Protestantism. In the United States, Protestantism was taken for granted. There was no reason to raise the issue of other ethics, especially Catholic and Jewish ethics. The title of Herberg's 1960 book—*Protestant, Catholic, Jew*—reflected "the way we were." Of course Catholic and Jewish influence was present and powerful, but more under the surface. There was still anti-Catholicism and anti-Semitism. Until John F. Kennedy in 1961, we had not had a Catholic president; until Joseph Leiberman in 2000, we had not had a Jewish vice presidential candidate.

Protestant Ethic Seems to Embody—Seems to Have Become—American Values

This thought about the lack of incentives to examine competing ethics can be extended a bit. In many ways, the Protestant ethic—and Protestantism itself—seemed to embody American values toward work and achievement. Stemming from Calvinist traditions, it spoke to getting ahead, of hard work, of individual responsibility—of all the things that seemed to be American values. This link between the Protestant ethic and American values is not surprising. After all, given the course of historical development, Protestant values *were* the founding values of American society. The Protestant worldview had ample time to develop unimpeded. It became almost equal to the American worldview. Entering such a system with a different religion could be construed as being un-American. Raising the possibility of other values might have seemed vaguely disloyal. For this reason, neither nativists (adherents of the nineteenth-century movement favoring native inhabitants) nor newer immigrants (later-arriving Catholics and Jews) would want to risk articulating an ethic which might put them in a more questionable position then they already were in.

Catholics Arrived Late in U.S. Immigration History

Catholic values have played a part, as they do now, in the development of American society. Because Catholics arrived relatively late in U.S. immigration history, however, the battle was an uphill one. White Anglo-Saxon Protestants were the first Europeans to arrive on these shores, and they established a dominant position that endured for almost 200 years. There were always a few Catholics and Jews in America, but they did not arrive in significant numbers until the nineteenth century; hence, calling attention to differences would be, perhaps, best avoided. This attention would be especially difficult if there were differences in values or a variation in emphasis concerning different goals. Differences in timing may have contributed to or augmented the reluctance to examine religion-based differences. These differences required that Catholics challenge the powerful influence of a dominant value system. In addition, Catholic values were not only later arrivals in America; they also differed somewhat from Protestant values in their social implications. These factors might have led American scholars to search for similarities, rather than differences, among religious groups.

Catholics Came to America in Part because of the Protestant Ethic

The foregoing point assumes that Catholic thinkers and scholars would want to articulate the ethic associated with their own religious background. For several reasons, this assumption may be false. One reason is that the immigrants came because of the individualism and freedom that American society—American Protestant society—offered them. That reason was not the only "pull" to encourage Catholic immigration, of course. There were pushes as well: The famine in Ireland (in the mid-nineteenth century) was a significant push. To the extent that Catholics, like all people, have some ambivalence within their own ethos, however, discussing it in the wider society might have been hampered. In some ways, the American Catholic Church would become a "reverse reformation." In the original Reformation, the evils, abuses, and difficulties of unimpeded Catholicism were challenged by Protestantism. The reverse occurred in the United States when Catholicism, tempered by its struggles with Protestantism in Europe, arrived to challenge the dominance of unimpeded Protestantism. The shape of this challenge would take time to develop, however, and would not be articulated as a separate ethic until later.

American Values Emphasized Assimilation and Fitting In

The values that characterized America emphasized a commonality, a oneness, in spite of structural differences and evidence to the contrary (e.g., the status of women, Native Americans, African Americans, and Asian Americans). We proclaimed that "all men are created equal," using language that is (now, though not at the time) supposed to communicate that "men" includes women. After all, this was the melting pot. Why would thinkers articulate differences when commonalities supposedly were valued, even if their own experience did not make those values manifest for them?

Anti-Catholic Prejudice

Furthermore, there was tremendous anti-Catholic prejudice in America in the middle of the nineteenth century.[2] Nativists (i.e., white Protestants who had arrived earlier) recognized the potential of "different values" and sought to oppose and control them. This element is the hostility and rejection that Catholics and Catholicism have encountered in a country that had been dominated by Protestants for more than 200 years. This situation reversed the historical position of Catholicism; one might say that it provided the Catholic Church with another great challenge (one was simply surviving through centuries, while countless other human enterprises came and went; another was the schism with the Orthodox church; and the Reformation was yet another). As recent immigrants, Catholics' religious practices were sharply different from the practices of the dominant Protestant religions as they had developed in the United States. Some of the features that distinguished American Catholicism from the established Protestant communities included ornamented churches, celibate priests (who wore peculiar clothes), ownership of local church property by distant authorities, and extranational allegiance (to Rome), with its potential for disloyalty. Not only were the immigrant Catholics poorer than the so-called "natives"; they also had to face organized nativist opposition, and anti-Catholicism flourished as a political orientation for a considerable time.[3] The Know-Nothing Party was anti-Catholic in orientation. Billington (1964) in *The Protestant Crusade* details many of its activities. In *The Symbolic Crusade* (1963), Gusfield argues that in the 1920s, part of the Prohibition movement may have been an attempt to make newly immigrant—and drinking—Catholics take the morally low ground while native WASPS took the higher (and drier) ground.[4] This issue arose in the 1928 presidential campaign. Al Smith was a mayor (New York), a Catholic, and a Wet (a "wet" was more or less anti-Prohibition or prodrunkenness). His defeat sealed the fate of Catholic presidential nominations until that of John F. Kennedy. Even then, in 1960, there was considerable suspicion of Kennedy's religion and much talk of a "red phone" to the Vatican over which Kennedy would get his "orders." Given that anti-Catholic sentiment existed in abundance, it is understandable that Catholics might adopt a low profile.

Stressing Religious Differences Politically Incorrect in the American Context

Considering our value system—which presumably supported religious freedom—discussing religion-based value systems may not have been culturally appropriate or, in today's argot, politically correct. It might have been more acceptable to talk about ethnic rather than religious divisions. One could speak about Irish Catholics as Irish, Italian Catholics as Italians, and so on, without raising the specter of religion. Although this approach might break down with respect to Germans, who were more evenly divided between Protestants and Catholics, it might have been sufficient for most uses.

Catholics and Protestants alike may have wished to continue this fiction. For Protestants, their interest was not in lionizing Protestantism but in "civil-izing" their religion such that it could be regarded as equal with Americanism itself. Thus transmuted, mainstream Protestantism would not have to be considered a religion. It could simply be regarded as the appropriate American thing to do, be, say, think, or believe. For Catholics—especially for those who hoped to join the melting pot—there is little incentive to call attention to religious differences.

Stressing Religious Differences a Poor Strategy for People Interested in Religious Amalgamation and Healing Christian Schism

There are other reasons to ignore religion-based differences. In a society that values pluralism, and where ecumenism is pursued, it might be more appropriate to stress similarities and commonalties rather than differences and disjunctures. This point is one that Gregory Baum suggests has consumed the brunt of his work (see Appendix A). People who are seeking church union of one kind or another (merger, fusion, reduction of schism) would tend to minimize differences rather then highlight them. Thus, from the point of view of people supporting one Christian church, recognition of differences among churches in general—and a Catholic ethic in particular—might well have been counterproductive.

Anti-Intellectualism in Catholicism Made Catholic Development of Catholic Ethic Less Likely

The authoritative structure of the Catholic Church and its history of clerical "know-it-all-ism" made for a certain anti-intellectualism among Catholics. Although there were pockets of free thinking, convergence with the teachings of the times and with Rome continues as a force in Catholic culture to this day. It is not necessary to document a vigorous hostility to ideas, or even a neutral posture toward them. The pervasive authoritarianism of the church structure (notably under the pontificate of Pius X) created what might be called a "hostile environment" for ideas and supported a "chilling effect" for intellectuals and thinkers. Andrew Greeley, for example, makes clear throughout his sociology and his novels the difficulties of numerous church postures. Thankfully, these strictures (which have been more relaxed since Vatican II) have inspired rather than silenced him. Greeley is unusual, however. Others who might have thought about and articulated a Catholic ethic may have been discouraged.

Catholic Value System Was Value Rich, Not Value Free

Catholic value systems take an embedded, value-recognizing approach to thinking about the world. The Catholic value system—especially the sociological approach to it—was value rich, not value free. Academics talked of a Catholic sociology—hardly a phrase designed to win acceptance in a social science that was making every effort to be objective and value free. Indeed, much of Catholic sociology, where some of these ideas might be explored, focused on the social concern traditionally involved in Catholicism and what I have called the Catholic ethic. Baum comments, "For the Catholic sociologists, the social ethics perspective was defined by the philosophy derived from the Church's social teaching" (1989, 719).[5] The whole point is that articulation of a Catholic ethic would require exploration of themes that raised questions about American values.

Catholicism Believed to be Permeated with "Foreign" Influences

Immigrants to America were expected to renounce their homelands. After all, that was why they left, was it not? Yet Catholics (and, perhaps, Jews as well, although the mechanisms were different) were considered subject to a foreign power in Rome. To some extent, that assessment was true: Roman ecclesiastical authority did influence American Catholics. In *The Americans: The Colonial Experience* (1958), Daniel Boorstin talks about the conflict about who owned church property. American tradition (such as it was in colonial times) suggested that the congregation—those who had contributed to the church and built it—owned the church. In the episode Boorstin recounts, it was revealed that the church itself (Rome) owned church properties. That incident confirmed and reflected "American" (i.e., Protestant) fears that Catholics might never be "American."[6]

The "American" tradition was not only about congregations owing church property; they also appointed the pastors. Again, Catholic practice was different. Local parishes did not appoint their priests (Morris 1997).

"Dark Sides" to Each Ethic

The Catholic ethic and the Protestant ethic each has great strengths. The Catholic ethic supports community and connection and providing a helping hand without a lot of questions. It is an accepting, even tribal or clan-type, belief system. It connects to a worldwide organization of great strength and power.

The Protestant ethic celebrates entrepreneurship and personal responsibility in religion and in life. It supports ambition and contains psychological drivers ("salvation panic") that push the individual. It supports the products of work and the importance of money.

On the other hand, each ethic has downsides. Acceptance dulls achievement; achievement delegitimizes a person's personal worth. Helping is good, but if the emphasis is on the giver (no questions asked) rather than the receiver, that can create problems. Sometimes help does hurt, in that it deprives the recipient of opportunities for growth. Providing help also sometimes sustains the status quo and does not press for more structural answers to questions of need. Moreover, clan cultures remember offenses. Sometimes offenses can be nurtured for years.

The only point here is that every system of social values advances some interests and retards others. Pushing the Catholic ethic may have had the result of exposing some of the problematic aspects it has.

Conclusion

The Catholic ethic—the hidden ethic—has not surfaced for several possibly interconnected reasons. The bottom line seems to be that Protestant values in a sense *became* American values. These values had more than 200 years (from 1620 to approximately 1850) to settle in and develop before Catholics and Jews arrived in any numbers. Catholic and Jewish values certainly have made their mark in the American kaleidoscope of culture in the past 150 years. Much of the support for the "welfare state" comes from that value base. We must bear in mind, however, that those values, even now, have not been here as long as Protestant values had already been here when *they* came. Catholic values stood juxtaposed to Protestant values. Indeed, as I outline in more detail subsequently, those values were at some odds to American values. This difference, added to the other reasons, tended to suppress exploration and explication of the "Catholic value system."

Some more detailed thinking has been suggested in portions of this chapter. This is only a beginning; more work is needed. Sometimes—as in the case of the dog who did not bark—the absence of things is as perplexing, and interesting, as the presence of things.

PART II

Pillars of the Catholic Ethic

The Catholic ethic has several properties that define it and facilitate its helping orientation. Although I do not claim that these features are a complete list of Catholic ethic properties, it would be surprising if more extended studies did not include aspects of each of these elements. These features are as follows:

1. An instrumental attitude toward money
2. An instrumental attitude toward work
3. A strong family orientation
4. "Fault-forgiveness"—acceptance of the natural cycle of fault and forgiveness, sin and redemption
5. Otherworldly orientation
6. An overarching structure that legitimizes dependency and makes it acceptable to approach that structure with problems and to receive sustenance from that structure for those problems.

Each of these features is present in the Protestant ethic as well, but with a different twist. The Protestant ethic has a transformational view toward money and work. It has a strong individualistic orientation. There are either/or tendencies in it (either you are saved or you are not) as opposed to shades of gray. The Protestant ethic has a "this-worldly" orientation and an ecclesiastical structure that emphasizes independence.

If we consider all of these points together, an additional point emerges clearly: Each point affects the others. One might think of it as a rope made up of six strands. Obviously, a considerable amount of attention must be given to unraveling the strands, noting their points of interconnection and the implications of those points.

Thinking of the Catholic ethic (and the Protestant ethic, too, for that matter) as a rope that weaves its way through the years suggests that the period of time one looks at a particular section of rope matters a great deal. The appearance of the rope may not be exactly the same at every point in time because different strands might be thicker (have greater emphasis) at one point in history than another. Even "ethics" get reinvented within their overall framework.

To be operational, however, ethics must be realized as *culture* (a package of beliefs and actions that serve as an operating policy and practice). This realization creates a couple of issues. One is that the practical directions of parts of the ethic are not always completely straightforward, if ever. Consider, for example, "otherworldliness." It could cut two ways. Focus on the otherworld may make it easier to be helpful in this world because status and position in this world per se is less important. On the other hand, the opposite of that argument must be considered as well. If status in this world is less important, why bother helping at all? This tension must be "re-solved" continually.

The second issue is really one of subculture. It involves adaptations to specific locales—the hyphenated-Catholic culture. As I have mentioned already, different groups of Catholics may have different mixtures of the elements of the Catholic ethic. There actually are many Catholicisms rather than one. Spanish, Irish, French, Polish—to say nothing of regional variations within countries—all exist and grow. The Catholic ethic exists nowhere in isolation. All organizations and enterprises are modified by the contexts in which they exist.

American Catholicism, if there is such a thing, grew up in and was subdominant to American Protestantism, if there is such a thing. Catholicism in Europe was a founding religion, more or less, but was tempered by the Reformation and changed irrevocably by it. In contrast, the Catholicism of South America in important respects is pre-Reformation Catholicism, transferred there before Catholicism had been tempered by Protestantism. The same mosaic, then, under different refraction, looks more different still.

Recognizing variations—historical variations in social values, tensions in cultural realizations, and subcultural variations in hyphenated local response—does not gainsay the theme, however. The Catholic ethic—*sui generis*—is worth attention.

CHAPTER 3

Work and the Catholic Ethic: What Work Means

Work is essential to any human community. Food must be gathered and prepared, children must be cared for, shelter must be constructed, and so on. In consumer communities, community members *consume* their work—that is, each worker uses most of what she or he makes; what is "sold" is only the small surplus. Here, "work" as it is commonly understood involves the full range of human tasks. In producer communities, however, workers create only a small fraction of what they need. Almost their entire work product is sold. The money from these exchanges is used to buy other necessities of life. In these communities, "work" is commonly understood to mean something like "the activity you do for 'pay'"; it involves a tiny fraction of human tasks.[1]

In the former case, work has self-evident meaning. People acting produce and consume product. Work is important not only because of its immediate benefit but because it is an integral part of community. In the latter case, the meaning of work is more impersonal—a point sociologist Georg Simmel made about the introduction of money as a medium of exchange. Meaning is more indirect. Work may be more individual and the immediate rewards—daily needs and community—more removed. The difference in the meaning of work is a key difference between the Protestant and Catholic ethics (Poggi 1993).

In part this difference in meaning can be tied to the fact that the Catholic ethic and the Protestant ethic began in different work communities. The Catholic ethic was formed within the producer community, where work was obviously important—you could not live without it, so it did not need special support. Work was a community-sustaining activity.

The Protestant ethic was formed during a period of specialization and differentiation, involving individuals heavily in "new work" (merchants, burghers). Their work was less visible and less traditional. Hence, it required the special emphasis we have come to know as the "work ethic."

Work Orientation of the Catholic Ethic

Work was important in pre-Christian and early Christian history, as well as in all other societies. After all, societal resources are created through work.[2]

The rules of Jewish helping (Hamel, 1990) indicate that a portion of the product of work (part of the orchard, fruits and dates that had fallen, etc.) was to be left for poor people. Collection of alms and taxes indicates that there was surplus to distribute. In the ancient world, however, work was something to be completed or avoided. Princeton University president Harold Shapiro (1982) quotes an old Yiddish proverb about value and importance of work: "A job is fine, but it interferes with your time!" Well-off people worked less, not more, than others. Indeed, one dimension of poverty for them was to lack enough resources for appropriate leisure—leisure involving ceremony, study, and community activities. In other words, there was tension between the values of work and the values of leisure, and leisure had a positive, important social value. In our time, leisure has an ambiguous status, unless we call it "recreation" and its purpose is to make one more fit for work, more efficient at work, and less likely to quit.

Among early Christians, work did not have sacramental status; it was not the way self-worth was indicated or proven, and it may have had social, but not personal, definitional elements. It was a social engine, not a sacred one, and was neither ritualized nor ceremonialized.

One way to think about the Catholic ethic culture of work may be to compare it with bathing. Baths are good. They clean you up. They help you to relax and feel better. They do not, however, bring you closer to God. Baths have not become ritualized in this culture. In some cultures, however, bathing has more meaning. Baptism, however (or ritual baths in other cultures), has ritualistic, transformational, properties.

Think about having a cup of tea. Tea is good. It is refreshing and has healthful properties. In American society, however, drinking tea is not accompanied by ceremony or meaning. In Japan, however, tea has become culturally important, and the place where tea is served, the preparation, the implements, even the clothing has become ritualized. Each element is both itself and other things as well. Much about the way the tea ceremony is conceptualized and performed reveals something about Japanese character.

Bathing and tea-drinking have not been culturally significant among most Americans because social processes have not added meaning to them. They are not inherently different. In certain societies and certain contexts, however, bathing has become ritualized and sacramental.[3] In other settings, so has tea drinking.[4]

In short, the Catholic ethic regards work as ordinary, useful, necessary, and required for most of the reasons already mentioned, but not all of them. Work is not ritualized, however, as it is in the Protestant tradition, and does not have sacred personal and transcendental meaning, nor does it become the *sine qua non* of social acceptance.

Work in the Catholic ethic produces things for your use, but it does not stop there. Work is not for you and you alone. There are two (or three) other consumers: God and the community. In the Catholic tradition, workers, by their labor, also serve God. This point is important because it gives a different meaning to work than the one that characterizes the Protestant "work" ethic. Here, work is a service, not a badge. And everyone who expends energy does work.

God is not the only other consumer, however. The community is a consumer. Work is not simply for your own resource development; it is needed to create something of value. The Catholic ethic takes aim at the "greed" factor—the idea that your interests are the only ones that count. Contributing something useful for today and tomorrow is important. In this sense, the here-and-now community and the community-of-the-future might be considered two different, though obvious linked, consumers.

Although the Catholic ethic does not ignore personal interests, it regards the important elements of community (God's community and the human community now and in the future) as central to a proper understanding of the meaning of work. That is the Catholic version of the work ethic.

Work Orientation of the Protestant Ethic

Perhaps no concept is more closely associated with the Protestant ethic than the idea of work. Sometimes it is even called the Protestant work ethic. Revolutions make the mundane meaningful. Through the concept of the "calling" developed in the Protestant ethic, all work became

God's work. The daily routine of production took on an additional layer
of importance and significance:

> But one thing was unquestionably new: the valuation of the fulfill-
> ment of duty in worldly affairs as the highest form in which moral
> activity of the individual could assume. . . . The only way of living ac-
> ceptably to God was not to surpass worldly morality in monastic as-
> ceticism, but solely through the obligations imposed on the individ-
> ual by his position in the world. That was his calling (Weber [1906]
> 1956, 80).[5]
>
> *The effect of the Reformation as such was that, as compared to the*
> *Catholic attitude, the moral emphasis on and the religious sanction of*
> *organized, worldly labor in a calling was mightily increased* (Weber
> [1906] 1956, 83; emphasis added).

Work became a sacred calling and became ritualized. Trivial or unpleasant tasks may not be work that anyone wants to do, but it is much
more meaningful if it is part of your spiritual calling and follows a ritual.

Yet a prowork attitude may well get out of hand and become
all-consuming (or mostly consuming). Work has a sacred value and is regarded as useful not only because of its link to income but because to
the extent that work represents effort and application, it has a value in
and of itself. "Idle hands are the devil's workshop" would be an appropriate phrase to associate with the Protestant ethic. On a more mundane
note, one might say, "Happy day is busy day."

Work also has symbolic and indicative benefits that reflect on the
worker's morality. It becomes a proxy for righteousness; the phrase,
"She is a hard worker" carries the full force of moral righteousness and
justification in a Protestant ethic tradition. Saying that is the same as
saying, "She is a good person." Conversely, of course, "An idle mind is
the devil's workshop!"

Salvation through Works/Salvation through Work

In the Catholic work ethic, work was useful in many ways and for many
things. There, however, work and "good works" were closely related.
Whereas "work" (activities in your occupation) had nothing specific to
do with your salvation, "good works" (helping work) could and often
did earn salvation credits. It was part of the God-as-bookkeeper model
of the salvation economy. Good works were one way that you could

gain a leg up on salvation. In the Catholic ethic, "good works" have positive salvation value. Because one's salvation status is not fixed, one can earn salvation credits through good behavior, helping works, and good works. There were other ways as well: Acting out the sacraments and saying prayers also were to your credit.

In the Protestant ethic, good works are supported and encouraged, but they have no salvation value as such. The Protestant Reformation did away with the ledger theology of the medieval Catholic Church, in which salvation status (called states of grace or states of sin) depended on the balance of the sins recently committed counted against the amount of celestial credit one had stored up and the amount of celestial credit one could amass through personal prayers, the prayers of others, and indulgences (earned or purchased).

Catholic Ethic Work Orientation and the Spirit of Community

What does this difference mean in terms of the spirit of community? In the Catholic ethic tradition, work is important because it has positive functions. The kind of work or the success in work is not an indicator of anything especially positive about you as a person. Work is not a litmus test for good intentions, either. Furthermore, one does not let work *interfere* with community—meeting and socializing with friends, for example. Work is a support of community, not your community. You get work through friends, rather than friends through work.

In the Protestant ethic tradition, you *are* what your work produces. You are entitled to keep your work product and acquire more. Work also is regarded as a test of moral character, as well as the vehicle through which income is provided.

Failure to work—being unemployed—becomes, to some extent, a moral failure and open to moral examination and moral criticism.[6] Seeking work becomes an important moral test.

Catholic Ethic Work Orientation and the Helping Impetus

Work also has implications for community helping. In the Catholic ethic, the less-emotional attention to work makes helping easier. St. Francis expressed this perspective well: "Everyone deserves a share."

Although individual motivation for work is a factor, in discussions of poverty much attention also is given to structural reasons for joblessness, such as structural unemployment, volatile labor markets, or disability. The Catholic ethic supports workers' rights to earn living wages, to organize, and to share in what the earth has to offer (Henriot, DeBerri, and Schultheis, 1990). It regards work as a process to produce wages and questions the acceptance of huge differences in access to resources. The Catholic ethic does not see a sacred link between work and holiness. Hence, demanding that work produce higher wages is not subverting a sacred liturgy; it is simply doing the obvious.

From the Protestant ethic perspective, work is the means to help yourself. If you do not work, perhaps you should not eat. The fear is that supporting people in need might encourage dependency and undermine the sacred value of work.

Conclusion

There are, then, two approaches to the meaning and purpose of work. The Catholic ethic regards work as "ceremonial," secular, transactional, and instrumental. Work is considered good, to be sure, but primarily because *people do it*. It occupies time. It provides things to do during the day. It provides income. It helps you meet people and creates a social setting. Work is community based.

The Protestant ethic regards work as "ritualized," sacred, transformational, and transcendental.[7] All work becomes God's work, ennobled through the concept of the calling. It thus becomes a moral vehicle through which you are judged as a person.

CHAPTER 4

Money and the Catholic Ethic: What Money Buys

"Money! . . . Money Money Money Money Money Money Money."[1] Money is such an explosive topic. It has an almost sacred theme in American culture (and, to some extent, worldwide). Asking how much money one makes or has is one of the "no-nos" in regular conversation because, of course, it is more than a resource question. Survey researchers know always to put the income question last in questionnaire administration. Apparently people will share family secrets, sexual practices, and illegal acts they have committed but frequently balk on sharing their salary.[2] It seems as if by talking about money one would reveal one's inner value—or the lack thereof. Indeed, the double meaning of the financial planner's question, "What are you worth?" nicely sets up the relationship between cash value and moral value. The question, of course, refers to net financial worth, but other meanings of the word *worth* include ideas such as caliber, excellence, merit, quality, stature, and value.

This discussion refers, essentially, to the high end of the scale. What of the bottom end—of poverty? Today, poverty is an especially hot topic. We are counting poor people, seeing how many there are, and whether they are women, children, ill, and so forth. Mostly we use a financial level for poverty; in the main, when discussions of "the poor" come up, deficits of money are the indicator of selection. There can be other kinds of deficits, however; the word *poor* also has multiple connotations. A second kind of deficit has to do with being in a sad, pitiable condition. If one says, "The poor soul!" one is expressing pity. Finally, there is the implication of low quality. "A poor job" refers to something that is badly done; "a poor product" refers to an item that is not well made.

Wealth and poverty, then—both of which have to do with money— also have to do with value. The very language we use to discuss wealth/ poverty/money is bonded to implications of moral stature. The Catholic

ethic and the Protestant ethic take different approaches to these connections in general and the meaning of money in particular. These different approaches to thinking about money/wealth/poverty create important differences in how one thinks about the relief of poverty and the
sense one has about the use of money as a central instrument in that
relief.

Money Orientation of the Catholic Ethic

In the history of Christianity, there has been a suspicious, tentative attitude toward money and wealth. Money was recognized as good, but its
paramount value was questioned. "In Israel, there was a firm tradition
that God was a protector of the poor. God does not show favoritism toward the rich" (Meeks 1986, 71). Jesus suggested to His disciples that
they give up their possessions and follow Him—and they apparently
did. Biblical injunctions to be a Good Samaritan and stressing the difficulty of a rich man getting into the Kingdom of Heaven also are part of
ancient wisdom as well as common folklore today.[3]

Money and wealth, in short, were not sacred or regarded as special
categories of property or attribute. This view was not distinctly Christian. Christianity absorbed and continued other traditions, adding new
elements only occasionally.

The key point is that, in the Catholic ethic, money never became
symbolized as anything but a means to an end—namely, provision for
human need. It did not signify anything except the ability to provide
daily bread. Money used as a product to produce more money (usury)
was frowned upon. If one were well-to-do, questions about the sources
and uses of money arose, perhaps because there was a social and personal ethos with respect to wealth, including money. One could use it,
but one also had a responsibility to use it for the good of the community
to some extent. There was a sort of dual demand on wealth—one's own
right to it and the obligation to use it as a community trustee.[4]

In sum, wealth/money is *a means to an end; wealth is part personal,
part communitarian; and poverty is not a great state to be in, but not
shameful either.* These are the key points that reflect the Catholic ethic
attitude toward money. Money does not transform one's status from un-
acceptable to acceptable because money is not a dimension along which
acceptability is measured. Money and wealth have no symbolic, transformational, or proxy powers. Wealth is like other measurable attri-
butes: age, weight, and bowling score. It may be better to be younger,
slimmer, and have a higher bowling score, but whatever the values we

attach to those measures, they don't reveal a person's value, inner character or nature, or proximity to God.

Over time, however, money becomes an issue. Catholics who are wealthy are not entirely comfortable with wealth. One example of this uneasiness is contained in a series of lecture and workshop notes by Father John C. Haughey, called *Virtue and Affluence: The Challenge of Wealth* (1997). The workshop was for Christians, not just Catholics, although Haughey is a religious order priest (Jesuit). "I had never had to worry about money, having promised at the ripe old age of nineteen a perpetual vow of poverty—to own nothing" (1997, vi). Haughey's view, which comes through loud and clear in the text, is what I consider the Catholic view to be: Money is to do things with; for wealthy people, *that* is the measure of one's soul. Having money means little in and of itself. "What is the purpose of the abundance of grain? It is the same as the purpose of all financial and material bounty—that all may share in it!" (Haughey 1997, 20). It could not have been said more eloquently.

Money Orientation of the Protestant Ethic

The foregoing view is distinct from the Protestant ethic view, which tends to regard money and wealth as indicative of inner election and thus sacred status. In the Protestant ethic, money is good, but more than simply good—money is symbolically good.[5] Having money means success, and success is a proxy for God's favor, evidence of being among the elect. In a perspective that celebrates "wealth-fare," "wel-fare" obviously is problematic. Where money is a central symbolic resource, providing money to others carries many more burdens, questions, problems, and difficulties than it would if money had a different social standing.[6]

The Reverend William Lawrence captures the Protestant ethic view well: "In the long run, it is only to the man of morality that wealth comes," and "Godliness leads to fortune" (1948, 69). As Weber says:

> In fact, the *summun bonum* of this ethic, [is] the earning of more and more money. . . . It is thought of so purely as an end in itself that from the point of view of the happiness of, or the utility to the single individual it appears entirely transcendental. . . . Man is dominated by the making of money, by acquisition as the ultimate purpose of his life ([1906] 1956, 53).

There were four specific religious movements in America—the so-called New Thought movements—that emphasized secular success. Lawrence's candidates are the Unity School of Christianity, the work of Ralph Waldo Trine (and his book *In Tune with the Infinite, or, Fullness of Peace, Power, and Plenty*, 1910), the Mormons, and the work of Edward Bellamy and his utopian novel, *Looking Backward: 2000–1887: Or, Life in the Year AD 2000* (1900). This list, of course, does not count Russell Conwell's *Acres of Diamonds* (1915), which celebrated the availability of cash in the backyard of "everyman."

The key concept is predestination, which creates salvation panic. A person's character is inexorably, indelibly, elect or nonelect. Because God is infinite, God's judgments are infinite. The individual therefore cannot alter her or his celestial destiny, but one can find out what one's celestial status *is*. Inner character is revealed through outer success. As Haughey says, "It turns out that the personal identity of the wealthy is forged much more directly and intimately from their wealth than is the case with the rest of the population" (Haughey 1997, 2). (See also Schervish, Coutsoukis, and Lewis 1994).[7]

Catholic Ethic Money Orientation and the Spirit of Community

Within the Catholic ethic, money is a community resource as well as a personal resource. It supports schools, the parish, missions, and "charities." It is not only yours. To a certain extent, you are a trustee of those resources.

Money does not separate its trustee from the community, either. The community is made up of people who have more and people who have less. More and less are features of community membership. Community comes first. There is not one community of people who have money and another community of people who do not. Acceptance in the community does not depend on possessing wealth. Moreover, because community acceptance is based on being a good community member, rich or less rich, personal acceptance (sense of self worth, self esteem) is similarly non–wealth-driven. Richer people are not better people.

Catholic Ethic Money Orientation and the Helping Impetus

The Catholic ethic money culture makes providing help for people in need a relatively ordinary, uncomplicated task. There are two basic reasons for this relaxed attitude. One is that needing help within a Catholic ethic community is simply being a part of that community. Needing help does not stigmatize you. The other reason is that providing money is not fraught with symbolism.

Needing money is not bad. It may happen to any of us at any time. Hence being "poor" is not symbolically problematic; it is just like breaking your arm. Your arm is injured; you need help until it gets better. You do not have to be a "worthy poor person" to get help.

The Catholic ethic money culture also makes it easier to provide alms and cash because the vehicle for assistance has no symbolic value. Hamel says, "It has not been possible to show that Christian helping was different in nature from other forms of social aid" (1990, 240). In golf, for example, people who do less well receive a handicap—a score adjustment that enables them to compete equally with players of varying skills. No one objects to a handicap; in fact, it was devised to enhance competition. That competition, however—with its winners, losers, and point spread—does not indicate anything about a person's inner character or sacred status. The same argument for a handicap could be made for helping; in a sense, the Catholic ethic attitude toward money is similar to the attitude toward handicaps in golf. Because money is not a fetish, one is not giving away anything *more* than money, and the loss of a little money is not a big deal. In a sense, then, the attitude toward money speaks not to the views of the recipient (attitude of altruism) or to the helping acts (tradition of helping) but to the *medium of helping.*

Perhaps the best place to begin a brief examination of this question is to speculate about why money became an instrumental object, rather than a sacred one, in the Catholic ethic tradition. One reason may be because the tradition began in a noncash economy, in which other goods were considered sacred. Bread and wine—staples of life—became symbolized and were elevated to sacred status. Although money existed, and coin of the realm was passed, it did not have the universality that some goods did. Jesus, after all, did drive moneychangers from the Temple.

In addition, there was an arm's-length attitude toward goods themselves. The invitation of Jesus to His followers to leave their goods behind is an example.

Hamel talks about early conceptions of poverty and helping as encompassing many of the foregoing points:

Various situations of poverty existed in Roman Palestine and in the rest of the Roman Empire. There were two broad categories for which our words "poverty" and "indigence" are approximations. The wider category included those with some income, but without the means, especially leisure, necessary for such social activities as entertaining, education, and political and religious service. . . . The narrower category included all who had lost this minimal degree of security and were dependent for their food, clothing, and lodging on organized helping and the evocation of feelings of pity (Hamel 1990, 239).

Alms, then, were a key kind of aid, and they often—perhaps mostly— were in-kind. Money did not really become a factor until the "monetization of poverty" in the Middle Ages. "The mendicants set forth the idea of sanctification through cash expenditures. . . . The monetization of alms marks a new stage, not only in the economic development of helping but also in its moral and social aspects" (Mollat 1986, 155–56). Of course the mendicants were working more in urban areas, and money had many advantages: It gave poor people who received cash alms some freedom of choice and allowed for some degree of secret almsgiving.

Finally, over time, the church developed a negative view toward certain aspects of money itself. For example, it condemned usury.

The development of a money economy—the monetization of alms that Mollat (1986) cites as part of the monetization of everything—occurred when money became a "store of value." As things become important in the world, they usually attract the attention of important institutions—and the growth of a money economy stirred interest in the Catholic Church. The fact that the church questioned money (a dominant ethos) and that it also was a store of value (a subdominant ethos) created a need and an opportunity for the Protestant ethic. Money was there, it was important, and it had been rejected by the dominant ethos of the times. Where could a new ethic find a better medium? Transformational changes often emphasize what has been underemphasized or even cast aside—the cornerstone from the stone the builders rejected—and that might be, in part, what happened in this case.

Conclusion

The Catholic ethic view of money, then, is ambivalent to suspicious. Money is good, as a lot of things are good. Having it does not make you good, better, or best, however; not having it does not make you bad, worse, or worst. Money is a tool, not a transformer.

Money is not a signal, either. It is not a proxy; it is not a scorecard in the game of life—either this life or the next. Money, in the Catholic ethic tradition, is like a bowling score. A bowling score measures success *at bowling*. It would never be considered to indicate moral character. Being a better bowler has nothing to do with being a better person; neither does being richer mean you are a better person. In the Catholic ethic tradition, money, like work, is a tool to provide necessary goods and services. It is not, however, a signal or sign of divine interest. Some people do well financially; others do less well. That is just one of the many dimensions along which folks differ, however. Furthermore, members of religious orders often take vows of poverty along with other vows. Such vows are not required in all orders and do not necessarily apply to the church itself. A high salary indicates nothing more than a high bowling score does: A high salary indicates success at a job; a high bowling score indicates success at bowling. In a Catholic ethic framework, neither case suggests celestial favor. There are other, more concrete routes to such favor.

This chapter outlines the central elements of the Catholic orientation toward money: its instrumental, not symbolic, value makes it more possible to provide help with money. The "dole" has no ominous significance. If help is needed, help is given. The result of this ordinary view of money may have been what first attracted the attention of Max Weber.

Because money is only instrumental in value, using it to help others is not only a minimal problem; it really is the right thing to do. You may need similar help one day yourself: Help is a kind of social investment.

CHAPTER 5

Family and the Catholic Ethic: All in the Family

The Catholic ethic tradition stresses the importance of family. This emphasis is an important part of the spirit of community. This orientation makes individual achievement more difficult because of the separation from family that achievement often implies. Because of this commitment to family, however, community-based helping to families is made easier. Community help to families is more palatable in the Catholic ethic tradition because of its commitment to family.

Family Orientation of the Catholic Ethic

The ensemble self approach that I mention in chapter 1 is a fulcrum around which the Catholic ethic family orientation is constructed. Within the Catholic ethic, one's very self-concept is formed within a cauldron of "the other." From the parishioner's family to the Holy Family and back again, the family, not the person, is the unit of community.

The well-known Catholic priest, novelist, and sociologist Andrew Greeley has talked often about the importance of the Catholic family, in his novels and his scholarly work. In fact, a central theme of Greeley's novels is Catholic families and their workings.

Family connection can be oppressive as well as helpful, however. It often is used to justify foolish sharing of resources or tolerance of abuse. Greeley writes of a son who is visiting his family on Christmas vacation:

> The priest received a call from a parishioner, whose oldest son, home from first year at an Ivy League law school, had brought a girlfriend home without warning. The woman was five years older than their son, did not wash or use deodorant, was foul-mouthed, in-

sulted the other children, and smoked marijuana. "You should not put up with this behavior," the priest said. "But he's our son!" the father replies (1991a, 280–81).

Greeley takes the family context as the natural, obvious center of action and activity. Others do as well. Msgr. Joseph Gremillion, who has long been involved in peace and justice activities, comments:

Vatican II strongly reaffirms a—perhaps the—basic tenet of Catholic social teaching: The family is the foundation of society. In it the various generations come together and help one another to grow wise and harmonize personal rights with the other requirements of social life. All those, therefore, who exercise influence over communities and social groups should work efficiently for the welfare of marriage and the family (1976, 111).

Several positions that the Catholic Church has taken—though vigorously opposed by many Catholics and non-Catholics—tend to support the family emphasis. Although most religions encourage members to marry within the group, the Catholic position on divorce—despite its widespread flouting among Catholics—remains steadfast in favor of families staying together. Although many otherwise devout Catholics ignore the church's official views on abortion and birth control, these views reflect a strong emphasis on family over individuals.[1] Although the hierarchy's opposition to female priests and women's issues generally reveal one of the oppressive sides to a strong traditionalistic family orientation,[2] the Catholic tradition is profamily, even at the cost of great unhappiness to individual family members. This point is made by Charles Morris in his wonderful *American Catholic* (1997). The position of the church makes sense if one steps away from the standard "conservative" and "liberal" packages.

The Catholic view, then, is "traditional" if traditional means the superiority of men and subdominance—or, as some people might say, subjugation and exploitation—of women. Support for the family has not been extended to include acceptance of new types of families, including unmarried couples, merged families, and gay and lesbian couples. Within its traditional context, however, the Catholic ethic's support for helping and the welfare state, for family allowances and children's support, is consistent with its devotional practices and beliefs. Nadler emphasizes the other side of help-giving and stresses the importance of help-seeking behavior: "[H]elp seeking is a culturally determined phenomenon, *which is affected by the degrees to which a sociocultural system emphasizes competitive or cooperative values"* (1986, 980). Nadler raises a point about the attitude of altruism that I have not discussed—the "other side of altruism," as it were. For every giver, there must be a receiver. Within the Catholic ethic tradition, receiving help is acceptable, just as it is within the Jewish ethic tradition. Within the Protestant ethic tradition, however, accepting help may and probably does engender stigma and scorn.

Individualistic Orientation of the Protestant Ethic

In contrast to the family orientation of the Catholic ethic, the Protestant ethic is individualistic, reflecting the personalization of the religious experience. "The concentration was on the individual self and its experience. The sense of sin was sharply personalized: *It is I who am the lost soul, sinful and defiled, in need of cleansing and renewal"* (Welch 1972, vol. 1, 28; emphasis added).

The functions of individualism and its enhancement within the Protestant ethic generally were positive. After all, acquiring and amassing resources requires one to take some resources from other members of the family or community. In a competitive environment, a guilt-free approach to competition surely was a plus.

On the other hand, this perspective supports the kind of individualism that allows exploitation of others and provides barriers against sharing. Ryan (1981) calls this kind of belief system "counterfeit equality"—meaning that the community, even the family, may lay no legitimate claims on an individual's resources. There is neither a sense of communal resources nor any obligation to share resources with others except through individual philanthropy.

The individualism of Protestantism and the Protestant ethic would find itself at home in a system that was comfortable with the "each tub sits on its own bottom" approach. Its family orientation might be sketched by Robert Frost's expression: "Home is the place where, when you go there, they have got to take you in!" (1971, 156).[3]

Catholic Ethic Family Orientation and the Spirit of Community

An emphasis on the ensemble or the family group leads naturally to groups of families—communities. The reverse also is true. Emphasis on the community finds more focused intimate expression in the family context. Family extends through generations and gradually includes members of the church congregation, ethnic group, local neighborhood, and larger community. Family and community become interconnected in ways that emphasize the bridges, not the fences.

As much as we might think of family orientation as obvious, it was not always thus. Support for "the family" was uncertain in the Greek and Jewish traditions. Hamel comments on the lack of attention given to children in some periods: "Little children, especially daughters, hardly appear in the sources. Jewish marriage contracts did occasionally stipulate that the husband was to provide care for his daughters, *whose right to maintenance was not clearly established.* . . . Children are rarely mentioned in Greek marriage contracts and inheritance clauses that come from other areas of the Mediterranean" (Hamel 1990, 41; emphasis added). Perhaps the weak emphasis on family in other traditions led the Christian community to become, in a way, a family. Meeks speaks of the "unusual emphasis on solidarity and intimacy of Christian fellowship":

> The rhetoric of this letter [St. Paul's] is so composed as to arouse the affection of the readers for one another, and for Christian groups in other places, with whom and with which they have had some direct or indirect connection. . . . More than a metaphor is involved here, for the Christians are evidently expected to cherish fellow members of the sect with the same care as they would natural siblings . . . (1986, 129).

This tradition of family/community solidarity grew over the years and has maintained itself with vigor to the present day. This is the tradition that Greeley evokes and invokes. Clearly, part of what appeals to readers of Greeley's novels is their evocation of the familial context of the Catholic parish in American ethnic communities. One can almost feel the sense of solidarity emanating from the pages of his books. It is the same feeling that Chaim Potok captures with regard to Hassidic and other Jewish communities in his novels (e.g., *The Chosen,* 1967) and that the series of mystery novels by Harry Kemelman (e.g., *Friday the Rabbi Slept Late,* 1964) evokes as well. The sense of solidarity and loyalty in the Italian families portrayed in the *Godfather* series reveals another facet of the emphasis on family. (The Mafia itself also is known as "the Family.")

It is this "community sense" that is often meant when one speaks of the Irish Catholic community, German Catholic community, Polish Catholic community, Italian Catholic community, and so on. The fact that the members of the group and people who are not members speak of these groups as if they were communities helps to make them communities and reflects the recognition that, to a considerable extent, they already are communities.

Catholic Ethic Family Orientation and the Helping Impetus

An emphasis on the importance of family and community over the individual is more likely to be pro-helping for several reasons. Most important, family orientation relies on a context of connection, and connection implies and is based on help.[4] In the Catholic ethic tradition, the individual, the family, and the community are parts of an integral whole, or mosaic. Family members support each other—which is one reason why families and communities might have been formed in the first place.

In "ideal" families, husbands and wives (or partners) meet each others' emotional and sexual needs in a secure context in which trust is present and vulnerabilities can be shared. Moreover (perhaps somewhat less now than before), grown children support older parents, who in turn pass on family resources. Because the family is where most individuals gain experience in giving and receiving care, an orientation that emphasizes the importance of family also supports the giving and receiving of aid. Indeed, as Harry Murray points out in his discussion of the Catholic Worker movement, socialization in the family was actual preparation for social responsibilities: "What the Catholic Worker position implicitly argues is that any member of society is capable of performing many of the tasks now claimed by various professions simply by virtue of being socialized" (1990, 5).

An emphasis on family also supports the importance of aid itself. Indeed, giving and receiving aid between relatives is not extraordinary. The concept of aid is inherent in the concept of family. Aid is considered a gift that is provided out of affection and a desire to help; it emerges out of a concern for connection and closeness, rather than a calculus of exchange.

Family orientation is not always positive. However, an emphasis on the importance of connection as opposed to an emphasis on the importance of personal sovereignty distinguishes it from other orientations. Helping others and receiving help from them is a natural element of the family orientation

The helping that occurs in the family extends into the community in the natural course of events. The Catholic ethic tradition and sense of family and community it endorses does not encourage an adversarial relationship between nonpoor people and poor people.[5] Because family and community are inclusive, sympathy and help for others is more likely.[6] The hospitality houses developed and maintained by the Catholic Worker movement are one example of community-oriented helping offered within the family context of a house where the helpers live.

Family and community helping are not problem-free, as each of us knows from our own experience. Help is hard to give. There is a story about two mothers watching the child of one try to tie his shoe. He could not do it and started to howl in frustration. The other mom spoke crossly and said, "For heaven's sake, why don't you help him?" "I *am* helping him," the child's mother replied. Murray (1990) points out in his work on Catholic hospitality houses that he was chagrined to find that even among the helpers—motivated by the best intentions—there were conflicts and contentions.

As helping expanded, it moved from the practices of helping—which were done in the community—to the policies of helping. Again, a documentary analysis supports an emphasis on helping within a family context. In Coleman's 1991 collection, *One Hundred Years of Catholic Social Thought,* one of four parts (one-quarter of the book) is about the family.

Conclusion

The Catholic ethic, then, is a family ethic. To be sure, the family it envisions is the "traditional" family.[7] Family extends to community, and helping each other is a part of the warp and woof of the family/community exchange. This orientation makes individual achievement more difficult because of the separation from family that it implies and perhaps requires.

Family is not all positive, of course—though, as I suggest, it sounds odd to point a finger at "family values." To the extent that family commitments do blunt entrepreneurship and the need for individual achievement, those commitments may have problematic aspects. To the extent that, in its traditionalism, the family fails to support the accomplishments and aspirations of both genders, it may be problematic. Family can be clannish if overdone: Acceptance is rich for the in-group and nonexistent for others.

These potential problems notwithstanding, a family orientation is a rich tradition. It provides support and helping. It may not be the place that, when you go there, they have to let you in; it may be the place you wish to go because it is warm and welcoming.

CHAPTER 6

Fault-Forgiveness and the Catholic Ethic: I'm OK, You're OK

One of the historical differences between the Catholic ethic and Protestant ethic approaches to the world had to do with the nature of sin and the way in which sin can be removed. Sin happened, of course, and it mattered because it affected one's salvation status.

The question hinged on what, if anything, one could do about it. The Catholic approach had emphasized that humans had and did sin but that we had some ways of removing the stain of sin from our souls. Pushed to extremes, of course—as may well have happened just before the Reformation—was the "commercialization" of salvation status in crude ways, particularly through the purchase of indulgences.[1]

The Protestant view—initiated by Luther—rejected this approach, arguing that humans could be saved by grace alone and that grace was a gift from God. Journalist Gustav Neibuhr puts it this way:

> Luther, a German monk born in 1483, became convinced that salvation was a divine gift that humans could not earn. Declaring he felt "reborn" by this realization, Luther also became fiercely critical of the medieval church's practice of selling "indulgences," by which believers understood they could purchase a divine remission for sins. In 1517 he nailed his criticisms to a church door in Wittenburg, Germany, a gesture considered to be the opening shot of the Reformation (Neibuhr 1998, A1).

Although the doctrinal issues of salvation by works or grace have now reached a level of accommodation, the values underlying each perspective continue to remain distinct. I call the Catholic ethic view "fault forgiveness"; I call the Protestant ethic view "fault acceptance."

I add the word "fault" because it goes a step further than sin, as it were, and addresses the issue of responsibility. This issue remains at the core of an ongoing dispute between Catholics and Lutherans:

The most important [difference] according to the document is the Lutheran belief that a person can both be forgiven by God and still be a sinner. Catholics believe that a person, once forgiven, has an inclination to sin but is not permanently a sinner in God's eyes (Neibuhr 1998, A1).

This emphasis on fault, and the permanence of responsibility, is a cleavage between the two ethics.

Fault-Forgiveness Culture of the Catholic Ethic

The Catholic ethic accepts a cycle of sin and redemption. Without supporting sin, it recognizes that sin will occur and that individuals may fall into sin and may come out of sin. The Catholic ethic tradition recognizes that good people stray and believes that absolution should be available to them. If to recognize sin is to accept it, then there is a degree of acceptance of sin in Catholicism.[2] Catholics believe, however, that sin—or evil—is at work in the world, fighting with good. Despite their belief that the outcome is certain (good [God] wins), Catholics believe that the struggle against evil continues in this world and that in some people and in some settings, evil and sin are stronger than good influences.[3]

Hence, there is a cyclical element in fault and forgiveness. The second difference is indicated by the specific, institutional mechanisms available to make the transition from a sinful, fault-filled state into a "graceful," sin-free, fault-free state.[4] Catholics can avail themselves of the Sacrament of Reconciliation (historically referred to as confession), which purges the soul of sin—literally making it all clean and brand new again.

On a day-to-day basis, the Catholic ethic tradition recognizes that sinners will need to be forgiven, will probably sin again, and will need to be forgiven again. This formula is one illustration of the Catholic ethic tradition's concept of the changeable, developmental character of the soul, rather than its inexorable nature. Catholics regard the soul as a tally of the battle between good and evil fought in each individual. At every moment in the Catholic world, some individuals' souls are being darkened by sin while others' are being cleansed by grace. This view of the soul does not make sharp distinctions between sinners and other believers.[5]

A quote from one modern Catholic, former Chrysler chairman Lee Iacocca, illustrates the point. Speaking of the possibility that Chrysler had gotten off track, Iacocca said, "If we went astray—you know people do go astray now and then in many areas—man, we got focused in a hurry." The headline of the article, which ran on the front page of the *Wall Street Journal,* read "With Chrysler Ailing, Lee Iacocca Concedes Mistakes in Managing: 'I'm Confessing My Sins Here'" (Ingrassia and Stertz 1990, 1). Iacocca's remark expresses one of the fundamental characteristics of the Catholic ethic tradition: a belief that sin is something that happens—and something that can be fixed. That Iacocca mentions it in an interview suggests that he expects others to recognize it as well.

Mechanisms of Redemption

Given that sin is widespread and that help mechanisms are necessary, what forms shall they take? Catholicism has well-established mechanisms to absolve sinners, practiced in the sacrament of penance/reconciliation—now the sacrament of reconciliation. Although this sacrament has taken various forms over the years, penance/reconciliation/reconciliation essentially involves confession and absolution—a process in which a priest is a central figure.[6] Iacocca's use of the phrase "I'm confessing my sins here" reveals the emphasis Catholics place on coming clean. For absolution to work, sincere remorse, prayer, and an effort to make things right generally are crucial.[7]

The penance/reconciliation system employed by Catholics includes several interrelated elements.

1. Penance/reconciliation is open to and needed by everyone; we all need help of one kind or another.
2. The sinner and his or her statements are accepted as genuine at face value; it is the requirement of true repentance by the sinner. If repentance is not genuine, forgiveness will not occur, ritual notwithstanding. The practice of penance/reconciliation assumes that sinners are sorry, however; they are not required to prove it. This acceptance of people at face value extends to questions about whether individuals are worthy of help: The help of the confessional is available to anyone who comes. Thus, distinctions between people who are "worthy" of help and those who are "not worthy" of help become irrelevant. Need is need.[8]
3. A significant feature of penance/reconciliation in the Catholic tradition is atonement: Something must be done to undo the consequences of sin to secure forgiveness. Although prayer is one element of atonement generally mandated by the confessor (six "Our Fathers ... "), parishioners usually are advised to take steps

to relieve the suffering their sins may have caused. Although they cannot undo the bad, they can make bad better.[9] Helping to make "bad" better creates a connection between the spiritual world and the temporal world.

4. Catholic religious practices include mechanisms that provide other than spiritual relief.[10] Penance/reconciliation among Catholics often mixes spiritual and personal problems. The confessional often is a place where personal weaknesses are considered in their social impact; anger, despair, and other mental states are considered as occasions of sin. Confessions often combine absolution for sins and pastoral counseling for personal problems, and Catholics have become accustomed to receiving practical help with problems along with spiritual guidance.[11] Over the centuries, priests often have been better educated than their parishioners.

The Confessional Exchange

In addition to the spiritual benefits of the confessional exchange, ritual also generates some structural consequences of importance.[12]

Legitimacy of the Helping Process

One consequence of the ritual of confessional exchange is that it legitimates the helping process. Whether the help needed is sacred, secular, or some combination may be secondary to the "metamessage" of the process. The sacrament of penance/reconciliation makes it acceptable for good people to get help—which makes it acceptable for good people to have problems with which they need help:

> As any Catholic Priest will bear witness, the confessional is a place to which many penitents carry more than their sins; they frequently bring their personal and domestic problems. Thus the reception of the sacrament of penance afforded a natural channel for guidance and direction (Ellis 1969, 59–60).

Universalism

An additional influential feature of the sacrament of penance/reconciliation is its universal application, encompassing all believers: All need it; no one is exempt. Even after discarding the narrow, immature construction of "sin" ("I failed to pray yesterday") maintained in the popular media—which few people would consider a reasonable approach today—most Catholics still believe that all individuals are prone to sin and that grace is something everyone needs. Thus, strict distinctions between the "needy" and the "nonneedy" are avoided.

Social Context of Sin Matters

Third, Catholics often consider sin in light of its "social" aspect, in which the treatment of others is the instance and perhaps the measure of sin.[13] Pride, anger, envy, covetousness, and other sins are defined by how they affect an individual's relations with others—an emphasis that stresses the hurt sinners cause. Such an emphasis also builds sympathy for others by building sympathy for the victims of the consequences of sin.

Make it Right

Penance/reconciliation also requires penitents to provide actual help to others to undo the consequences of sin. This focus on reconciliation not only stresses the act of helping, reinforcing its importance; it also stresses atonement as a process as well as an act.

Interpersonal

Another structural characteristic of the Catholic confessional process is that it is interpersonal, rather than intrapersonal. Although the process of penance/reconciliation typically involves helping others, it also includes the penitent's experience of receiving help from others. This dynamic further amplifies the changing roles individuals play in the Catholic tradition, from beneficiary to benefactor, from sinner to saint.

Finally, the confessional exchange provides a model for the secular counseling relationship. Psychiatrists, psychologists, social workers, and other counselors use similar techniques and many use some version of the fifty-minute hour (Linder 1954). Although the rituals of these helping professions are mostly devoid of sacred elements, they share with the sacrament of penance/reconciliation an underlying process of sharing fears and concerns and receiving support and advice.

Fault-Accepting Culture of the Protestant Ethic

The Protestant ethic—no doubt partly in response to the commercialization of salvation that so incensed Luther—moved to the other side of the street, as it were. From a great deal of control over one's salvation fate we move to no control. There are no organizational mechanisms that allow individuals to pull themselves out of the "slough of despond."[14] Here is Weber's description of the Protestant ethic:

> The God of Calvinism demanded of his believers not single good works, but a life of good works combined into a unified system. *There was no place for the very human Catholic cycle of sin, repentance, atonement, release, followed by renewed sin* ([1906] 1956, 117; emphasis added).

Furthermore, one bears this burden alone. It is consistent with the individualism of the Protestant ethic—and indeed may be a partial source of that individualism—that each person must struggle with his "fault" and deal with it as best she or he can. You are, potentially, never "okay."

One of the implications of being a fault carrier is that, because the sin cannot be excised, the carrier must be excised. Perhaps this impetus is behind the typical American response to trouble—we fix problems by firing people. When things go wrong, we like to find out who is at fault. In business and industry, the moment something goes wrong, the search for guilty parties begins. The underlying assumption is that some*one* (or more than one—several *ones*) *is responsible* for what happened. Once those individuals are identified and punished, the problem will be solved.

The concept of "fault carrier" also implies an internal, or character, issue rather than a behavioral problem. Perhaps stemming from a belief in predestination, character-defining designations often are regarded as immutable: "Jimmy's just that kind of boy." This permanence is in sharp contrast to the openness of American society. Perhaps the emphasis on openness is in response to, and a partial counter to, the closure of predestination.

Fault-Forgiveness and the Spirit of Community

One of the important implications of the belief that all humans are subject to a cycle of sin and forgiveness is the recognition that both sin and forgiveness are widespread: All humans can sin, and all can be saved. Because there is no internal inexorability, there are no divisions in the community. All are part of the community of potential sinners; all are part of the community of people in need of assistance.

There is a recognition that the person who is a sinner today may be a saint tomorrow, and the one who is a saint today may be a sinner tomorrow. Thus, there is no inexorability of position. The saint and sinner roles may be played—and probably are played—by all humans at various times of the day, week, month, and over our lifetimes. This cycle leads to a reluctance to judge too harshly because, perhaps, "there but for the grace of God go I."[15] Hence, prohibitions or questions about providing help to people in need do not excite moral passions. It is not only a sensible thing to do because these people need help; it also may be a prudent thing to do because you may be in the very same position shortly. Certainly nothing in your character prevents you from being in that position.

Because the Catholic ethic tradition is not prone to making crisp distinctions between good people and sinners or between people who need help and those who do not, negative judgments and hostile actions are tempered. As Iacocca suggests, we all go astray, so people who judge others too harshly might expect less tolerance for their own failings. "Judge not lest you be judged" expresses one of the dominant tendencies of the Catholic ethic tradition.

Not only should one temper one's thoughts; actions are to be restrained as well. Thought and action are different things. Thinking judgmental thoughts is one thing; taking negative action is something else again.[16] Here, too, the merciful culture of the Catholic ethic tradition urges temperance. Questioned by Pharisees about how to punish an adulteress, Jesus urged them to "Let the man among you who has no sin be first to cast a stone at her" (John 8:1–7, *New American Bible*, 1971). When the Pharisees left the woman unpunished, Jesus told her: "Nor do I condemn you. You may go. But from now on, avoid this sin" (John 8:11).

To regard this process as natural makes it difficult to believe that there are sharp divisions between people with problems and those without. Needy individuals and those with plenty are not really very different, any more than people who are tall and those who are short. That needy person, however, in a spin of fate could become rich. This tradition differs from one that regards poor people as someone apart—in Tracy's (1989) words, "the other"; in Joyce Carol Oates's terms, "Them" (1969); or in Michael Katz's terms, *The Undeserving Poor* (1989). In the Catholic ethic, however, statuses are not permanent. The world is a fickle place, and the mechanical observation that "what goes up must come down" has its counterpart in social terms as well. The "high and mighty" can quickly become the "low and powerless" and may need the assistance from others that they are now providing for today's needy. Following the same logic, today's altruist may have been disadvantaged yesterday. The Beatitudes suggest just such an "inversion" of status. "Blessed are the meek, for they shall inherit the earth" is a different ethic from one that suggests aggressiveness, domination, and cornering the market.[17]

Whatever differences there are between individuals pale in comparison to the commonalties among people. This sense of natural relations between humans not only creates a bond between poor and well-to-do people, it also means that mechanisms to help others are natural as well.[18] Thus, community embraces us all.

Community also is the place where one gets assistance. There is the local priest and the local parish. There is the corporeal (earthly) community of friends and neighbors and the heavenly community of all the saints and martyrs. The community not only knows about sin; it is there to lend you a hand. Thus, in sin and before God, you are not alone; you have community help.

Catholic Ethic's Fault-Forgiveness Orientation and the Helping Impetus

The community orientation has implications for the helping orientation impetus. First, the fault-forgiveness cycle itself *is* a kind of helping. Absolution for sin is provided strictly within the rituals and under the authority of the Catholic Church, but help can be provided by anyone—a point Murray (1990) makes in his discussion of hospitality. The fault-forgiveness culture of the Catholic ethic tradition not only assumes a *process* of moving between sin and absolution, it also assumes that the process is *natural*. Because it is a process rather than a destination, a sinful path can be reversed, and suffering individuals can be helped.

Expanding on these celestial concerns, groups affiliated with the Catholic Church typically have adapted this principle to provide help to people with earthly problems as well. From leprosariums to soup kitchens, hospitals to homeless shelters, helping has been a part of the Catholic ethic tradition. (At Catholic high schools such as Brother Rice in Brimingham, Michigan, students must fulfill service requirements: ten hours for freshmen, up to forty hours for seniors.)

In addition, the Catholic mechanisms of confession and forgiveness prefigure—in some cases, with amazing directness—helping activities in general and welfare-state activities in particular. In the most general sense, of course, mechanisms that provide help in one area can be regarded as a subtle support (and perhaps overt support) for providing help in another area.

More than that, however (as has been discussed by various people in the mental health field), the parallel between confessing sins to a priest and receiving help in the form of absolution is not dissimilar, in some essentials, from the pattern of psychotherapy and counseling. This process involves sharing concerns and difficulties with a therapist and receiving in return understanding and support, as well as a sounding board to explore new options and alternatives.

Conclusion

The fault-forgiveness culture of the Catholic ethic looks to a cycle of sin and forgiveness. The individual can and should take responsibility, but there is a community around to help out. This part of Catholic ethic culture has many elements that make helping natural and ordinary, on one hand, and temper hostility toward needy people, on the other. This aspect of the Catholic ethic works first as a powerful and compelling notion that establishes the perspectives and points of view that guide daily decisions. In addition, it works as an influence on behavior because of the rituals of confession and the requirements of penance/reconciliation. The set of assumptions that are the foundation of the Catholic penance/reconciliation system make the Catholic ethic more sympathetic and understanding of poor people and more willing to offer practical help to improve their welfare.

CHAPTER 7

Otherworldliness and the Catholic Ethic: Where Change and Achievement Can Really Matter

All religions have some interest in and perspective about the "life" beyond life as we know it. Orientation toward Heaven (otherworldly) or Earth (this-worldly) is a defining characteristic of any religion, but uncovering how these orientations are determined and how they influence action are not easy tasks. The Catholic ethic's otherworldly perspective emphasizes the extent to which one can influence that "next" life and the extent to which that life is the "real" life toward which one goes. This perspective is opposed to the Protestant ethic's "this-worldly" orientation, which suggests that this life is the "really-real" life, and the afterlife is a reward.

An otherworldly orientation directs individual believers to focus on life in the next world and diminishes the importance of temporal concerns. The prospect of Heaven—eternal life with God—is of paramount focus in the Catholic tradition. Catholics are expected to remain slightly detached from this world, in the hope of finding better conditions in the next world. Indeed, one of the criticisms of liberation theology that some Catholic thinkers have raised is that it focuses too much on conditions in this world.

A this-worldly orientation stresses the importance of conditions during life. Individual believers' attention is directed more to the here and now, partly because one cannot possibly influence the status one has after death.

The Catholic and Protestant ethic traditions differ with regard to the control one has over one's salvation status. In the former, one can influence one's salvation status; in the latter, it is more problematic. In the former, the emphasis is on creating one's salvation; in the latter, the emphasis is on discovering one's salvation. The difference is the difference between "works" and "work. . . . " The Catholic ethic, then, is focused on the otherworld because there is something Catholics can do about it. The Protestant ethic is focused on this world because it reveals something about the next world. These orientations are different in tone, approach, and impact, and they generate variations in approaches to human conduct.

Weber ([1906] 1956) placed great importance on the difference between Protestants' this-worldly orientation and Catholics' otherworldly orientation. Because of the this-worldly orientation of the Protestant ethic, measures of success in this world—especially those connected with money and work—take on more meaning for Protestants, stress the individuality of success, and make the idea of sharing more difficult. For Catholics, whose historic focus has been otherworldly, symbols of success in this world are less sacred, community more enhanced, and helping more evident.

Otherworldly Cultural Focus of the Catholic Ethic

There is an otherworldly emphasis within the Catholic ethic tradition. As Mack, Murphy, and Yellin write: "The Catholic ethic propounded a culturally established emphasis on otherworldliness; the rationale for the performance of tasks was other worldly" (1956, 295).

There are several ways to understand this emphasis. For one thing, the Catholic ethic developed during a period of fixed social structures. For many practical purposes, change in the here and now was not possible for the individual. Change, like pyramid and cathedral construction, was something that happened over hundreds of years. Hence, a focus on change in one's salvation status made sense. In a relatively fixed social structure, the needs for individual accomplishment could be addressed through otherworldly achievement.

This focus on the then and there, however, creates lowered emotional connection with the here-and-now. Perhaps part of the reason Weber ([1906] 1956) saw differences in the achievement trajectory of Catholic and Protestant regions was that, for Catholics, the here and now was not all that meaningful.

The otherworldly focus reflects another perspective on change, however. Its perspective on the process of change is long term and systemic, rather than short term and individualistic. Its perspective on the method of change is bit by bit and transactional, rather than all at once and transformational. And its perspective on the location of change is in God's world, not our world. The energy of achievement is pushed into the celestial world rather than the corporal world.

This-Worldly Cultural Focus of the Protestant Ethic

The Protestant ethic has a this-worldly orientation. It is not that there is less concern about the afterlife; rather, there is little that can be done about it. For that reason, emphasis should be placed on the here and now—doing what one can to make this life better for you and yours.

Novelist Louis Auchincloss captures this emphasis well. In a family's story that weaves throughout the course of American history, he begins in the Plymouth Bay Colony. Part of the dialogue he develops is between the colony's Governor, Winthrop, and one of the members of the colony, Master Hutchinson. Hutchinson is wondering whether doing good works (recall the earlier discussion on this point) could possibly matter. Winthrop replies that what you do in this fleshly life does not matter to your salvation. Hutchinson then asks why, if this were so, should anyone behave? Though fictional, art seems to reflect life in this language:

> The Governor: The reason it matters how a man behaves himself even in this remote and isolated community is that God will help him HERE. Here, Master Hutchinson, in this fleshly life in the Massachusetts Bay Colony. Concern yourself not with the hereafter. Leave that to God. He made a covenant with this colony that if we should follow his precepts He would protect us here, in the wilderness. And He has! (1976, 23)

Of course, if ways in which one can control the afterlife are limited, the energy of competition is forced or directed into the here and now. If one adds to this mix the idea that success in this life is somehow a proxy for success in the next, one has a powerful motivational system for here-and-now achievement.

Change in terms of location is in the here and now. That is what one can control. The process of change is swift (one can see it in one's life and career). And the method of change is dramatic (transformational and all at once) rather than bit by bit.

This World and the Next: Salvation Status and Social Status

The focus on this world and the next is always connected to concerns about salvation status and social status. I regard these two concepts as parallel. For the Protestant ethic, salvation status is questionable, unknowable, and uninfluenceable. It is no surprise, then, that anxiety about it becomes transmuted into energy in the here and now and into social status. Social status, in turn, becomes sacred status: The social ladder becomes Jacob's ladder.[1]

For the Catholic ethic, on the other hand, salvation status is clear, knowable, and malleable. It is not surprising, then, that this world loses a bit of luster, and achievements are muted. We are, after all, a "cup o' dust."

In a strange way, the two systems—the salvation system and the social system—interact. For the Catholic ethic, developing within an aristocratic system of generally fixed (or "sponsored") status, all that was available for the expression of mobility impulses was the sacred realm. Hence, we can easily understand why one would regard that realm as more valued and "this world" as less valued. The Protestant ethic's development appealed to people who already were in new statuses in this world and those who sought legitimacy and reassurance that the source of their status (commerce, money, resources of that kind) was legitimate. Hence the "inversion," as it were, of Catholic ethic thinking: The next world was fixed; this world was what one could influence and change.

Otherworldliness and the Spirit of Community

Otherworldliness does help, however, in creating a spirit of community in this world. For one thing, if this world and its goods are less vital to one's sense of self, cleavages between and among community members are lessened. Even tensions between community members and non-community members potentially can be enhanced. To the extent that difference and inequality corrodes community, an emphasis on the next world mutes differences in this world. To the extent that there *are* differences in this world—you have more money than I do, you have a bigger house than I do, you have more crops than I do—they are more "matter of fact" and not imbued with any meaning.

For some people—and this is the area of voluntary poverty—the journey is made easier if one packs lightly. The goods of this world can weigh us down. The idea of actually embracing poverty—voluntary poverty, or vows of poverty—is emblematic of an otherworldly orientation. Although the idea of choosing to make do with less seems antique in our consumer times, in fact many Catholics and other Christians still choose to forgo comfort and luxury to pursue spiritual values.

The "salvation creation" perspective, as opposed to the "salvation discovery" perspective, also adds to community orientation in this world. It does so in two ways. First, it places everyone on a common journey. To be sure, sojourners move at different rates; some have a better journey (or seem to) than others. Yet we are all on the road together. Each of us can understand the other's quest. And it is a quest. Working and acting together is a great way to build community. Second, the community is not divided into elites (the saved) and masses (the unsaved). Such distinctions between the "okay" and the "not okay" break the connective tissue that sustains community.

Catholic Ethic Otherworldly Orientation and the Helping Impetus

Community itself sustains the helping impetus, of course. There are some more specific contributions, however. If the things of this world are of lesser importance on the grand scale of things, then sharing them also is of less importance. Hence, helping does not take from one's vital resources—resources, yes, but not crucial ones.

Being on the journey together also stimulates helping. We are all heading in the same direction along the same path. If someone should fall or stumble, one would naturally bend down to give that person a hand; if one subscribes to the Catholic ethic, one would not think that helping another somehow harms oneself or makes onself less worthy. On the other hand, people who live the Catholic ethic do not seek to help only others who are "worthy." On the great path curving upward to heaven, all are worthy.

The Catholic Worker movement is an example of how the simple life becomes, also, the helping life. Catholic worker houses (a legacy of Dorothy Day) still scattered across the United States are one example of this tendency:

Catholic Worker homes usually adopt three major activities: hospitality (the provision of food, clothing and shelter, usually in skid-row areas); direct nonviolent protest against social injustice; and publication of newspapers and newsletters. The hospitality involves actually sharing one's own home with the poor; full-time volunteers live in houses and, in the "richer" houses, may receive $10 or $20 a week stipend. The houses . . . have no paid staff (H. Murray 1990, 6).[2]

Certainly not every individual who is influenced by the Catholic ethic tradition is serving as a volunteer with the Catholic Workers, but the philosophy of voluntary poverty that has sustained the group has enabled it to continue its selfless service to poor people since 1930. Priests in religious orders, moreover, take vows of poverty. Clearly, part of the Catholic ethic tradition deemphasizes the value of earthly success. To that extent, it could allow its adherents to share more with others.

Also involved here is what in *The Catholic Ethic in American Society* (Tropman 1996, 106) I called the "heavenly calculus." I was referring to the ideas about salvation structure (amount, access, process) that religious perspectives communicate. In the Catholic ethic, the "other world" is open to all. There is plenty of space in heaven. It is not restricted, therefore, in the "zero-sum" sense in which your salvation may "bump" me because you have taken one of the slots.

This "Garden of Eden" (plenty for all) salvation perspective of the next world supports helping in this world because it becomes a way to *think about the resources in this world.* The elements of transactional and transformational change also relate to helping. The Catholic ethic transactional change perspective regards life as moving in "baby steps." Hence, a helping hand with this step or that step is not a big deal. As the church, priests, and other religious help us, we in turn help others. Salvation is a non–zero-sum game.

For the Protestant ethic, salvation seems to be more limited. Slots are on the scarcer side and cannot be earned. My salvation may very well take a slot you were hoping for. Moreover, whatever the process, we go alone. My hypothesis is that our view of the "salvation economy" influences and structures our view of the "world economy."

Conclusion

The Protestant and Catholic ethics must find ways to express the competing values of achievement, individuality, and entrepreneurship, on one hand, and equality and community on the other. Imaginatively, the ethics trade off their locales for the expression of these values.

For the Catholic ethic, the achievement motive is expressed in the "then and there"—in the next, sacred, world. That is where individuals are in a contest for salvation status. In one sense it is not much of a contest because there are plenty of awards to go around. For the Catholic ethic, community is here, among everyone on the wagon train winding into the sky. Progress is slow but steady—a perfect example of transactional change.

For the Protestant ethic, achievement and entrepreneurship are features of this world. They do not influence one's status in the next world, but they serve as "indicators." One waits and hopes to receive grace in this world—that heavenly gift that reveals the recipient as one of the elect. This is a perfect example of transformational change.

CHAPTER 8

Structural Features of the Catholic Ethic

I have approached the Catholic ethic as a value system. And indeed it is. Out of the value system come cultures—belief/behavior packages—that exist for a while at periods of time and enact the structure of "operational" Catholicism. The implication of these structures is significant.[1]

Structural Elements of the Catholic Ethic

Several particular elements of Catholic culture are worth noting because they deliver an impact that accelerates the impact of the Catholic ethic. The ones I have selected do not represent a complete list, but as I look at the picture, they are of great importance: historical vitality; globalization; formal organization format; subsidiarity; and, in America, Catholic schools and nativist opposition.

Historical Vitality

The Catholic Church is one of the world's oldest organizations. Connect to it, and you connect to history itself. The very stability of the organization in a vital state is an amazing organizational achievement. The oldest corporations in America—General Electric, for example—are scarcely 100 years old. Firms and corporations seem to die almost as fast as restaurants, yet here is an organization that is 2,000 years old. This success alone adds weight.

Globalization

Organizational Catholicism has maintained itself worldwide—today we would say "globally." It has outposts throughout the world and keeps in touch with them through emissaries; trips to and from Rome; and radio, television, and computer connections and the like. No one can have

74

missed the peripatetic Pope who traveled all over the world at the end of the twentieth century, making and keeping connections. The church was "global" before it was popular for corporations to become global. It is meaningful to grow up as a citizen, parishioner, or member of an organization of worldwide scope that permits worldwide identification and has worldwide authority.

Formal Organization Format

The Catholic Church is, among other things, a formal organization. It has buildings, people, and resources and is capable of carrying out a wide range of tasks. The church organization has functional and staff subsidiaries. National churches, dioceses, and parishes are functional subsidiaries. Orders represent cross-cutting staff functions. Indeed, Pascal and Athos (1981) suggest that much of the West's corporate organizational structure has been modeled on that of the Catholic Church. In this sense, the church represents an organization whose weight and might can support or oppose various policy proposals and social programs. It is capable of acting—and does act—as an organizational entity, independent of collectivities and individual believers. Papal encyclicals and bishops' letters are examples of the multitude of vehicles through which the church's official platform is pursued. At various times in its history, the Catholic Church has started crusades, launched inquisitions, and hired lobbying firms to advance its organizational aims. I heard recently that the Pope is going on MTV! Any discussion of the Catholic ethic must include some mention of this organizational element of the Catholic Church.

Subsidiarity

One of the important organizational principles of the Catholic Church is the principle of subsidiarity. Essentially, this means that higher organizational levels should not undertake tasks that can better (or best) be accomplished by lower-level units. This idea was rediscovered by Peters and Waterman in their book *In Search of Excellence* (1982). They called it "loose tight properties"; they meant that successful organizations did a few key things centrally and let the subunits (those close to the problems) deal with the problems.

Catholic Schools

Catholic schools are a prominent feature of the landscape in the United States and elsewhere in the world. Until the advent of charter schools,

Catholic schools represented the only real large-scale alternative to the public education system in the United States. This system ran from kindergarten to the doctoral level. This vast network of education and interaction was a place for identification, perspective, and community—and for the norms of the Catholic ethic to be worked out on a daily basis.

Nativist American Opposition

In chapter 2 I discussed the importance of nativist opposition with respect to the pressures it generated toward keeping the Catholic ethic idea hidden. It also had another effect, however. Hate creates fences—"pales"—within which the lived life goes on. It strengthens and isolates.

Catholic Structure and the Spirit of Community

Each of these elements (as well as others) enhances and supports the spirit of community. They act independently and interdependently to create community connection and crystallize community continuity.

Historical Vitality

Church creates a certain comfort level. One has a sense of the connections over time. These connections may be most obvious in Europe, where cathedrals seem to be around every corner. One sits in a church—perhaps Saint'Antimo in Montalcino, Italy, built by Charlemagne in the eleventh century—listening to Gregorian chant in its dark coolness and thinking how old this church is, and then thinking that as old as it is, the church *already* was 1,000 years old when it was started. That is connection; that is community.

Globalization

The church is worldwide. All over the world, Catholics have similar and recognizable devotional practices. Even when local languages were different, the use of Latin in the liturgy (until relatively recently) gave Catholic travelers in foreign churches a sense of being at home—similar, perhaps, to how an American might feel at a McDonald's restaurant in Tokyo. The universal character of the Catholic Church means that the same or similar values are embraced in many places around the world, despite local differences in languages and cultures. Dominant values create community.

The fact that there is a worldwide culture of Catholicism does not mean that there are not many differences as well. Hofstede (1980) provides one of the few international, cross-cultural examinations of Catholic identifications and values as part of his investigation of a large multinational firm. In *Culture's Consequences: International Differences in Work Related Values*, Hofstede finds that, controlling for intranational or ethnic factors, religious commonalities and differences in subculture are of some importance. The truth is that hyphenated Catholics (Irish-Catholics, Hispanic-Catholics, etc.) have community and subcommunity, culture and subculture.

Formal Organization Format

The formal organizational structure of the church embodies the phrase that was a favorite of my seventh-grade teacher, Mildred Mundt. "A place for everything; everything in its place" was her mantra; it did provide a sense of order. The formal organization aspect of the Catholic Church—as distinct from its Catholic ethic value system—has a place for everyone. It has officials, pronouncements, and directions, and it tells you what to do. For many people, that kind of structure is anathema; for many others, it is a source of comfort. It is community through organization.

Subsidiarity

This principle of keeping action at the lowest level is a kind of empowerment. In this respect the Catholic Church is a successful formal organization, keeping individuals at work locally while making policy globally. Hence, parish councils (local community) match the strength of the formal organization connection (global community).

Catholic Schools

So much of the music we remember comes from the years when we were teenagers. The reunions we attend are high school and college reunions. Those years—the period between our family of origin and our family of creation—are when community seems especially strong. This is where Catholic schools come in. By creating opportunities for interaction and identification, schools are institutions that build community as well as provide education. Students in Catholic schools are exposed to the values of the Catholic ethic tradition in some of their classes and through the values expressed by the members of religious orders who teach at and lead most of these schools. These mechanisms of socialization augment other influences to support the values of helping and tolerance for human failings. When Catholic schools are linked with a parish, as has been typical in America, they underscore communal elements of the Catholic ethic tradition.

Nativist American Opposition

Good fences may make good neighbors, but fences keep one interacting with one's own. Opposition intensifies in-group identification and interaction. Like it or not, opposition builds and sustains community.

Catholic Structure and the Helping Impetus

Each of these dimensions not only enhances community, it sustains helping ideas and actions.

Historical Vitality

Part of the history of the Catholic ethic is the history of helping. I detail some of these historical efforts in chapters 9 and 10. The overall point is that helping behavior—from travelers' aid along pilgrimage routes to leprosariums to Catholic Charities USA to Caritas—is that helping is integral to the Catholic ethic.

Globalization

The global connection supports global helping. There are the "missions," of course, but I do not consider activity to create converts as helping behavior in the sense discussed here. Many of the missions, however, were "charitable" in nature. Mission priests and nuns would give homilies at Sunday mass (as part of a fundraising tour) and ask for support. Other parish collections sought aid for people far away, as well as those close to home. Prosocial helping was not just for the family next door; there is a global connection.

Formal Organization Format

The Catholic Church (the institutional church) is a large organization with many levels of authority, from the parish to the Vatican. Directions about behavior and belief come from all levels of the church, and its bureaucracy resembles any other modern corporation or government. It has departments and levels, reporting relationships, flows of authority and information, and trained functionaries (i.e., priests) to speak for the church, subject to its imperative authority in Rome. In terms of organizational structure, the Catholic Church is a large-scale, need-meeting system. Among its other features, it provides support to people in trouble and offers them forgiveness and grace as well as more practical help.

Catholics are accustomed to this structure—and were accustomed to it long before the welfare state was invented. The development of the Catholic ethic's support for progressive community helping policies may have found its genesis within the structure of the Catholic Church itself: Catholics as a group are accustomed to a large need-meeting bureaucracy of an ecclesiastical sort, and that kind of group might be more accepting of a large need-meeting bureaucracy of a welfare state sort. The departments of social services in most governments are much like secular versions of the Catholic Church. Local welfare offices are not unlike parish churches, where individuals make contact with vast organizations that help needy people. One provides practical help with food, shelter, and clothing; the other offers spiritual help. Catholic parishes continue to provide practical help to their members, of course—from sanctuary for political refugees to business contacts for well-to-do people. It is true, however, that the growth of the welfare state apparatus has reduced the need for parishes to continue to provide as much practical help as they had in the past.

In some ways, then, the Catholic Church apparatus and its operation and purpose are parallel to some functions of the welfare state. Individuals who are accustomed to the Catholic Church's structure would not find the welfare state structure alien. In many instances, of course, the Catholic Church structure was a precursor to the actual welfare state, meeting both sacred and secular needs.

Subsidiarity

In the helping department, subsidiarity balances the pressures of globalization and the pressures of formal organization. In the first case, the pressure for global connection and assistance is balanced by pressures to help here at home, in one's own parish. In the second, the presence of hierarchy does not mean that "hierarchy does all." As with the Catholic Worker movement, individuals are challenged to do helping works, not just support the activity of good works.

Catholic Schools

Church, school, and neighborhood communities overlap perfectly for most children and their parents, reinforcing social ties and encouraging mutual assistance. The togetherness of the typical American Catholic parish—described so well by Greeley (1991a)—was interwoven with the connections between church, school, and neighborhood.

Nativist American Opposition

Opposition to you and yours usually means that those who hate you are unlikely to help you. This prejudice forced the Catholic community—parishioners and hierarchy alike—to intensify the impetus for helping that already was present in a network of Catholic helping institutions. Much of this helping was of a social service nature. Some, however, was of a political nature, provided through city political machines. This is where the "private regarding" political orientation came into serious play.

Conclusion

In the daily and weekly experience of Catholics—the "habits of the day," to paraphrase Bellah (1986)—there are underlying messages of support and encouragement for the helping process, for the giving and receiving of help. There are structures in place to make that happen, and there is the shared experience of immigrant oppression—at least in America, at least figuratively—that helps to solidify bonds between individuals and to support the principle, already established in other ways, of interpersonal helping. The global manifestation of the institutional church and the very presence of helping activities worldwide combine to manifest and reinforce the Catholic ethic.

PART III

A Cultural and Structural History of the Catholic Ethic and Community Helping

These two chapters consider the Catholic ethic and the spirit of community from two connected perspectives—social values and social structure. I suppose my sociological training has encouraged me to place these perspectives into two separate chapters; they could have been in a single combined chapter as well. There is linkage between the material, of course, because values and structure, beliefs and actions are not all that separable.

There are two reasons for this parallel approach. First, although what we think and what we do are connected, they are not identical. The current business question for executives (and for rabbis, priests, and ministers, I would imagine)—"Does he walk the talk?"—has a lot of meaning. Second, important social thinkers have taken positions on the importance of one or the other. On the culture (talk) side we can start with Plato and touch base with Sigmund Freud and Max Weber. Each of these thinkers (and many others) started with ideas and regard behavior as a kind of product. On the other hand, the "walk" side, we can invoke Aristotle, Karl Marx, and B. F. Skinner. These thinkers (and others) took the position that the concrete comes first, and ideas and values follow. Thoughts are somehow a product of the empirical situation in which you find yourself. Each side has made good points; neither side is anywhere near conclusively right. Both ideas and structures seem to have some independent importance; hence the dual treatment.

A Preferential Option for Poor People

The bottom line suggests, to me, that Catholic culture and structure stress community and the helping that is, for Catholics, inextricably interconnected. Not everyone needs help equally, however; some people need more than others. The Catholic ethic conception of community is "family-like" in some respects. By this I mean that within the family— our families—we parents provide different kinds and amounts of help to our children as they need it. If one of the kids needs more, we provide that for them up to our ability. The Catholic ethic is like this. It tends to be *most* sensitive to the neediest members of the community. This approach recently has been called "a preferential option for the poor." That phrase just means that special attention should be given to putting the last first.

Several questions arise here. One is, "How long has this been going on?" Is it recent? How has it played out historically? What are the views of the Protestant ethic on poor people? Weber ([1906] 1956) says nothing about them directly. How are poor people to be regarded?

Helping Traditions in the West

Societies have always helped their members. Conceptions about what help was, how much was needed, how the transaction was conceptualized (a gift, or a loan), and how much one was obligated to "share" are the subject of endless discussion. Figure III.1 lays out a picture of the historical flow.

Figure III.1 suggests that Catholic helping developed out of Jewish, Greek, and Roman traditions, at least, and developed through the 1,500 years or so until the Reformation. Latin American Catholicism is depicted as breaking away *before* the Reformation. At that time, Christianity split into Protestant and Catholic streams—with England, the United States, and Sweden representing the Protestant stream and Spain, France, Italy, and Ireland, among others, representing the Catholic stream. Each of these "ethnic Catholic" areas may have had its own specific version of the Catholic ethic in general and its helping components in particular. The next two chapters provide a historical overview of helping, with an emphasis on the Catholic ethic perspective.

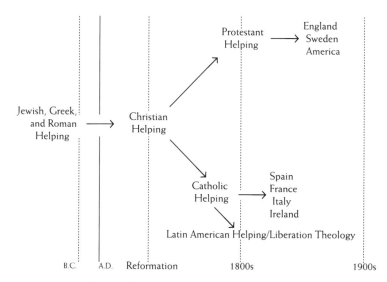

FIGURE III.1   *Development of Helping Traditions in the West*

Community and Poverty

As cultures create themselves, problems of need, distribution, and justice always come to the forefront. It is likely that all groups address the same kinds of questions. What am I entitled to? What should I/we do about people who have less? How much less is okay, and at what levels does less become not okay? How should we think about poor people? Should one praise them or damn them? Is their condition to be understood as a result of the operations of the universe or as the result of their own actions? Do we suffer or benefit from being near poor people? Are "they" like "us" or different from us?

The Catholic Church as a culture—as a set of beliefs, norms, and values—espouses community, with special reference to helping and kindness toward others, understanding of others' weaknesses, and support for people in need. Biblical verses that are familiar to Catholics support this contention: "Love thy neighbor as thyself"; "Faith, hope, and charity—and the greatest of these is charity"; and the stories of the Good Samaritan and the Prodigal Son are just a handful of examples of the underlying theme that has flowed through Catholicism over its history.[1] Given choices, the Catholic ethic "chose" to favor poor people.[2]

The Protestant ethic, on the other hand, chose to emphasize achievement and success. It has a preferential option for the successful. This does not mean that the Protestant ethic is directly "antipoor," although, in a parallel way, as many questions (often of a negative sort) are raised about poor people within the Protestant ethic tradition as are raised about rich people in the Catholic ethic tradition. Indeed, there are good reasons to believe that the Protestant ethic *is* antipoor, in important ways, just as the Catholic ethic may be, in some ways, antirich.

Each tradition, one might say, has different views toward poverty and success.[3] These views are outlined in Table III.1.

In each case, however, the dominant view has a powerful subdominant view active within it. The dominant and subdominant views of poor people within both traditions are displayed in Table III.2.

In sum, two views of poverty run intertwined throughout history. One of these views is positive—the *Dignitas Pauperum Christi* (the dig-

TABLE III.1   *Dominant Catholic Ethic and Protestant Ethic Orientations toward Poverty and Success*

View	Catholic Ethic	Protestant Ethic
Poor people	Preferential option	Potentially problematic
Successful people	Possibly problematic	Probably the elect

TABLE III.2   *Dominant and Subdominant Cultural Perspectives about Poor People in Catholic Ethic and Protestant Ethic Traditions*

View	Catholic Ethic	Protestant Ethic
Dominant	*Dignitas Pauperum Christi*	Unworthy poor; morally questionable
	All are equally saved/ saveable	Nonelect
	Fair Share	*Fair Deal*
Subdominant	Wretched of the earth	Worthy poor

nity of the poor of Christ)—in which it might be correct to say "that the place of the pauper was already among the elect" (Mollat 1986, 113). This view was espoused by two influential thinkers (St. Francis and St. Dominic) whose writings still guide much Catholic thinking. "Both men saw Nature as a marvelous creation designed to serve the needs of all mankind. All men were in essence equal, and all were *equally redeemed by Christ; hence all enjoyed equal claims upon a patrimony originally held in common*" (Mollat 1986, 120; emphasis added). This is the essence of the dominant Catholic view. There is a subdominant view, however, that considers poor people abhorrent, loathsome, and the like— and perhaps not from "our" tribe/clan/ethnic group.[4]

On the other hand, there is a view that suggests that, in a twist on what Fitzgerald said, "the poor are different" (to which Hemingway might have replied, "Yes, they are broke!").[5] As the former view stressed the causes of poverty and giving all persons a "fair share" (Ryan 1981), this one emphasizes the causes of poverty and stresses a "fair deal." From this tradition arose the distinction between the "worthy poor" and the "unworthy poor" that is so conventional now.[6] Understanding the dominant and subdominant elements, as well as the fact that both traditions are drawing from the same sources, helps to explain some of the apparent problems for anyone who thinks that a historical tradition is unambiguous. Berger worries about this problem in his discussion of the "Bishops' Letter" (National Conference of Catholic Bishops 1986) and the more conservative response by William E. Simon and Michael Novak, *Toward the Future: Catholic Social Thought and the U.S. Economy* (1984).[7] Berger comments:

> The bishops claim that the application of their ethical presuppositions and their method of reasoning to the subject at hand constitutes a major contribution. . . . But Simon and Novak, drawing on

the same ethical presuppositions and the same method of reasoning, have come to very different conclusions. The fact that Catholic moral teaching is so flexible as to lend legitimacy to such opposed perspectives on reality raises serious questions about the alleged contribution of this method of moral reasoning (Berger 1985, 35).

This puzzlement obtains only if one takes a unitary view of the situation. From the analysis presented here, one could argue that the bishops are coming out of the dominant Catholic tradition, whereas Simon and Novak are coming out of the subdominant one.

Conclusion

Looking at more than 2,000 years of history, the picture I see is that the Catholic ethic and the spirit of community have as a dominant feature a collective perspective that offers a hand to people in need: "There but for the Grace of God go I." Metaphorically, a rising tide lifts all boats. There is a subdominant theme of individualism and "success"—especially, I sense, among American Catholics. The Protestant ethic and the spirit of capitalism, on the other hand, have a dominant individualistic perspective. Metaphorically, "each tub is on its own bottom." It contains an important subdominant theme of lending a hand, especially to the worthy poor. As we take a brief tour through historical values and behaviors toward disadvantaged people, I explore these themes.

CHAPTER 9

A Social Values Perspective on the Catholic Ethic and Community Helping

Poverty will always be with us. Human society always seems to have some people with more and others with less. Sometimes the difference arises from natural disasters, disease, and other acts of God. Sometimes it is related to human acts, from war and its aftermath to exploitation of the powerless by the powerful and—on more than one occasion, no doubt—deficiencies of motivation and aspiration in individuals. Occasionally, lack of resources is voluntary, such as in a situation in which a person, for religious or ethical reasons, gives them up. Whatever the explanation, people with less than they needed for their times have been called "poor." Throughout history there have been many names for and many divisions of poor people, but as a group, they are always with us. Above all else, perhaps, the spirit of community requires attention to the least of its members.

The Early Church: Poverty Is a Worry

In the times of the early church in Roman Palestine, two kinds of poverty were recognized. The distinction is familiar to people working in and among disadvantaged populations today: "The distinction [was] made in antiquity between the 'needy' (those in a desperate situation) and the 'poor' . . . " (Hamel 1990, 92).[1]

There were many different approaches to poverty. Hamel comments, "The help extended to poor people in most situations of need took many forms, depending on the religion, culture and social situation of the benefactor and the beneficiary" (1990, 212). It is important to understand the traditions out of which the Catholic ethic grew. They were, in historical order, Greek helping, Roman helping, Jewish helping, and Christian helping.

Greek Values

Because the Greek culture was a defining culture of ancient times, what they thought is of interest to all and has had enduring impact. Obligation to help per se was not present—a contrast with the Jewish tradition. Nor, it appears, did poor people have rights. Instead, there was an exchange mentality, in which richer individuals provided assistance in exchange for "friendship, obligations from others, honor, and sometimes even quasi-divinity" (Hamel 1990, 219).

Jewish Values

Jewish helping arose out of a biblical tradition and has flourished in Jewish tradition to this today. Although this tradition did not exalt poor people, there seems to be no history of aversion to poverty. Unlike the Catholic vow of poverty, however, there is no sense of aversion to wealth in Judaism. Therefore, although poor people were not exalted, there is a commandment in Jewish tradition that sharing should occur. Hamel comments, "The most frequent word used by the rabbis to express helping, *seddaqua,* meaning 'righteousness' or justice, reveals a basic attitude, *namely, that of the donor's obligation and the poor's right*" (1990, 216; emphasis added). Rights included freeing of slaves in the sabbatical year, forgiveness of debts in the jubilee year (fiftieth year), access to common grazing land, the tithe for the poor, and so on.

Roman Values

Some of the early helping in Rome showed the influence of Greek views. One point of importance, however, was the urban nature of Roman helping. In some ways, the Roman games were an urban poverty program, keeping unemployed people off the streets and entertained. This theme of concern for the urban masses, as well as the centrality of *urban* elements in poverty thought and relief, arose again in the Middle Ages when the mendicant orders went into cities to help people in poverty and municipalities began to develop programs to aid poor people.

Public giving was part of the imperial tradition, and it was the emperor's function, in part, to provide—as Trajan had done—not only for feeding his people but also for overseeing what we would call recreational facilities and leisure activities and generally enhancing the "quality of life" (Mollat 1986, 19).

Christian Values

More to the point in terms of the origins of the Catholic ethic is "Christian helping." Again, Hamel is useful here:

> We have already seen that the various traditions in the gospels present Jesus as encouraging the traditional duties of Judaism. He himself practiced alms and strongly recommended it to his disciples. *But a new aspect is that he is presented as the center of every demonstration of love: "As you did it to one of the least of these my brethren, you did it to me." This theocentricity allowed the new Christians to see people other than their kin or neighbors as potentially worthy of the kind of helping that did not produce any return* (1990, 220; emphasis added).

The early Christians continued and developed the theme of "love your neighbor as yourself" (Meeks 1986, 150). By the end of the second century, the need to perfect both soul and actions, and the different realms that these spheres represent, had developed. Meeks quotes Irenaeus, a bishop at the end of the second century:

> [Because] man is an animal made up of soul and body . . . there is both bodily holiness, the safeguard of abstinence from all shameful things and wicked deeds, and holiness of the soul, the preservation in its integrity of faith in God (1986, 155).

One should be pure in thought and exemplary in action. The attitude of altruism stems from this injunction.

The early Church, then, emphasized the ideas that poverty was a fact of life; that it was to be treated charitably, positively, and even in a semisacred way; and that believers had the duty to give alms to help people in need. Although there might be problems in working with poor people, those problems needed to be overcome. James of Vitry (ca. 1224) commented that caregivers should possess "the courage of a martyr to overcome one's repugnance at the unbearable filth and stench of the patients" (Mollat 1986, 102).

This view—that poverty was a part of life and helping was a part of life—is what I call the *natural* view of poverty. There seemed to be no sense, at this point anyway, that poverty was useful or had supernatural connections and purposes. Nor was there a sense that poverty was *shameful* or that one should have contempt for poor people. These views would arise later.

The Middle Ages
Streams of Poverty Thought:
Natural to Supernatural to Shameful

The natural view of poverty continued to develop up through the Middle Ages. Mollat's *The Poor in the Middle Ages* (1986) deals with the history of thought and action about poverty from the fifth century to the early sixteenth century. He argues "that if personal helping was the basis for all helping, interpreting the meaning of personal helping within the context of social life in general is a delicate matter" (1986, 154). There is room for disagreement about the view that personal helping is the basis for all helping, but the point about "interpreting the meaning of personal helping within the context of social life" is exactly correct.

This later Christian/Catholic thinking about poor people built on, yet transformed, the imperatives of Greek, Roman, Jewish, and early Christian doctrines. The natural view of poverty became the supernatural view of poverty: Helping got religion. Three important points in thinking about poor people are of great importance to the Catholic ethic.

The natural view of poverty (that it was a part of the human condition) seems to have characterized thinking about poor people from ancient times until around the twelfth century. The "poor of Christ" exemplifies this view. In the thirteenth century, St. Francis and St. Dominic also argued that the poor might be closer to God ("Christ's poor"). This view is in contrast to the one developed within the umbrella of the Protestant ethic, in which having money was a symbol of Godliness. Under the Catholic ethic, it was harder for a rich man to get into heaven than a camel to go through the eye of a needle (Mollat 1986, 21). Misner comments,

> According to Christian teaching, the fact was that God placed a few persons high and many low in social standing for gracious reasons of his own. There was even a certain advantage in *not* being placed high up, since leisure and wealth carried with them the potential for dissipation, vice and abuse of power that the limited circumstances of the common folk tended to rule out (1991, 16).[2]

Second—and perhaps because of the "close to God" element—the historical helping injunctions became celestial imperatives. Helping now had salvation credit. The good that helping could do for the recipient in relieving the suffering that person experiences had been matched, or perhaps exceeded, by the good it could do for the giver. "Salvation, like investment, was a matter of debits and credits, and in neither the spiritual nor the temporal realm were people willing to put all their eggs in one basket" (Mollat 1986, 265). Perhaps more than anything, the attitude of altruism stems from this thinking, this transformed and energized view of helping and of poor people. "The obligation to be charitable antedated the Church, *which made charity a condition of salvation. . . .* Theologians asserted that the property of the Church constituted the 'patrimony of the poor'" (Mollat 1986, 38; emphasis added).

In the Catholic ethic tradition, charity aids the giver. The performance of good works is supported within the culture of Catholicism. Potentially, good works become part of the "celestial (salvation) balance sheet" that is reviewed when one's celestial (salvation) fate is determined.

Third, the "patrimony of the poor" sets an institutional imperative parallel to the personal one. The church becomes a trustee of substantial assets and must use those assets to benefit poor people. This tradition of institutional helping can be observed repeatedly over the course of history. It has been especially well articulated in the past 100 years through the so-called social encyclicals that began in 1891 with *De Rerum Novarum* (Of New Things).[3] The fact that there has been recent expression of these themes does not mean, however, that they are recent themes; they are involved in the very roots of the founding of Catholicism.

This is not to say, by any means, that the church has always lived up to the "patrimony of the poor" duties, any more than endorsement of the phrase "all men are created equal" created equality. Both principles, however, in their own realms, create the conditions for claims, generate expectations, and build a platform for proscriptions. One might say that these views, though built on past ideas of helping and of poor people, transformed and extended that past in a powerful way, adding a supernatural and institutional element to thinking about poverty.

Now it was the Protestant ethic's turn. As is always the case, where there is an "on the one hand" there is an "on the other hand." Among all the positives about poverty, there are other views. In fact, there is a hostile subtext to thinking about poor people—a contrapuntal baseline, as it were. It was not because of poverty, exactly, however. It was for status reasons. Mollat points to this hostility and links it to inappropriate social climbing: "Hostility to the poor is reflected in the literature from around the year 1200 in the theme of the low-born upstart who seeks to force his way into the upper strata of society" (Mollat 1986, 85).[4] This hostility, it seems, became transmuted into a dislike of poor people themselves. "By the end of the fourteenth century the idea of the poor as a 'dangerous class' had come close to supplanting the image of the pauper as God's chosen and a symbol of Christ" (Mollat 1986, 266).[5] Indeed, the very connection between poverty and God became inverted:

> What did hideous tramps and fierce bandits have in common with Christ? How could people tolerate rebellion and violence against the established order and the will of God? What justification allowed able-bodied men to go begging, contrary to the natural law of labor? . . . For was not poverty the result of sin? And were not paupers disposed to sin repeatedly? . . . Poverty, at first feared, then discredited, was now derided (Mollat 1986, 254).

That thinking set the stage on which the Protestant ethic played out. Wealth and work moved to center stage. Poor people became the shameful poor, poverty an occasion of sin.

Issues in Early Poorthought

This history and the struggles around doing good contain many of the issues that remain with us today. One is the attempt to fit poor people into some kind of category system.

> What was the dividing line between "able-bodied?" Here though, sorting had practical rather than moral connotations. Byzantine law and morality regarded the capacity for work as a defining criterion. Vagabondage and unemployment were political problems; physical and mental disability were moral problems (Mollat 1986, 19).

Thus, very early in thinking about poor people, categorization of poor people emerged. The issue of work as one criterion for this classification was present but essentially unremarkable. This *moral matter-of-factness* with respect to work and categories is a part of the Catholic ethic today.

A second issue is urban poverty. The cities always seemed to have more poor people than other places, even though in the Middle Ages there were relatively few cities. It might be that then, as now, greater concentration of poor people leads to greater need and calls forth greater effort. The idea that greater visibility also may create a greater sense of menace, with respect to the urban place and poor people in it, would emerge more strongly later, though it was present in Roman times. Emphasis on the need of poor people in urban places is a characteristic of the Catholic ethic today.

A third issue relates to the entitlement that poor people "have." What are poor people "owed" from those who have more? The answer has to do with power and the relationship of poverty to accessing the means of sustenance. Mollat argues that "in the eighth and ninth centuries poverty . . . connoted not so much inferiority to the wealthy as subordination to the powerful" (1986, 20). Emphasis on labor support and the right of the working man to a "living wage" stems, in part, from these early approaches. The point, of course, is to get that living wage. The idea contained here, however, is that there is some obligation on the part of people who have more to help those who have less. Indeed, within the feudal system there were obligations incumbent on feudal lords for the care and protection of their serfs.

Finally, as always, there were practical details. The duty to give alms, for example, was not without problems. One problem, of course, was, "How much?" Often the phrase "out of surplus" was used as a measure for alms, but surplus was construed to exclude expenses necessary to maintain social status. Another question was how far toward poverty one should go to relieve poverty. In addition, of course, there were questions of how much poor people "need" and what they would do with the benefits they received. Misner comments, for example, that "One was not expected to impoverish oneself or one's family; one should maintain the style of life appropriate to one's station while from the surplus or excess, as it was called, supporting the needy" (1991, 17).

The Modern Period: Different Strokes for Different Folks

Our historical tour has taken us through the Reformation. One of the things that the Reformation re-formed was the view of poor people, which got reformulated along with the view of the rich. The voluntary poverty of historical Catholicism was now regarded as "odd." Weber points out, "To wish to be poor, it was often argued, was the same as wishing to be unhealthy" ([1906] 1956, 163). Because of the development of the idea of predestination, the world was separated into the invisible church of the elect and, of course, the nonelect:

It was an aristocracy . . . a gulf which penetrated all social relations with a sharp brutality. This consciousness of divine grace of the elect and the holy was accompanied *by an attitude toward the sin of one's neighbor, not of sympathetic understanding based on consciousness of one's own weakness, but of hatred and contempt for him as an enemy of God bearing the signs of eternal damnation.* (Weber [1906] 1956, 122; emphasis added)

Two streams of thought moved forward (Catholic ethic and Protestant ethic), contesting between themselves and with the realities of the structural situation. In Europe, Catholic ethic thought generally dominated, building on the positive attitudes toward poor people that stemmed from the Catholic tradition. The Protestant ethic thus responded to, reshaped, and reprioritized the Catholic ethic.

Developments on the Continent

On the continent, a variety of measures and associations sought to put the Catholic ethic into practice through what has come to be called "the social question." Misner's study on Catholic ethic responses to the post-Reformation periods, *Social Catholicism in Europe from the Onset of Industrialization to the First World War* (1991), details the various approaches taken in European countries to social need. Misner reviews social Catholicism's activities in several countries, including France, Austria, and Italy throughout the nineteenth century:

It has to do with the tensions between groups characteristic of nineteenth century societies: the difficulty of reconciling the interests of the new classes of industrial bourgeoisie and their clientele on the one side with those of industrial workers on the other. It was not just a matter of rich and poor, but of a newly dominant mode of production, that, though highly efficient, redounded to the benefit of the few, as it seemed, and the social and economic decline or exploitation of a great number.

"Social Catholicism" has to do, then, with Catholics who take this problem as central. (Misner 1991, 39)

In 1891, the first of the social encyclicals (*De Rerum Novarum*) was issued. It became an important phase of the Catholic ethic in which the institutional church began to play a more aggressive policy role in articulating what the bases of community welfare policy should be.

Developments in England

In a way, England was a transitional case. Catholic first and Protestant second, it is the fulcrum between the continent and the states with respect to the spirit of community. It developed a series of "poor law" policies—beginning with the Statute of Laborers (1349) through the poor laws (1602), the "reform" of 1834, and the Royal Commission of 1909 to the Beveridge Report of 1942. England's "position" toward poor people was uneven, reflecting "dueling values" of helping and harshness. England was perhaps a mix of Catholic ethic and Protestant ethic ideas; it seemed to have been dominated first by Catholic ethic perspectives, then by Protestant ethic perspectives, and then emerged as a mix, with a welfare state tilt.

In the fourteenth century, the Statute of Laborers prohibited begging and alms. "The beggar, in the concern of the Statute of Laborers, was not a problem in destitution but a seepage from the supply of labor" (De Schweinitz [1943] 1961, 6). Nonetheless, from that point through the Royal Commission of 1602, there seemed to be a somewhat positive sense of community and helping, with the usual cautions. Suspicion crept in, however, and the Poor Law Reform of 1834 entailed a hostile and negative set of policies. The essence of the 1834 perspective and approach may be best captured in a comment by Benjamin Disraeli about the poor law "reform" of 1834.[6] "It announces to the world that in England poverty is a crime" (De Schweinitz [1943] 1961, 124).

As might be expected, the problems of the harshness of the 1834 reform (no more "outdoor relief"—poor people had to go into workhouses and poorhouses, among other things) created pressure to "reform the reform." Another Royal commission made its report in 1909. This report took a more positive view toward helping, although the majority view based this helping within the "private" sector—a sector organized and orchestrated by the relatively newly developed Charity Organization Society. Conflict and tension continued in England, and the "negativism of 1834" was replaced with a "system of help in the Royal Commission Report of 1909." In that report, however, there were majority and minority segments—twin streams, as it were. One stream (the majority) was for retaining much of the voluntary system that had developed, with some specific improvements. Much of what we call "social work" and "voluntary agencies" developed during this period. The Charity Organization Society—models of which appeared almost immediately in America—was the cornerstone of this movement. "Friendly Visitors" went out to aid the worthy poor. The minority report took a governmental aid approach. It was authored essentially by Beatrice

Webb and, stemming from Fabian socialist thinking, set the stage for the welfare state. After 1909, many of its ideas got worked into programs; the remaining ideas would be almost completely enacted through the Beveridge Report of 1942 and became the basis of the "welfare state" activities of Britain in 1942.[7]

Developments in America

In America, however, there were no historical constraints. "There *was no old order*" (Reid 1995, 2208; emphasis added). Although the Poor Laws became the basis for the American approach, "In general, the colonists did not pursue the administration of the Poor Laws with the same vigor or anxiety as did their English counterparts" (Reid 1995, 2208). They regarded poor people as a part of the social order, not a threat to it. The philosophical basis of responsibility, however, was based on a package of ideas, including "individualism, personal responsibility, the moral importance of work and distrust of collectivism and centralized government" (Reid 1995, 2209).

The early period in America was characterized by voluntaristic efforts. This was followed by (and existed with) indoor relief, such as poorhouses, almshouses, and "houses of correction."[8] Attempts at national public responsibility failed in 1857 when President Pierce vetoed the "Ten Million Acre" bill—a congressional act that would have provided land-grant mental hospitals. Pierce's reasoning was that if the federal government provided for this group it would have to provide for all needy groups. This view held sway until the Social Security Act was signed on April 14, 1935.

Although the federal government largely stayed out of the "welfare" picture until the Social Security Act was passed, it did have some involvement. After the Civil War, the Freedman's Bureau attended to some of the issues that affected former slaves; the federal government also paid pensions to (northern) Civil War veterans and their families. Both of these programs were discontinued, however. In 1912, given interest in child labor, the Children's Bureau was formed in the Department of Labor. Aside from these efforts, however, "government action" was at the state and local level. There was public relief, as well as programs for insane, delinquent, homeless, and destitute people. Public responsibility was reactive and limited, however.

In what has come to be typical American style, private action grew up alongside, and as a supplement to, public action (much as private pensions have grown up along with, and as a supplement to, Social Security.) In lieu of public responsibility, a private "volunteer" organization of helping developed through personal aid, religious orders, scientific charity, and Charity Organization Societies.[9] Every year public and private officials gathered in a national conference—variously called the Conference of Charities and Correction and, later, the National Conference of Social Work—to exchange ideas, review issues and perspectives, and present papers.[10]

Throughout this period, a perspective developed that emphasized suspicion of poor people. (I discuss this development somewhat more in chapter 10.) This point of view included an increased connection between "poverty" and "criminality" (charity and correction), a sense that poverty was caused by the moral weakness of drinking (hence Prohibition), the development of the "worthy poor" concept, and an increasing sense of "blaming the victim" (Ryan 1971). Jane Addams worried about this trend. She felt that this perspective on poor and needy people ignored the virtues that they have (what today we would call the "strengths" perspective) and might cause "helpers" to approach poor people with distance and disdain.

Developments in America: A Buffalo, New York, Example

An example from nineteenth-century Buffalo, New York, may be illustrative. Many Catholics arrived in Buffalo in the middle of the nineteenth century via the Erie Canal. The American Catholic Church, as many observers have pointed out, helped these immigrants, and the Catholic ethic was alive and well, though under much suspicion from nativism. Gerber mentions "the simultaneous praise for the activities of the Sisters of Helping *and* the nativistic cautions" (Gerber 1984, 125; emphasis added). The Sisters ran the *only* hospital that served people of all faiths and classes! The nativistic element tried, but failed, to provide relief for poor people:

> The organized, private, Protestant response to poverty was bedeviled by difficulties in raising funds, and perhaps even more, by the impossible effort, through home visitations of relief applicants, to separate the "worthy" from the "unworthy" poor. The passions for rooting out the latter impaired the ability of the Protestant-organized Buffalo Association for the Relief of the Poor, which was the most active and well organized of all antebellum Protestant relief organizations, to reach people too proud to have middle class American investigators snooping about their homes and into their lives (Gerber 1984, 131).

This Protestant ethic perspective is in contrast to the Catholic ethic perspective. The Sisters were already running a hospital without regard to "worthiness." They did more than that, however:

> When angry groups of unemployed led by Irish workers and ward politicians gathered in the depths of the 1857 to 1859 Depression to demand "work or bread" from municipal officials, *Protestants had special reason to be grateful that the Sisters of Helping were giving out food to everyone, "worthy" or not, at their soup kitchens* (Gerber 1984, 131; emphasis added).

Perhaps these actions belong in chapter 10. I describe them here to contrast the "culture of disdain" for poor people to the "culture of acceptance" that characterized religious efforts to help poor people in Buffalo. Gerber goes on to point out that even when Buffalo did develop a hospital for poor people, its death rate was much higher than at the Sisters of Helping hospital. He notes that the dominant culture was hesitant about helping poor people not only because of aversion to them but because the very processes of help were suspect: "Indeed, what was done for them, in the form of helping, was widely believed to create dependence and sap initiative" (Gerber 1984, 132).[11] Moreover, the papers were full of condemnation: "For expressions of *contempt for the poor, particularly those begging, accepting helping, residing at the poorhouse or engaging in 'work or bread' demonstrations*, see *Buffalo Commercial Advertiser*, June 15, 1858, August 22, 1859, January 27, 29, February 15, 1860" (Gerber 1984, 133; emphasis added).

The pressures of modernization, the need to help Catholic immigrants, and the concerns the church had for disadvantaged people were continuing and strong, and now—at least as far as mid–nineteenth-century Buffalo was concerned—sharply different from those expressed in the Protestant tradition. The Protestant domination of the world was starting to be an issue, however. The Protestant advance, about which Max Weber would write shortly, was in full speed. Between 1870 and 1910, for example, of 13 countries for which there is economic growth data, 9 of the top 10 were heavily Protestant (Inglehart 1990, 60).

Catholic Social Thought

It was in this context—social Catholicism in Europe, tensions and reform in England, private social welfare in the United States, and the development overall of industrial capitalism—that in 1891 Pope Leo issued *De Rerum Novarum*. This document was the first in a continuing

arc (to the present day) of papal encyclicals and other documents—
loosely called "Catholic social teaching"—that deal with the condition
of people, the rights of the state, and so forth (Henriot, DeBerri, and
Schultheis 1990). Although the messages themselves, over the years,
have reflected an evolution and reconfirmation of the Catholic ethic,
there are basic themes that remain throughout—reflecting, as it were,
the Catholic ethic. Henriot, DeBerri, and Schultheis (1990, 20–22) sum-
marize them as follows:[12]

- Link of religious and social dimensions of life; God is in the World
- Dignity of the human person; women and men are made in the
  image of God; what happens to people is important
- Political and economic rights; all people have basic rights (voting,
  free speech, food, shelter)
- Option for the poor; preferential love should be given to poor
- Link of love and justice; love of neighbor is necessary, and must
  be manifest in action as well
- Promotion of the common good; individual rights are experi-
  enced within the context of the common good
- Subsidiarity; the closest institution to the problem should solve it
- Political participation; participation in decision making is a key
- Economic justice; the economy is for the people of the earth
- Stewardship; all property has a "social mortgage"; people need to
  respect and share earthly resources
- Global solidarity; we all belong to the human family
- Promotion of peace; peace is the fruit of justice

This summary articulates a broad perspective about the Catholic
ethic and its view of community and helping. The dignity of the person,
the presence of economic rights, options for poor people, the link between love and justice, economic justice, and stewardship are all there.

Vatican II

The social values story does not end here, however. While the "arc of
encyclicals" was being developed, other things were happening in the
church as well that lend support to the Catholic ethic concept. The Second Vatican Council (in the 1960s) also continued the tradition of the
encyclicals and promoted changes in *attitude and methodology* (culture
and structure, to use the terms here) that were reinvigorating for the
Catholic ethic. Henriot, DeBerri, and Schultheis (1990) make the point
that humanization, justice, and preferential options for poor people

were key elements of the Vatican II thrust, which underscored the prohelping and propoor traditions within the Catholic ethic. Henriot, DeBerri, and Schultheis quote from *The Church in the Modern World*— a segment used to close Vatican II in 1965:

> The joys and the hopes, the sorrows and anxieties, of the women and men of this age, *especially those who are poor or in any way oppressed*, these are the joys and hopes, the sorrows and anxieties, of the followers of Jesus Christ (Henriot, DeBerri, and Schultheis 1990, ix; emphasis added).

There could hardly be a better statement of the procommunity, prohelping views of the Catholic ethic. Following up on these initiatives, the energizing of South America through the development of liberation theology is an example of the Catholic ethic as well. Cardinal Arns specifically described the propoor theme of Vatican II as inspired by the Holy Spirit. Such a connection reinforces the Catholic ethic as not only the will of the church but as the will of God (Arns 1985).

Twentieth-Century America

Let's go back, however, to the United States—the "bastion" of the Protestant ethic. The American Catholic Church was articulating a mission to poor people that, among other consequences, would lead to the establishment of the National Conference of Catholic Charities (now Catholic Charities USA). Its code of ethics emphasized the Catholic ethic:

> The good news of the Gospel, the goal of helping and justice to all people in this life, and the scandal of the human suffering present in this world, pose a challenge to the church as the people of God. Ultimately, this challenge occasions a central mission of the organized church, which constitutes the particular, though not necessarily unique, mission of Diocesan Catholic Charities and its affiliated agencies and institutions (National Conference of Catholic Charities 1983, 11).

The Catholic Charities USA vision reads as follows:

> Believing in the presence of God in our midst, we proclaim the sanctity of life and the dignity of the person by sharing in the mission of Jesus given to the Church. To this end, Catholic Charities works with individuals, families and communities to help them meet their

needs, address their issues, eliminate oppression, and build a just and compassionate society (Catholic Charities USA 1997, 7).

This vision leads to a mission statement as follows:

> The mission of Catholic Charities USA is to provide service to people in need, to advocate for justice in social structures, and to call the entire Church and other people of goodwill to do the same (Catholic Charities USA 1997, 11).

Thousands—probably hundreds of thousands—of statements by Catholic religious leaders over the first two-thirds of the twentieth century in the United States reflected the Catholic ethic sentiment. Perhaps no document more clearly defines the Catholic ethic for today than the "Pastoral Letter on Catholic Social Teaching and the U.S. Economy." Issued in draft in 1984 and subsequently discussed and approved by the American bishops (there was a parallel Canadian effort), it not only outlines the essence of the prohelping/propoor views of Catholic culture, it makes several specific policy suggestions as well (though they are offered as illustrative). One must see the bishops' letter as a contemporary expression of the Catholic ethic. Although it was appropriate for the time and place of its issue, it is stimulated by and draws from a 2,000-year tradition of concern for the community and for disadvantaged people.

That enduring prohelping quality of the Catholic ethic was criticized by Berger (1985). In "Can the Bishops Help the Poor?" Berger made several criticisms; two are basic. First, he is troubled that "Catholics . . . should find so little to learn from the American experience . . . " (1985, 33). Berger feels that economic development and prosperity, more or less, and the democratic/capitalistic processes that produce them, help poor people better than "helping." Second, and more interesting from the perspective here, he faults the bishops because their social program is, well, Protestant! "For in their political and ideological positioning, the Catholic Bishops are following in the well-worn footsteps of official mainline Protestantism. If their pastoral letter reads in places like a translation from the Swedish it is also, minus a few papal quotations, reminiscent of the social action pronouncements of the United Methodist Church" (Berger 1985, 35).

With respect to the first criticism, Berger seems to be articulating the individualistic perspective, which is what I think he means by the lessons of the American experience. He misses a couple of points himself, however. At the general level, he misses the conflict between individual and community-based perspectives on social life. Second, he misses the fact that capitalistic processes of "self-help" do not work the same for all groups. For Catholics in America, lack of acceptance rather than inclusion was the norm. Acceptance came later. The "melting pot" (Zangwill 1922, 69) turned out to be at least three pans, not one. Whatever "melting" occurred tended to proceed within the main religious groupings of Catholic, Protestant, and Jew (Kennedy 1944). The Bishops were working not only out of the historical Catholic ethic but out of the American experience as Catholics had experienced it as well.

The charge of "Protestantism" is even more interesting. There is no question that there are prohelping perspectives and positions within the Protestant tradition. Berger's criticism ignores the larger truth, however, that community social concern is a dominant part of the Catholic ethic and a subdominant part of the Protestant ethic.

Conclusion

The Catholic ethic enacts the spirit of community through a positive and inclusive conceptualization of poor people. The Catholic ethic—at least the prosocial/propoor/prohelping elements—has proven to be robust. An attitude of altruism is represented by the fact that it is alive and vigorous.

From the early part of the fifth century until the early part of the sixteenth century, ideas about poverty and helping shifted, reversed, transformed, and finally, with Protestantism, split into the aforementioned twin "streams." In essence, a negative and suspicious view toward poverty and poor people developed and matured. This view would coexist with the more helping view. With the advent of Protestantism, the negative view became, for Protestants, dominant and the more helping view became subdominant; for Catholicism, the traditional view was retained and mixed with a strong measure of the newer, more suspicious view.

An excellent summary is provided by Charles Curran:

> The cannons of distributive justice are complex; but the great emphasis in distributing the goods of society is given to the basic needs of individuals, whereas in distributing burdens, emphasis is placed on ability. . . . So, too, distributive justice is recognized as the need to distribute the goods of society so that all can enjoy the minimum of the goods of this world which is necessary for living a decent human life (Curran 1988, 415).

CHAPTER 10

A Social Structural Perspective on the Catholic Ethic and Community Helping

Aside from what people and institutions value and think (their attitude), there also are actions they take (behaviors). From the examples of Jesus' helping to liberation theology, ways to help the community generally and poor people specifically have challenged religious doers. The importance of inclusive community is an old idea, continually reinvented for contemporary times (whenever contemporary is). The key for liberation theology—and, indeed, what has been a key question for Catholicism all along—is how to translate these values into action. "Without implementation, an analysis of the causes of poverty would be little more than an intellectual exercise" (Levi 1989, 35).

Questions about action—what action to take, when, and how to decide each of these issues—remain among the great problems of the human condition. Over its long history, Catholicism and the Catholic Church have expressed their prosocial commitments to community through an impressive action record of helping and being involved with poor people. Levi points out that "for nearly two thousand years churches have had a quasi-monopoly in the Western world on dealing with poverty" (1989, 1).

Consider, for example, the medieval monasteries and the care they provided for sick people, travelers, and poor people in their districts. There may have been self-interest as well as other interests: The church owned a great deal of property, and one author (Mollat 1986) has suggested that the provision of helping activities, whatever its other benefits, served as a demonstration to the surrounding community that the church was not spending its resources completely selfishly. To this example one can add the vows of poverty taken by many religious orders. Such vows provided visible evidence of a communal orientation. Other religious orders, specifically designed for community helping and building purposes such as nursing or teaching, provide further examples.

In addition, Catholic churches traditionally have had Poor Boxes to collect alms in the back of the church—from the community of the faithful to the community of the faithful. The St. Vincent de Paul Society (Catholic men who do helping works) is an example of an organization that aims to provide community-building relief, especially to poor people. In the United States, Catholic Charities USA and local affiliates and related groups provide a network of services to Catholics and non-Catholics.

Liberation theology is based on the past as well. Levi, for example, notes that, "Actually, the major points of Liberation theologians on poverty are not so entirely new. There is considerable congruence in the positions taken by several popes, some nineteenth century theologians and the liberation theologians on the causes of poverty" (Levi 1989, 39).

The Early Church—Poverty Requires Helping

Christian patterns of community helping emerged out of the Jewish and Greco-Roman traditions, just as the patterns of thought did. Early practices, therefore, as well as early thoughts and opinions, have influenced and become part of the tradition of helping. As Hamel points out, "Many Hebrew-Aramaic and Greek texts make it clear that material poverty existed, that it was sometimes very deep or very extensive, and that it was a serious concern of religious and civil leaders" (Hamel 1990, 210). Concern, of course, is one thing, actions are another. Some maxims expressing rules of conduct emerged, however. "Do unto others as you want others to do unto you" is one. It implies the relationship aspect mentioned in chapter 9 and thus circumscribes helping actions to people who might return it. On the other hand, "Love thy neighbor" removes this "exchange consideration." Although "the 'Golden Rule' is . . . the heart of Christianity" (Hamel 1990, 212), it still allows a quibble over who your neighbor might be. Of course, there also are the touchy issues of what should be done for non-neighbors—people who just need help. Hamel points out that the story of the Good Samaritan actually is a story of a "typical non-neighbor" (1990, 214).

Greek Helping

Obligation was not a part of the helping tradition in Greece. It seemed to be the love of the attention that helping got that motivated, if motivation occurred at all. Although in some cases no reciprocity was expected, these acts were important for the receiver: "providing water or fire, directions, proper burial, a small coin for a beggar, or a piece of bread" (Hamel 1990, 219).

Jewish Helping

Within the Jewish tradition, there were many examples of the tradition of action in which Christianity developed. Jewish farmers, for example, were expected to leave part of their field unharvested, to be used by poor people. There was a sense of obligation to share. Public helping also was available, but even then there was a sense of ambivalence about public aid. "Poor people were encouraged to stay away from these funds: their sense of shame was called upon. . . . Extreme merit was assigned to people who, though entitled to use public helping funds, did not come forward to claim them" (Hamel 1990, 218).

Roman Helping

Public giving also was part of the Roman imperial tradition. To a certain extent, the Roman Games were a public welfare program. "Bread and circuses" provided a way to entertain and feed urban unemployed people in an appropriate context.

Christian Helping

Taking the example of Jesus to heart, Christians developed helping actions quickly, building on traditions of Jewish, Roman, and Greek helping. The early church was characterized by members helping poor people. Which set about "alleviating the physical and social humiliation of the poor" (Mollat, 1986, 21). Gregory of Nyssa (The Desert Father) exhorted, "Let us feed and clothe Christ" (Mollat 1986, 22). Some early monks and priests apparently impoverished themselves to provide resources for this injunction, but there was an actual embracing of poverty by monks and priests through vows of poverty as time progressed. The vows taken by some religious orders today continue this early tradition.

The Medieval Church

Documents suggest that in the sixth century, churches were enjoined to spend between one-quarter and one-third of their resources on poor people (Mollat 1986, 38). In addition, poor people were treated in hospitals operated by religious orders and housed in monasteries. Indeed, Hincmar reminds one of his bishops that a key duty was "to receive the poor or other guests in hospitals, kept open for the purpose and staffed with the necessary personnel" (Mollat 1986, 45).

Much of this helping, though certainly not all, was carried on in Benedictine monasteries. For example, monasteries developed an almonry— a specific place where poor people were sheltered, and which apparently had its own budget. By the twelfth century, however, "the Benedictine monasteries did not have as much of a monopoly on helping assistance to the poor as they once had" (Mollat 1986, 87). New problems had developed, and the monasteries had become (in contemporary social service parlance) a "four walls" program, run within the confines of a building. Settlement houses, Jewish community centers, and other building-centered programs are modern examples. In some sense, these programs may be considered offspring of the monastic programs.

Then as now, however, such programs did not reach everyone. "[T]he monks rarely saw . . . the most miserable of the poor: the social marginals and intransigents who lived in the forests or roamed the countryside, and the tramps and prostitutes who inhabited the growing towns" (Mollat 1986, 86–87). The comment sounds chillingly contemporary. Then, as now, "outreach" was required, and monks and preachers began to go out of the monasteries to take care of poor people.

In an age of pilgrimages to religious sites, hospices[1] were located along routes, and aid and shelter were extended to travelers. Rivers were an obstacle, "so, in that progressive age, the 12th century, helping was married to technology in the building of stone bridges" (Mollat 1986, 92). In addition, secular orders received bequests and gifts and administered them for poor people. So numerous were the helping entities that, "If the locations of helping institutions were marked on a map of Europe (in the 12th century . . . [only a] few empty spaces would stand out" (Mollat 1986, 100).

There were many specific helping activities, including almoners, almonries, orders, begueinages, and secular societies, forming an impressive tradition. By the thirteenth century, mendicant orders began to seek out poor people in the cities. Early social policy began to be considered:

> [T]he Dominican Giovanni of Vicenza . . . was assigned the task of reforming the communal statutes of Bologna and Verona; . . . others were assigned the same task in various other cities. These men . . . incorporated provisions favorable to the poor in the new statutes (Mollat 1986, 126).

By the fourteenth century, the Vatican finally became involved:

> Somewhat slower to act than the lesser bishops, the pope finally created an official department of paupers in the curia at Avignon. . . . The papal almonry became known as the Pignotte, doubtless from the small loaf that used to be distributed to the poor . . . (Mollat 1986, 136).

Princely almonries also developed, as well as more secular societies—the Hospitallers, for example, whose motto was, "Our lords the poor, our lords the sick." Each church had a "poor table" that was both an actual table set up next to the church to distribute goods to poor people and an organization that received and managed goods and money to benefit the poor (Mollat 1986, 139*ff*).

Institutions—especially hospitals—continued to multiply, and almost no town was without a hospital and a leprosarium. Merchants were added to the church and aristocratic authorities as providers of alms. In addition, a whole range of people contributed "common alms" to existing helping institutions. Some even left money to poor people in wills.

All of these provisions were unable to make much of a dent in the level of poverty—a familiar song today. As Mollat (1986) points out, the rise of merchants and business, and the rise of money, was associated with the development of a class of poor people that was not well understood then and, one might add, not well understood now: the working poor, or paupers.[2] The working poor were people who had a job but did not make enough from that job to live on. As Mollat notes, "Plague, famine and war, disastrous as they were, were only stations of the cross in the passion of the pauper" (1986, 207).

Any contemporary scholar of social service systems would be amazed at the extent to which the basic components of the helping mosaic were in place by the fourteenth century. Perhaps that was because the causes of the need for help were the same then as now: war, illness, and social exploitation, as well as individual differences in ability, interest, and motivation. Although "the poor ye shall always have with you," it might be more accurate to say, "the causes of poverty ye shall always have with you."[3] What is impressive here is consistency and continuity, rather than differences and variations. Inglehart comments, "Old 'worldviews' are remarkably persistent, shaping human behavior long after the conditions that gave rise to them have faded away" (Inglehart 1990, 426). What he does not say is that, sometimes, conditions don't fade away; they emerge again and again, always with the same message: "Plague, famine, war . . . only stations of the cross . . . " (Mollat 1986,

207). The point to be made here, before we consider the advent of the Reformation, is that a focus on the structure of poverty relief is, in a way, a focus on a result. The causes and roots of poverty were much the same then as they are now.

The "Re-Formation" and Poverty Strategy

In offering new options for belief and faith, the Reformation re-formed actions toward poor people. It was transformational change (Eisenstadt 1985). Simultaneously, of course, it reconceptualized community, helping, and the poor:

> The poor in cities became, of course, more visible and troubling, as it had been to Roman rulers many years before. The worsening of rural and urban conditions led to protests by the poor, and periodic uprisings had to be suppressed. It is no wonder that the poor came to be thought of as a "dangerous class" (Mollat 1986, 226).

Carter Lindberg, professor of church history at the School of Theology at Boston University, says it well:

> The medieval worldview, formed by a "piety of achievement," idealized poverty as the preferred path to salvation, actualized by either voluntary poverty or alms to the poor. As Little states in his essay, "The most sensitive actions remained moral, either by patronizing the poor (giving alms) or identifying with them (embracing voluntary poverty). The material effects on actual conditions were, in either case, necessarily modest." Urban efforts to respond to widespread poverty were thus stymied by the religious endorsement of poverty. The early Reformation in Germany, exemplified by Luther, undercut the medieval religious legitimization of poverty when it displaced salvation as a human achievement with salvation as a divine gift. Towns were now free to engage in a new field of discourse regarding social issues such as poverty and, with the active cooperation of Reformers, such as Luther, they developed and passed new legislative structures for social welfare (Lindberg 1994, 177).

Luther developed the concept of the "common chest" idea of community aid. In Wittenberg the town passed the Wittenburg Order of 1522:

Of the seventeen articles in this legislation, all but three are concerned with alleviating the plight of the poor. A common chest was established for poor relief. . . . Funding was provided from the endowments of discontinued religious institutions. . . . If this funding was not sufficient article eleven provided for a sort of graduated tax. . . . Begging was abolished . . . " (Lindberg 1994, 187).

This "common chest" has come down to us to this very day in the idea of the Community Chest movement—now called the United Way. Help was provided for poor people, but some of the new discourse was not all that positive. Begging, a traditional source of income for poor people, was now gone. "The Reformation church orders mandated that only the truly needy should be supported, all others must either leave or work—a theme repeated in countless later pamphlets under the overworked motto that he who does not work shall not eat" (Lindberg 1994, 188).

This division into worthy and unworthy poor was only one kind of classification. Many poor people were perceived as "choosing" poverty. (This idea is not as strange as it might seem: There were many people in religious orders who chose lives of voluntary poverty; it is part of the available models for people to observe and select from.) Other approaches had to do with the causes of poverty. Various designations were used, such as "fiscal paupers," "beggars in search of their daily bread," "rural and urban paupers," "vagabonds," and so forth. This classification approach led to the association of poverty with criminality, then to the need to police poor people (Mollatt 1986, chapter 12). This approach did not sway everyone, of course, but it reflected the increasing dominance of behaviors and concerns that had always been present (Hamel 1990).

Thus, poverty relief efforts after the Reformation split into two groups: the Catholic group and the Protestant group. Catholic helping continued much as its previous trajectory would suggest. In thought and action, support efforts to aid poor people continued. Within the Protestant arc, a more negative view had developed.[4] We can see the results of these two views as we look into the nineteenth century.

The Nineteenth Century

The nineteenth century is a good place to explore the development of "modern" action concerning social action and social aid. This period bore the brunt of industrialization, and a new cause of poverty—industrialization—was added to the substantial traditional list.

To be sure, Protestantism would do away with the Catholic idea that good works and the suffering of the poor cooperate to bring about redemption. But both Catholic and Protestant traditions, nourished in the same soil, hold that helping is the primary instrument for the rehabilitation of the poor (Mollat 1986, 299–300).

The Protestant Helping Stream

The "Protestant stream" can be illustrated additionally by the development of the Poor Laws in England (see chapter 9). The English Poor Law of 1602–1603 codified practices that had developed throughout the sixteenth century in England into a reasonably coherent set of public provisions for disadvantaged people. These provisions, I argue, stemmed from the Catholic ethic tradition, combined with the feudal and monastic traditions.

Times changed, however: "The Reformation wiped out every vestige of Catholic beneficence in England. The monasteries, with their associated hospitals, asylum houses, and schools were confiscated for the benefit of the king, his retainers and favorites" (O'Grady 1930, 1).

Perhaps in part because of this transformation, over the next 200 years there was increasing negativity toward poor people in England. Tensions between helping poor people and punishing them were very distinct, as detailed by De Schweinitz ([1943] 1961).[5] A "survival of the fittest" mentality grew, marked by policy reversal, upheaval, and, finally, the negative and hostile "Reform of 1834," in which "outdoor relief" (helping people in their own homes through money and supplies) was ended and poor people were placed in poorhouses or "houses of correction." That measure represents the peak of the hostility to poor people detailed by Mollat (1986)—whereby they became ostracized, criminalized, policed, and about as far from Christ's Poor as one could get. The horrors of the period are documented in Dickens' novels.[6] The Reform of 1834 occurred at the point of industrialization of England, when the perils and difficulties of the industrial transition were perhaps most acute and society exercised minimal control on the abuses of capitalism.[7] This "backward" step in the conception of poverty and the activities of government to help poor people must have greatly exacerbated the conditions that Marx saw and may have helped him form his ideas about the oppressive and exploitative nature of social systems.[8]

The Reform of 1834 set in motion the general poverty relief system we have today, at least in the West. Because governmental organizations' activities were limited, "private" activities developed; social work was central to this effort. The Charity Organization Society developed in England and moved to America, beginning in Buffalo, New York, in 1882. The Quakers maintained an important helping focus. The Salvation Army was founded and remains to this day a powerful helping organization. The tensions in England between public and private, governmental and voluntary ultimately were resolved in favor of public structures (the so-called welfare state) through the Beveridge Report and the need to provide governmental services to people injured by World War II. Whether private or public, however, these approaches tended to address the immediate problems faced by needy people and paid less attention to the structural causes of poverty.

The Catholic Stream

A detailed treatment of Catholic responses to the social question during the nineteenth century is provided by Misner (1991) in *Social Catholicism in Europe* and by Cort (1988) in *Christian Socialism.* Ashford's (1986) study, *The Emergence of the Welfare States* also is extremely informative.

Essentially, this stream involved seeking to develop responses to the exploitative challenges of the developing industrial system. Social reform was one development. A second was the rededication of traditional charities.

> The greater part of church people's active response to the needs of the age was . . . in the age-old works of mercy: direct succor for the poor and for those [the working poor] whose traditional livelihoods no longer supported them. This was done by reconstituting the helping institutions of the church on a new basis, now that the old ones had been swept away (Misner 1991, 35).

Perhaps "swept away" is too strong a term. The old systems were no longer adequate, and new vehicles had to be developed.

What were some of these new approaches? Religious socialism was one. It suggested that the church ally itself with revolutionary movements—an idea not well received by the Pope. Social reform for the "new poverty" was advocated in the Chamber of Deputies in France in 1840. On the private side, the Society of St. Vincent De Paul was founded. Patronages were set up (these were clubs of moderately well-to-do French people who sought to find apprenticeships for poor people).

These and other social works were not sufficient, however. The Revolution of 1848 is ample evidence of the problems and tensions of the age. Afterward, patronages increased, Christian factories began to develop, and corporations of tradesman and workers emerged.

There is no question that there were "liberal" and "conservative" elements within the social Catholicism of the nineteenth century. For our purposes, however, the key element is that there was a consistent, concerted attempt—through traditional and new modes—to meet human need.

Catholic culture, then, had a tradition of action. Even if it was not as vigorous as it might have been—confounded as it was by protecting its own institutional interests, national and class divisions, and checkmates—social Catholics, as well as the church itself, worked to aid disadvantaged people throughout the nineteenth century. The main helping vehicles of the social Catholicism were methods such as the following (see Levi 1989):

- *Helping:* One was the act of helping itself. Although divisions of opinion about the specifics occurred throughout Europe, "everywhere helping continued to play a part in the search for answers to the Social Question, and continues to do so today" (Levi 1989, 56).
- *Catholic Lay Association:* A second was the Catholic Lay Association, which is like the Knights of Columbus or the St. Vincent de Paul Society. There was a strong tradition of this kind of effort, stretching back to the Hospitaliers and the guilds.
- *Catholic Social Action:* A third was Catholic Action, a social movement that manifested itself sometimes as a political party, sometimes as a helping organization.
- *Catholic political parties and labor unions:* Catholic political parties and labor unions represent a fourth approach. Sometimes they were one and the same; sometimes they were distinct entities.
- *The state itself:* Finally there was the state itself. Levi (1989, 50) points to the fact that the church used the developing political power of the state, as well as associations and parties, to influence the social agenda. According to Wilensky (1981), this approach had a powerful impact.

Approaches to Poor People and Helping Them: Connections to the Protestant and Catholic Ethics

Obviously there are several different approaches one can take to providing help to people in need. One way to think about help is the distinction between institutional help and residual help (Wilensky and Lebeaux 1956). Institutional help means that help is part of the warp and woof of the community structure. This describes the Catholic approach. The residual approach, on the other hand, considers the individual the first line of helping—God helps them who helps themselves—and provides resources only when one's own are completely exhausted. That is more in line with the Protestant ethic approach.

Another approach looks at levels of cause and help, rather than the structure of how and when help is provided. One approach is to look at the individual level of cause. In this case, the "problem" is thought to be located at the level of the individual who "has" the problem. Freud looked at problems in this way. Much medical analysis is like this as well. This approach tends to resonate well with the individualism of the Protestant ethic.

Another approach, however (favored by Max Weber and Karl Marx), looks at the system as having important causal power. System-level causality fits well with the communitarian perspective of the Catholic ethic. For Weber, the causal elements were ideas—the Protestant Ethic, to be exact. For Marx, the cause of social phenomena, especially the exploitation of workers, was structural and depended on one's position in the social order.[9]

Marx was not the only thinker who was developing a structural explanation of the problems of poverty, however. Catholic thinkers before Marx were developing a structural critique of the existing social system as a causal factor in poverty. One of these thinkers was Phillipe Buchez, who developed a two-class theory of poverty (Levi 1989). Other vintners worked in this vineyard as well.

Although a great number of labels were attached to these individuals, they shared a common ground. They all searched for alleviation of industrial workers' distress. They all realized the novelty of the situation—especially the system-caused, rather than divine, nature of poverty (Levi 1989, 12).

Of course, when one sees and articulates poverty as the result of people and polities rather than the individual "victim," it presents a great problem. The people and polities in power who benefit from the status quo are unlikely to agree or want to do anything about it. Hence, the "blame the victim " strategy is an excellent way for people in power to avoid taking any responsibility for people who are powerless. It's *the poor's* fault. We do not have to do anything at all. Sen made the same point about famine: It is the result of a political act or series of acts—what Tuchman would call "folly" (Sen 1990; Galbraith 1984; Tuchman 1984).

There are ways other than the Protestant and Catholic ethics to look at poverty identification and helping diagnosis and strategies, such as institutional and residual, individual and system-level. Religiously connected language is one way to discuss these elements, but it is not the only vocabulary available.

Poverty and Poverty Relief in America

In America, relations between religious ethics were unlike those in Europe. America was—and to some extent still is—a land in which the Protestant Ethic was unchecked. There was no aristocratic or Catholic tradition for it to encompass. Indeed, Catholics and Jews, arriving later, provided the immigrant ethics butting up against a fairly well established "American Mind."

Poverty and its relief were localized, limited, and probably inadequate. Historians of Catholicism in America emphasize the important role the church played in aiding Catholic ethnic groups who were pouring into the country from Europe (Abell 1960, especially "Bibliographical Note," 289*ff*; Ellis 1969; Hennesey 1981). Though aid to immigrants was generous in spirit, as Gerber (1984) has pointed out, it also was an important element in Catholic motivation. The tradition of the Catholic ethic was important in America because governmental aid had not yet developed. There was episodic and uneven local assistance, but that fell far short of the need. By and large, however, efforts to fight poverty in America were largely "Protestant" in nature—characterized by low-level governmental involvement, high emphasis on voluntarism and voluntary localized efforts, suspicion of poor people, fault-finding, and individualized responsibility. America had a Society for the Prevention of Cruelty to Animals (SPCA) but no Society for the Prevention of Cruelty to Children until the turn of the twentieth century. Attention to children did not develop until a famous case was brought up in New York by the SPCA. Poor treatment of "Mary Ann" was brought forward by the SPCA on the sensible grounds that the abused girl in question was, after all, a species of animal! Gerber (1984) cites some of these developments (see chapter 9)—halting though they were—in Buffalo, New York. At about the same time (just before the Civil War), Dorothea Dix's influence peaked. The social reformer had been successful in securing support in many states for asylums for mentally ill people. The "Ten Million Acre Bill" that President Pierce vetoed in 1857 was "hers."

Poverty relief efforts with a moral flavor were more successful. The Temperance movement was one of the most successful, first in reducing the amount of alcohol consumption and then in securing a Constitutional amendment enforcing Prohibition. Interestingly, the Temperance movement actually started as just that: an attempt to control the amount of drinking, not to ban it. In the 1820s and '10s, however, drinking became imbued with a negative moral patina. Booze began to be associated with poverty—and then was suggested as a cause of it.[10]

In addition, the United States finally developed two assistance programs, both as a result of the Civil War. One was the Freedman's Bureau—a War Department office to aid freed slaves; the other was the Civil War Pension (also a War Department office), which was designed to provide benefits for (northern) Civil War widows. Both were allowed to lapse, in spite of arguments to continue and extend them.

Social work and training for social work began at this time. Among other developments, the Helping Organization Society—which had started in England because of the cutback in Public Relief as a result of the Reform of 1832—began to gain support in America. All of these efforts were private and relatively small, however, and they became the middle-class mission to poor people, with a reputation for "offering help with an upturned nose"; they cannot be considered to be within the spirit of the Catholic ethic. Furthermore, the "nativist" hostility to Catholics began to thrive at this time, as Billington (1964) outlines in *The Protestant Crusade*.

For these reasons, then, if help were to be given to poor Catholics, the Catholic community (communities, really) would have to organize it. Hospitals and religious orders continued to serve not only "their own," however, but others as well. In Buffalo, as Gerber points out, the Sisters of Helping "had, for a decade, operated the city's only hospital, public or private . . . which served people of all faiths, classes, and ethnicities" (1984, 125). When a poorhouse finally did get established (in a Protestant neighborhood), it

> was the subject of constant criticism by priests and other spokesmen for the immigrant poor, who reportedly received cruel treatment there. Major figures in the Protestant establishment complained about the very high mortality rate for the sick poor at the poorhouse relative to that at Sister's hospital (Gerber 1984, 132).[11]

The Catholic ethic had a rich tradition of helping patterns and action to draw on, beginning from the very foundations of (Catholic) Christianity and moving through the helping structures of the succeeding centuries.

The Twentieth Century

At the turn of the twentieth century, a new spirit of social help and social reform was in the air. The Social Gospel movement is one example, in addition to the policies advocated by the Bull Moose party and municipal reform, conservation, and progressive movements in general. Much of the impetus for these movements flowed from the subdominant commitment to helping within the Protestant ethic. The Social Gospel was a

Protestant movement, but it indicated that the climate of the country had changed. The Social Gospel looked to the system as much as to individuals for causes of poverty. Much of this effort, however, was stimulated as well by the large number of Catholics flowing into the country. By 1910, large numbers of Catholics and Jews had immigrated to the United States, and the Catholic ethic and the Jewish ethic were represented in larger populations—leading to a rebalancing impulse. These new additions to the "American character" made a difference; they must have been an encouragement to subdominant Protestant ethic impulses as well as forces in their own right.

Furthermore, Catholic helping behaviors were politically important later, in establishing the social acceptance necessary for the New Deal and the Social Security Act to succeed. True, Al Smith—a Catholic—lost the presidential election to Herbert Hoover in 1928, but the fact that he got the nomination in the first place showed how things had changed.

Charles Morris, in his masterful *American Catholic,* talks about the Catholic influence:

> The most influential American Catholic economic thinker was Msgr. John A. Ryan, sometimes called "Right Reverend New Dealer" by critics of his unabashed support for the Roosevelt administration. A priest of the St. Paul Archdiocese assigned to Catholic University and the NCWC [National Catholic Welfare Conference], Ryan was in much demand as a speaker and as a Congressional witness, elaborating Catholic principles in books like *The Living Wage* and *Distributive Justice.* He burst to prominence in Catholic intellectual circles in 1919, when he drafted the "Bishops' Program for Social Reconstruction," banging it out in five hours when an NCWC committee decided they needed to make a public statement. The "Bishops' Program" called for a long list of basic economic reforms, including a legal minimum wage, government sponsored health and old-age insurance, strict child labor laws, tougher antimonopoly enforcement, and equal wages for women. The radical reformer Upton Sinclair called it a "Catholic miracle" (Morris 1997, 151).

Ryan drafted the "Bishops' Program" in 1919. His ideas came to be part of the foundation of programs we take for granted today. The ideas were not just his, of course; he crystallized the helping elements in the Catholic ethic. Individual aid (old-age insurance) and systemic issues (antimonopoly enforcement) were part of the list. These two themes have always been part of the Catholic ethic, from the time when the laws of Italian cities were rewritten to attempt to influence social policy elsewhere in Europe (Wilensky 1981) to attempts to pass social security legislation in the United States. The action element of the Catholic ethic may be as alive and well today as ever (Abell 1960).

In the United States, the Catholic ethic tradition has left its stamp. The institutional development has been impressive. Catholic Charities USA is now the among the largest private social service organizations in the United States, with a total revenue of more than $3 billion.[12] There are other national groups—the Jesuit Volunteer Corps, for example—and more local ones. There are schools of social work at most Catholic universities. In Detroit, Focus Hope, founded by the late Father Cunningham, is an outstanding example.

On the social action side, the Catholic Worker movement, organized by Dorothy Day, took a more militant view that brought a sharper focus to the structural causes of much inequality (Miller 1982). Day was a fierce crusader for social justice (and a pacifist).

Perhaps one of the most important statements of current views of the Catholic ethic came from the American bishops—the Bishops' Letter of 1986 (National Conference of Catholic Bishops 1986). This document serves as cultural and structural evidence that the Catholic ethic is alive and well in contemporary society. Its content, viewed as an example of conceptualization of the problem of poverty, continues the attitude of altruism described in chapter 9. The fact of its existence; the fact that it circulated widely, among religious and nonreligious people alike; and the fact that the bishops debated it in public are all consistent with the Catholic ethic tradition of action. Moreover, some of the content of the Bishops' Letter is not just conceptualizing and preaching; it is laced with concrete suggestions and plans for action. Many people have chosen to fault certain suggestions. The bishops themselves, however, suggested that their proposals were made only to stimulate discussion and mix reality with the rhetoric; the calls to action do not have the same status as the more conceptual parts of the letter. It is within the tradition of the Catholic ethic, however, to express both parts—a conceptual, cultural approach to poverty and helping, as well as specific suggestions for action.

In at least one situation, however, the Catholic ethic urges restraint from action, rather than action. This caution concerns judgments about poor people—especially judgments that might be found under the more moralistic umbrella of the Protestant ethic tradition. The bishops comment:

We ask everyone to refrain from actions, words, or attitudes that stigmatize the poor, that exaggerate the benefits received by the poor, and that inflate the amount of fraud in welfare payments.

These are symptoms of a punitive attitude towards the poor. The belief persists in this country that the poor are poor by choice, or through laziness, that anyone can escape poverty by hard work, and that welfare programs make it easier for people to avoid work (National Conference of Catholic Bishops 1986, section 194).

The Catholic bishops captured very well the underside of views toward poor people—a view that is subdominant in the Catholic tradition but occupies a more dominant position in the Protestant ethic tradition.

In addition to the Bishops' Letter, there are other examples of action in the Catholic ethic. The Catholic social service system continues to fill a role in health care, operating major hospital systems throughout the world and across the United States. These and other Catholic helping organizations make a concerted effort to further the helping tradition.

For example, in a recent effort to determine whether the helping tradition has continued, the Catholic Hospital Association developed the "social accountability budget" to measure whether service is being provided to poor people. What accounting procedures permit an empirical assessment of service to poor people?[13] It is in the Catholic ethic tradition to ask such questions—and to develop procedures for answering them. The social accountability budget is a manual "which provides a set of guidelines and worksheets for planning and reporting community benefits, especially services to the poor" (Catholic Health Association 1991, 42). The Catholic Health Association also surveyed its members. Its major findings:

> 1) Catholic health care facilities have shown sustained and increasing commitment to providing care for the poor and (providing) other community services, despite growing fiscal constraint.
> 2) Many Catholic health care facilities are engaged in an explicit process to reinforce, measure, and plan for their contributions to the community (Catholic Health Association 1991, 42–43).

This result is surprising, in a sense, but it should not be when it is considered within the Catholic ethic tradition. It conveys several structural elements of the Catholic ethic. First, it represents action on behalf of poor people. Second, it includes the broader community, not just Catholics, in that scope. Third, it specifically assesses services to test what is being given and whether it is enough. The assessment reinforces the commitment and thus becomes a fourth point.

This action of the Catholic Health Association sounds like the medieval bishops Mollat (1986) discusses, who tried to spend one-fourth to one-third of their resources on poor people. Apparently, there has always been this concern about doing enough and looking to see whether enough was actually being done.

The idea of one-fourth of a parish's resources going toward poor people has a historical basis. Does it have any contemporary relevance? In at least one case, it certainly does. The diocese of Lansing, Michigan, presented relevant figures in its financial report of 1988–1989. The diocese's combined income for that period was just a little less than $3.7 million. The Catholic Charities Department controlled 24 percent of those monies—just below that medieval goal. When one adds the ministries budget of 12 percent of the total (including ministries to deaf people, campuses, the Hispanic community, and handicapped people), however, a total of 36 percent goes to prohelping efforts—right on the medieval money, as it were. That amount is impressive, and it is emblematic of the Catholic ethic tradition.

One last point about the Catholic ethic and prohelping action—with respect to Catholic education—must be made. Evaluating educational expenditures is always difficult for social services analysts because they fall into a middle ground. On one hand, providing educational services to a population is indeed providing a service and perhaps should be counted as such, like health services or universal pensions. It is an improvement in human capital that should count as much as counseling someone with a broken heart or fixing a broken arm. In the American context, however, unlike in Europe, education expenditures seem always to be factored out or at the very least reported separately. That may be because Americans just don't like social aid and prefer to rename it or legitimize it in some other way (e.g., veterans' benefits, tax expenditures). In any event, that question need not be settled here. Suffice to say that many scholars emphasize one part of the Catholic educational system as specifically relevant to a discussion of the Catholic ethic: the constant emphasis in Catholic schools on values and experiences/practices. Thus, Catholic education becomes, if not an occasion for helping, propoor action itself, a setting for teaching, showing, reinforcing, and legitimizing the Catholic ethic.

Liberation Theology

One of the most important contemporary movements for social justice and social change in South America is liberation theology. This movement emphasizes action aimed toward removing social, economic, and political inequalities. The movement raises several issues that are important in a consideration of the influence of the Catholic ethic in the twentieth century.

Liberation theology may be the most recent and most influential of religious developments proposing action on behalf of poor people. Levi (1989) argues that although much of liberation theology is a reworking of older concepts, there are some new ideas:

> Liberation theologians have introduced at least two novelties in their suggestions for remedies for poverty. One is assigning to the church and religion substantial responsibility for material improvements in life on this earth as a preparation for entering the Kingdom of Heaven. . . . The other novelty lies in their encouragement of action to translate principles into reality (Levi 1989, 61).

Neither of these ideas seems very new in historical context; each draws on that context. These are things that, in some ways, the Catholic Church has always tried to do. What does seem novel, however, is the aggressiveness and immediacy with which these goals are pursued, as well as the fact that the analysis and action target, and act on, privileged and well-to-do people. Social action within the church Ecclesiastical Base Communities and the People's Church also signal an identification with poor people and participation by poor people as preferred methodologies, each of which is innovative and powerful.[14]

Conclusion

The Catholic ethic has an impressive history of action toward social helping, a conception of community that enacts its sense of wholeness through prohelping, and, especially, propoor action. Although the fact that this confluence exists makes it seem as if it were obvious, such a link is really not obvious. There are many situations in which action does not match thought. America itself provides one example. Founded by people who sought religious freedom, the new communities quickly began to exclude people with different views.

A second point is that this pattern of action toward poor people has persisted over time and space. There certainly have been periods of waxing and waning, but the overall prosocial consistency is amazing for social institutions. Variations of these early efforts endure to this day.

By way of bringing this discussion together, let's consider the kinds of approaches developed under the Catholic aegis from a social services perspective:

- **Building-centered programs** such as monastic almonries exist today in "feed the poor programs" in many churches.
- **Social policy** (such as the propoor encyclicals and Bishops' Letters) continues to this day.
- **"Outreach" programs** designed to seek out poor people currently operate in the form of parish and local community development.
- **Hospitals** continue to offer service.
- **Aid to travelers and immigrants** operates today through Catholic Charities.
- **The Poor Table** can be seen in diocese and parish poverty relief efforts.
- **Religious orders** devoted to poor people continue to exist and work.
- **Secular helping societies** also continue to exist and work.
- **Wills and bequests** remain vehicles to aid churches and provide help through community foundations.
- **Papal and aristocratic helping** have emerged in governmental social programs and in religious efforts to help poor people in many specific instances.[15]

Third, Catholic culture was not characterized by the periods of negativism and poor hating that one so often finds. The Catholic ethic's prosocial emphasis and spirit of community was a tent to which the prodigal sons and daughters could, indeed, return.

PART IV

Expressions of the Catholic Ethic: Public Policy Opinion in Contemporary America

Several years ago I wrote a book called *Public Policy Opinion and the Elderly* (Tropman 1987). It involved an analysis of trends in American public opinion on policy issues in the third quarter of the twentieth century. As a way of looking at public opinion on policy issues, I introduced the term "public policy opinion." This phrase referred to something more than "just" public opinion, if public opinion is restricted to how people feel about things. The "policy" component invokes an action element. Public policy opinion looks at questions about what people would like themselves or someone else to *do* about a situation or a policy area. For example, would people pay more in taxes to support seniors? Would people pay more in taxes to provide health care? If you (the respondent) were doing the federal budget, how would you rearrange it among a range of social needs? And so on.

I am doing something similar in this section. I review a range of public policy opinion data from various sources (the National Opinion Research Center at the University of Chicago, the Gallup Poll, some published tables in Greeley's work) to look at the three major facets of inquiry we have been exploring in this volume: the Catholic ethic, the spirit of community, and the helping impetus.

Throughout I look, by way of dividing the data, at differences by major religious group (Catholics, Protestants, and Jews). More distinctions would be wonderful—ethno-Catholics; African American Protestants; Orthodox, Conservative, and Reform Jews. The only characteristic these data made available, however, was race; thus, I can distinguish between white Protestants and black Protestants. This distinction is of some importance because black Protestants are very different from white Protestants on social welfare measures, yet they would be numerically swamped within the larger group if they were not factored out. The overall result of these analyses is that, on empirical grounds, Catholic identification does make a difference, in the direction of community and the direction of helping.

CHAPTER 11

Let the Numbers Do the Talking

Is there any empirical support for the two main assertions of this study—that there is a Catholic ethic, and that it is of a helping nature? Perhaps the first question to ask in this context is, "What would the evidence look like, were we to find it?" In other words, it is not immediately clear what data would provide convincing evidence of the form and nature of the Catholic ethic. Therefore, the initial task of an empirical assay would be to consider this question.

What Would Evidence Look Like?

Empirical evidence in the social sciences typically relies on measurements of attitude and behavior, usually shown in numbers. Because attitudes and behaviors do not always agree, measurements of both are ideal.[1]

I use measures of "policy opinion"—reports of attitudes and behaviors from national samples of American citizens. The dependent variable (the thing to be explained) is various measures of community orientation and support for helping actions. The independent variable (the thing that does the explaining) is religious identification. Catholic respondents are more positive than others in terms of community helping measures.

It is not altogether clear, however, what kind of differences we should expect. For one thing, I am talking here about an ethic—either Catholic or Protestant—that exists in archetypal form, somewhat independent of what individual people may manifest. Indeed, one might ask (though I have not done so here) how close any given individual is to the ideal. With respect to actual respondents—Protestant or Catholic—I argue that they are subject to mixed and conflicting values (see Tropman 1989; see also chapter 13 of this volume) that would depress the sharpness of the empirical differences. Hence I shall seek—or be satisfied with—small but consistent differences over a range of measures, surveys, and approaches. More particularly, I shall look for *patterns* of difference. One must have more than one point to get a straight line, for example. In addition, I shall develop some index variables. In general, indexes composed of several indicators of the same dimension should perform better than the original measure because more information is captured. That turns out to be the case here.

Others may take issue with these approaches, and to some extent I do as well. In the beginning of any work, however, there is an absence of standards to apply, so one begins with an approach that surely will be changed later.

The Catholic Ethic

Is there some sort of focused and interrelated set of ideas, values, attitudes, and beliefs that characterize Catholics? Although on one level the answer would seem to be, "Well, probably yes," the concept of the Catholic ethic as such has not been previously developed in scholarly literature.[2] Despite the absence of the use of the *term*, scholars have tried to look at the *idea* of religious difference, focusing on Catholics.

One of the early sociological works on this topic, *The Religious Factor* (1963) by Gerhard Lenski of the University of Michigan, comes to the following conclusion (based on data collected in 1958):

> Our study has provided striking support for Weber's basic assumption—at least as it applies to major religious groups in contemporary [circa 1963] American society. As the findings . . . make clear, the four major socioreligious groups [white Catholics, white Protestants, black Protestants, and black Catholics] differ from one another with respect to a wide range of phenomena affecting economic, political, kinship, and scientific institutions. Furthermore, *these differences cannot be accounted for in terms of the economic position of either the individuals involved or the groups* (Lenski 1963, 357; emphasis added).

Several scholars, of course, have examined the ways in which various religions differ with regard to their sociological implications. There have been comparative studies of Christians and Jews, Catholics and Protestants, and so on.[3] Lenski also outlined expected differences between Protestants and Catholics, using data from the Detroit Area Study (DAS).[4] He was very explicit hypothetically about how he expected Catholics to behave:

> We may expect the behavior patterns linked with the Catholic group are likely to become somewhat more prevalent while patterns linked with the white Protestant group become less common. . . . Gradual changes in population composition [will] encourage many, or most, of the following developments:
>
> 1. Rising rates of church attendance in American society;
> 2. Strengthening of religious group communalism;
> 3. Strengthening of both the nuclear and extended family systems;
> 4. Declining emphasis on intellectual independence;
> 5. Increasing support for welfare state policies;
> 6. Increasing support for the Democratic Party;
> 7. Shifting focus from work group to kin group;
> 8. Slowing rate of material progress and perhaps also of scientific advance;
> 9. Rising birth rates;
> 10. Narrowing latitude for the exercise of the right of free speech;
> 11. Increasing restraints on Sunday business, and divorce, and possibly birth control; and
> 12. Declining restraints on gambling and drinking (Lenski 1963, 361).[5]

One of the most important features of Lenski's (1963) work was that the differences he found were not large. In a way, one might expect such a result, given the open nature of American society and the multiplicity of influences that obtain. Nevertheless, some people expect large differences or expect one variable to explain large proportions of the variance between several religions. Instead, we will have to look at such differences where they occur and not expect too much of any single variable—religion, race, gender, income, or any other factor.

A second point about Lenski's work is that he was so specific about his expectations that scholars have depended on his work since its publication. Several of his findings (on familism and welfare-statism in particular) support the point about the helping orientation of the Catholic ethic tradition, but for now we can regard Lenski's work as an early statement of the Catholic ethic values package.

Despite the meticulousness of Lenski's work—or perhaps because of it—other scholars have reexamined and challenged his findings. Greeley (1964), in particular, raised questions and objections. Howard Schuman reported an important replication in 1971. Schuman's study was important because it used the same survey approach that Lenski used (i.e., the DAS); Schuman was able to adopt many of the methodological and technical advances since the earlier research, however. Based on these adaptations, he wrote:

> Most of our conclusions about an intrinsically religious factor, therefore, must be negative. But not quite all, for a single question on work values, repeated in 1966 . . . did replicate Lenski's results; moreover, stronger results were produced in favor of the hypothesis than were apparent in 1958. Also the question seems theoretically closer to the conceptual meaning of the "Protestant ethic" than most of the other variables. . . . In particular, under a variety of controls, Protestants significantly more than Catholics rank as most important their attitude "that work is important and gives a feeling of accomplishment" (Schuman 1971, 45–46).[6]

Lenski (1963) and Schuman (1971) asked respondents to rank five values involved in choosing a job in order of importance: high income; no danger of being fired; working short hours, lots of free time; chances for advancement; the work is important and gives a feeling of accomplishment. Table 11.1 reports the results.

TABLE 11.1   *Detroit Area Study: Survey Responses of White Males Giving First Rank to "The Work Is Important and Gives a Feeling of Accomplishment" versus Other Values when Choosing a Job*

Year	Percentage Choosing "Protestant Ethic Response" ("Work is Important")		
	Catholics	Protestants	Jews
1958	44	52	48
1966	44	49	52
Social class (1966)			
Upper middle	58	68	ND[a]
Lower middle	44	47	ND
Upper working	38	40	ND
Lower working	37	37	ND

Note: For details on class categories, see Schuman (1971, 35). [a]ND = no data.

In sum, it seems that differences in work attitudes, lodged largely in the upper middle classes, are a significant source of difference between Protestants and Catholics.[7] Prevailing attitudes toward work held by Catholics could indeed be part of a Catholic ethic. Of course, Lenski could have been more right when he did the work; the world had changed by the time Schuman came along, and powerful processes of amalgamation were at work (Morris 1997).

Another follow-up to Lenski examined relationships between individuals, family and friends, and voluntary associations. McIntosh and Alston (1982) used a different data set—the combined National Opinion Research Center General Social Survey for 1974, 1975, and 1977 ($N = 3,278$). They conclude that religion plays an important part in national life:

> The principal thrust of Lenski's *The Religious Factor* is that religious life links Protestants and Catholics to secular life in different ways. We have found that religious life does provide such a linkage, but it operates largely in the same fashion for Protestants and Catholics (McIntosh and Alston 1982, 875).

The zero-order relationships between religion (a dummy variable: Catholics = 0; Protestants = 1) were not large, but they were statistically significant.[8] McIntosh and Alston comment again on social class: "What we have shown, however, is that what social class divides, religion unites. Religious commitment leads to greater secondary and primary ties in particular tying family, neighborhood and voluntary organizations together" (McIntosh and Alston 1982, 876).

In a way, one could think that the Catholic ethic is spreading. Because McIntosh and Alston's data are newer than Lenski's, they seem to indicate that Protestants, in this dimension—religious commitment being linked to ties to family, and so forth—are moving closer to Catholics; it is a hypothesis to consider. In any case, we can expect substantial mixing of attitudes in a country such as the United States. After all, Catholics have been converging with Protestants in terms of economic achievement (if not in work values), so some movement the other way is not out of the question.

Lenski's structural predictions were generalized and codified, though not directly, by the work of Andrew Greeley (1990). Greeley clearly believes that Catholics and Protestants *do* have different values. Members of each group "imagine" things differently, he says—a phenomenon he calls the "analogical imagination," in contrast to the "dialectical imagination" (Tracy 1989). Greeley extends this notion to outline a specific set of expected behavioral consequences rather than the "population tendencies" described by Lenski (1971):

> Catholics will be more likely than Protestants to value social relationships. . . . Catholics will be more likely than Protestants to value equality over freedom. . . . Catholics will be more likely than Protestants to advocate decentralization. . . . Protestants will value in their children the virtues of initiative, integrity, industry and thrift more than Catholics, while Catholics will value loyalty, obedience, and patience. . . . Protestants are more likely to emphasize personal responsibility (Weber's "worldly asceticism") than Catholics; they will also be more likely to emphasize the "work ethic" than Catholics, who will be more likely to work because they have to than because they want to (Greeley 1990, 47–48).

Greeley's (1990) thinking reflects and extends Lenski's (1971), and he does so with a much wider base of empirical data (using several countries) and more sophisticated analytic techniques. Greeley's predictions and results, summarized from his extensive review of empirical works, are displayed in Table 11.2.

Of 36 variables, 21 (58 percent) fell in the hypothesized direction. Of 63 betas—21 each for country (the United States, Great Britain, Ireland, Canada, and Australia), denomination, and denomination under 40 years old—all but three were statistically significant.[9] The betas ranged from .02 to .60. The median betas were .13 for country and .07 for denomination and for denomination under 40 years old. Thus, the distinctions were clear but were not really strong.[10]

Another way of looking at the matter might be to develop a religious "scale" to measure attitudes. There is a Protestant ethic scale but as yet no Catholic ethic scale.[11] Andrew Greeley has developed something similar, however, called the "GRACE" scale (a 7-point scale between forced choices of pictures of God: mother/father; master/spouse; judge/lover; king/friend) (Greeley 1990, 41).[12] Regarding the GRACE scale, Greeley says, "Religion, I saw, could be profitably approached as a predictor variable that is of some considerable importance in understanding social attitudes and behaviors" (1990, 43). Almost echoing Lenski's comments of decades earlier, Greeley comments, "The religious imagination, then, does contribute to people's social and political attitudes and behaviors, and its contribution cannot be reduced to either demographic or political orientation" (1990, 42). Could these effects be manifest within a concept called the Catholic ethic? The answer must be affirmative.

In his scholarly work, Greeley (1990) has shown that there is a distinctive Catholic "imagination"; it could be called a Catholic ethic. The Catholic ethic is global, like the Catholic Church itself. Greeley's multinational data and McIntosh and Alston's (1982) data from many ethnic groups within the United States showed differences between religious groups that, though significant, were modest in strength. Thus, thinking about the power of the Catholic ethic needs to be tempered; perhaps, by extension, thinking about the Protestant ethic should be tempered as well.

What of current differences and similarities between Catholics and Protestants in America? Data from the Gallup organization, taken from a Times/Mirror Gallup Typology Survey conducted May 13–22, 1988, provide one of the most complete pictures of these conditions. These data are displayed in Table 11.3.

The data presented in Table 11.3, which indicate important differences in every area, suggest the presence of a Catholic ethic. Some of the differences are greater than others, of course, but the *consistency of differences* suggests that Catholics, on the whole, think differently about things (more in some areas than others) than Protestants.[13] It is not really necessary to show that the differences are huge—just that they are significant and consistent. (After all, each individual is subject to many influences other than religion.)

Notice too that the confirmations come in the areas considered parts of the Catholic ethic—work, otherworldliness, fault-forgiveness, and understanding; these correlations indicate the characteristics of a Catholic ethic. The data do contain some surprises, however. With regard to family ties, Catholics were less family oriented than I (and others) would have thought. Obviously this area needs further attention by religious sociologists.[14] It also is necessary to point out (though the data are not included here) that white Protestants differ considerably from black (or African American) Protestants. In general, African American Protestants tend to be more "liberal" than white Protestants, although that is not always the case. Because of the complexities of those data, they require analysis on their own.

Indeed, this point is crucial. African American Protestants are a contrasting (or subset) subculture within the Protestant ethic, like the Quakers and the Salvation Army, or the Mormons. Elements of the African American experience—slavery, oppression, exploitation—no doubt were important formative forces in developing a helping ethic of their own.

Another relevant data set has been collected by the National Opinion Research Center at the University of Chicago in the General Social

TABLE 11.2   *Differences between Catholics (C) and Protestants (P) on a Range of Issues*

Issue	C	P	Issue	C	P
Equality vs. Freedom			*Spouse and parent*[r]		
1. **Freedom** vs. equality[a]		+	18. **Parent**	+	
1a. Changing society[b]		+	19. **Spouse**	+	
Fairness			*Marital success factors*		
2. **Fairness**[c]		+	20. **Marry1**[s]	+	
Social change			21. Marry 2[t]		+
3. **Change 1**[d]		+	22. **Marry 3**[u]		+
4. Change 2[e]		+	23. Marry 4[v]	No prediction	
5. Change 3[f]		+	*Divorce factors*		
Confidence in social institutions			24. Divorce1[w]	+	
6. Army, police, church, legislature, civil service	+		25. Divorce2[x]		+
7. Unions, press, legal system, education	+		*Child-rearing factors*		
Work factors[g]			26. Child1[y]		+
8. Work 1[h]	+		27. **Child 2**[z]		+
9. **Work2**[i]	+		28. Child 3[aa]	+	
10. Work3[j]		+	29. **Child 4**[bb]	+	
Tolerance factors			30. Child 5[cc]	+	
11. **T_1**[k]	+		31. **Child 6**[dd]	+	
12. **T_2**[l]	+		*Family revolution factors*		
13. **T_3**[m]	+		32. **Family 1**[ee]	+	
Morality factors			33. **Family 2**[ff]	+	
14. **M1 Life Ethic**[n]	+		*Religious factors*		
15. **M2 Personal Ethic**[o]	+		34. **Church**[gg]		+
16. **M3 Social Ethic**[p]	+		35. **Devotion**[hh]	+	
17. M4 Pacifist factor[q]		+	36. **Doctrine**[ii]	+	
			Weber factors		
			37. Postsecondary education[jj]	+	
			Durkheim factors		
			38. Cohesion[kk]		+

Source: Organized from Greeley (1989a).

+ = religious orientation that should be stronger.

+ /bold = hypothesis upheld.

[a]*Catholics* = more freedom.

[b]*Catholics* = prochange.

[c]Three variables (attitudes toward pay scales; control of business firms; and the right of workers to understand before obeying). *Catholics = Profairness.*

[d]Changes that would improve respect for authority and family life.

[e]Changes in emphasis on money, work, and lifestyle (directions unspecified).

TABLE 11.2   (*Continued*)

^fChanges in more [*sic*] respect for individual and technology.

^gHow would you spend time if work week reduced to a three-day week with same pay.

^hEmphasis on family, hobby, relaxation, study.

ⁱEmphasis on community service/small business of one's own.

^jEmphasis on avoiding boredom/getting another job.

^kReject immigrants, unwed mothers, members of sects, students, large families, and students as neighbors.

^lReject political dissidents of left and right.

^mReject criminals, heavy drinkers, mentally ill neighbors.

ⁿDisapproval of homosexuality, prostitution, divorce, suicide, mercy killing, premarital sex, adultery, and drug use; the "life-ethic factor."

^oDisapproval of lies, cheating on tax, welfare and transportation fare, and buying stolen property; the "personal ethic factor."

^pDisapproval of strikebreakers, political assassins, joy riding, fighting with police, not reporting an auto accident; the "social ethic factor."

^qDisapprove of killing in self-defense.

^rCommonalities between respondent and parent/spouse (Catholics have higher number of common elements/variables).

^sSimilarity of backgrounds: religion, politics, tastes, child-rearing attitudes, sharing of chores, and income.

^tHigh loadings on tolerance and respect.

^uHigh loadings on satisfactory sex and living away from in-laws.

^vHigh loading on faithfulness.

^wDivorce acceptable when violence, unfaithfulness, absence of love, unsatisfactory sex, and personality conflict are present.

^xDivorce acceptable when sickness, dislike of relatives, and financial problems are present.

^yPositive loadings on independence, leadership, imagination; negative loadings on manners.

^zHigh positive loadings on politeness, work, thrift, negative on respect.

^{aa}Positive on obedience, unselfishness.

^{bb}Positive on religion.

^{cc}Positive on self-control and patience.

^{dd}Positive on loyalty and duty.

^{ee}Emphasis on sexual traditionalism.

^{ff}Emphasis on traditional relations between parents and children.

^{gg}Satisfaction with the church's response to human needs.

^{hh}Measures religious behavior.

ⁱⁱAcceptance of traditional beliefs.

^{jj}Catholics less likely to seek postsecondary education.

^{kk}Protestants more likely to be lonely.

TABLE 11.3   *Protestant (P)-Catholic (C) Similarities and Differences (P-C), White Protestants Only (Percentage Agreeing with Statement)*

Statement	P	C	P-C
Otherworldly			
Success in life is pretty much determined by forces outside our control.	**38.3**	**43.9**	**−5.6**
Work			
Hard work offers little guarantee of success.	**29.2**	**32.8**	**−3.6**
The strength of the country today is mostly based on the success of American business.	**81.8**	**78.9**	**2.9**
Fault/forgiveness cycle			
We have gone too far in pushing equal rights in this country.	**51.3**	**45.3**	**6.0**
I think it's all right for blacks and whites to date each other.	**35.7**	**53.1**	**−17.4**
School boards ought to have the right to fire teachers who are known homosexuals.	**59.8**	**44.5**	**15.3**
Books that contain dangerous ideas should be banned from public school libraries.	**55.4**	**50.3**	**5.1**
There are clear guidelines about good/evil that apply to everyone regardless of the situation.	**84.3**	**75.2**	**10.1**
Family			
Too many children are being raised in day care centers these days.	72.4	71.8	0.6
I have old fashioned values about family and marriage.	91.5	85.8	5.7

Source: Interuniversity Consortium for Social and Political Research, University of Michigan (italicized question headings added), Times Mirror/Gallup survey, 2,294 U.S. adults, administered May 13–22, 1988.
Note: Bold items support Catholic ethic thesis.

Survey (GSS).[15] Some of these data examine general attitudes held by Catholics and Protestants, providing yet another way to approach the Catholic ethic question. In these surveys, Catholic/Protestant differences have to be assessed on measuring support for views that "the world is evil" versus "the world is good"; "human is evil" versus "human is corrupt"; "the good must act" versus "the good must beware"; and, in a test of one of Greeley's predominant notions, "God is not here" versus "God is here." These data are presented in Table 11.4.

TABLE 11.4   *Contrasting Worldviews of Protestants and Catholics; National Opinion General Social Survey, 1983–1989 Combined*

God here vs. not here

	Here (1–3) (%)	Uncertain (4) (%)	Not Here (%)
Protestants	73.9	17.1	8.4
Catholics	71.8	20.6	7.6
Index of dissimilarity = 3.2 percent[a]	N = 1,325		

The world is evil

	Evil (1–3) (%)	Uncertain (4) (%)	Good (5–7) (%)
Protestants	21.2	27.0	51.8
Catholics	13.5	26.6	59.9
Index of dissimilarity = 8.1 percent	N = 5,105		

Man is evil vs. good

	Evil (7–5) (%)	Uncertain (4) (%)	Good (3–1) (%)
Protestants	19.2	22.7	57.9
Catholics	9.7	21.5	68.8
Index of dissimilarity = 10.65 percent	N = 5,097		

Good must beware vs. good must act

	Beware (7–5) (%)	Uncertain (4) (%)	Act (3–1) (%)
Protestants	24.0	27.4	48.5
Catholics	14.6	28.3	57.1
Index of dissimilarity = 9.45 percent	N = 1,341		

[a]Index of dissimilarity is calculated by subtracting the Catholic percentage from the Protestant one (Absolute Difference), summing the differences, and dividing by 2. The resulting percentage difference can be interpreted as the percentage change either column (or row) would have to make to become identical with the other column. It ranges from zero, if the columns (rows) are identical, to 100 percent if the columns (rows) are completely different.

What do these data tell us? The most important point, revealed in the first segment of the table, indicates a difference of the sort Greeley (1990) suggests in terms of whether Protestants see God as removed from the world, whereas Catholics see God as present in the world.

On the basis of his [Tracy's] study, he suggested that the Catholic imagination is "analogical" and the Protestant imagination is "dialectical." The Catholic "classics" assume a God who is present in the world, disclosing Himself in and through creation. The world, and all its events, objects and people tend to be somewhat like God. The Protestant classics, on the other hand, assume a God who is radically absent from the world, and who discloses himself only on rare occasions (especially in Jesus Christ and Him crucified). The world and all its events, objects and people tend to be radically different from God (Greeley 1990, 45).[16]

The data do show a Protestant/Catholic difference, but not quite in the direction that Greeley seemingly would have wanted. A large percentage of both groups sees God as present (God is here) in the world (more than 71 percent); a minority in each group sees God as removed (God is not here) from the world (less than 7.5 percent). Apart from this finding, the small (3.2 percent) difference between the two views actually runs in the other direction—showing that Protestants are more likely to see God as present in the world. Greeley was not necessarily wrong, however. As we have seen (and the data in the remainder of the table suggest), there are important differences in Catholic and Protestant attitudes. The question might not be a valid measure of Greeley's construct, or Greeley may have slightly misconstructed the construct because he is certainly right in his main premise—that there are differences in how Catholics and Protestants see the world.

The next three sections of the table, which deal with questions about evil in the world, evil in humans, and the need to be wary, show consistent, definite differences between Catholics and Protestants. Catholics are more likely to think the world is good (by 8 percent), more likely to think that "man" is good (by 10.6 percent), and more likely to think that the good must act (by 9.4 percent).

Are these differences important? Almost certainly the answer is yes. It is hard to know how to think about percentage differences; we do not have a metric for doing it in social science data. We do have such a metric for auto loans, however, and that standard is a good one to apply here. Percentage differences of 3, 4, or 5 percent are low, just as they would be for an interest rate on an installment loan. Rates of 8, 9, or 10 percent are substantial, just as they would be on a loan, and rates closer to 18, 19, or 20 percent are high—and really quite striking. The differences here fall into the "substantial" department. They are significant, important, and definite. They certainly do not suggest completely different cultures for Protestants and Catholics; nor would that be expected, considering that they share the Christian tradition and many other structural features. There are differences between the groups, however, and these differences describe the nature and scope of the Catholic ethic concept.

The Catholic Ethic as a Helping Ethic

Some elements of a helping approach and support for welfare-state initiatives are suggested in the earlier data. The question about whether "the good must act" suggests that the impulse to translate Christian principles into action is present in Protestants and Catholics but is stronger among Catholics.

In their work on *American Piety,* Stark and Glock (1968) provide a contemporary picture of the attitude of altruism. They look (*inter alia*) at two measures, "doing good for others" and "loving your neighbor," as necessary for salvation. On both measures, Catholics exceeded Protestants (57 percent versus 52 percent and 65 percent versus 58 percent, respectively). Two caveats are in order, however. One is that the differences were not great. Second, there was a great amount of variation among the Protestant denominations, so "Protestant" is not a unitary category at all.

In more recent surveys by Gallup and Castelli (1989), a welfare-state measure was presented, testing support for increased spending for four types of programs: social security, health care, aid to homeless people, and aid for elderly people. The patterns of findings are similar to those in Stark and Glock (1968). White Catholics gave more support than white Protestants to each of the four spending programs—by 6 percent, 3 percent, 5 percent, and 3 percent, respectively (Gallup and Castelli 1989, 202). The pattern is still there, however. The Catholic ethic is alive and well, if converging, among American Catholics.

Other data from the Gallup poll illustrate differences between Catholics and white Protestants on helping-related questions. Relevant data are presented in Table 11.5. Items that support a prohelping/pro–welfare state orientation are in bold type.

In six of nine cases, the responses indicated a more helping orientation among Catholics—an orientation that supports government action to care for needy people. Although the differences between Catholics and Protestants are definite, they are not striking. The largest distinction, however, is in responses to the last question in the list: "The government should guarantee every citizen enough to eat and a place to sleep." On that item, there was a substantial difference: 59.4 percent of the Protestant respondents and 70.9 percent of the Catholic respondents were in agreement. Differences are present, and in the direction that I have hypothesized. The differences are modest, however, rather than huge—suggesting the importance of other variables.

Another test of orientation would be to ask people how they would reallocate government spending. After all, it is one thing to say that certain things should be done; it is quite another to shift allocations (and perhaps increase taxes) to bring change about. Admittedly, this exercise still measures attitudes, but it does ask individuals to do more than simply express an opinion. Resulting data are presented in Table 11.6. Again, results favoring a Catholic ethic thesis are in bold type.

TABLE 11.5   *Protestant (P)-Catholic (C) Similarities and Differences (P-C);
Welfare State/Helping-Related Questions, White Protestants Only
(Percentage Agreeing with Statement)*

Helping-Related Questions	P	C	P-C
The federal government should run only those things that cannot be run at the local level.	82.0	74.3	**7.7**
The federal government controls too much of daily lives.	64.3	54.6	**9.7**
The government is really run for the benefit of all the people.	51.6	58.1	**−6.7**
Business corporations strike a fair balance between making profits and serving the public interest.	43.6	41.1	2.5
There is too much power concentrated in the hands of a few companies.	77.2	77.8	−0.6
Our society should make sure everyone has an equal opportunity to succeed.	91.1	90.7	−0.6
It is the responsibility of government to take care of people who can't take care of themselves.	72.4	72.8	**0.6**
The government should help more needy people even if it means going deeper into debt.	48.4	54.4	−6.0
The government should guarantee every citizen enough to eat and a place to sleep.	59.4	70.9	**−11.5**

Source: Times Mirror/Gallup survey, 2,294 U.S. adults, May 13–22, 1988.

These data make clear that Catholic respondents want to increase governmental expenditures in all areas, indicating support for government operating as an agent in the community. Second, the larger distinctions tend to be in areas of human service concern, such as health care, assisting minorities, unemployment assistance, and social security. The results regarding aid for minorities are of interest because they correlate with a similar attitude toward racial harmony shown in Table 11.3 regarding interracial dating.

Other assessments would be in order, however, including an examination of the role of variables in an index of several components. Because any given question in a social research survey taps only one dimension of complex constructs, indexes—apart from their utility in data management—often actually provide better measures of complex constructs than single questions do. Pyle (1991) constructed an index variable on "helping orientation" of four questions available from the GSS.[17] One

TABLE 11.6   *Protestant (P)-Catholic (C) Similarities and Differences (P-C); Welfare State/Helping-Related Federal Budget Questions, White Protestants Only*

Question: "If you had a say in making up the federal budget this year, for which of the following programs would you like to see spending increased, decreased, or kept the same?" (Answer reported here: percentage saying budget should be increased)

Answer	P	C	P-C
Programs for the elderly	71.2	76.0	−4.8
Programs for the homeless	62.4	68.9	−6.5
Improving public schools	66.8	67.6	−0.8
Reducing drug addiction	64.4	70.1	−5.7
Improving nation's health care	67.4	72.8	**−10.4**
Programs to assist blacks and other minorities	22.2	38.0	**−15.8**
Scientific research	39.8	52.9	−13.1
Government assistance for unemployed	32.2	45.0	**−13.7**
Research on AIDS	65.5	72.4	−6.9
Social Security	58.0	66.8	**−10.8**

Source: Times Mirror/Gallup survey, 2,936 U.S. adults, April 25–May 10, 1987.

question, regarding spending on assistance to poor people, was subsumed under the rubric *Natfarey*.[18] A second was *Helppoor* (should the government improve the standard of living?);[19] the third was *Eqwlth* (should government reduce income differences?);[20] and the last was *Govless* (should government spend less on poor people?)[21] The index, *ALLDEVAR* (ALL DEpendent VARiables; 4 = "propoor;" 12 = "antipoor") comprises these four questions. The relationships among the index variables, ALLDEVAR, and their means are displayed in Table 11.7.

Table 11.7 reveals some of the value of an index. The average intercorrelation among the component variables is 0.30. Each variable is correlated with the index variable at a much higher level, however—an average of 0.72.[22] How does religious identification affect these variables? The notion of the Catholic ethic would predict that the mean score for Catholics is lower (more supportive of helping and welfare activities) than the mean score of Protestants, and it is. For these data, the mean for Catholics is 6.50 (the range is 4 to 12), whereas the mean for Protestants is 6.71. Although this difference is in the expected direction, it is certainly small. This difference is heightened, however, when race among Protestants is taken into account. The mean score for African American Protestants (5.72) is lower than that for Catholics, whereas the mean score for white Protestants is 7.21! It seems that a key corre-

TABLE 11.7 *Intercorrelation Matrix and Means, Four Welfare Indicator Variables and Index Variable, National Opinion General Social Survey, National Opinion Research Center*

Welfare Indicator Variable	[1]	[2]	[3]	[4]	[5]
[1] Natfarey (Spending to help poor) (1 = too little; 3 = too much)		0.33	0.23	0.24	0.68
[2] Helppoor (Should government improve standard of living?) (1 = government action; 3 = people help selves)			0.34	0.38	0.74
[3] Eqwlth (Should government reduce income differences?) (1 = should; 3 = no government action)				0.21	0.73
[4] Goveless (Government should spend less on poor.) (1 = disagree; 3 = agree)					0.73
[5] ALLDEVAR (All dependent variables) (4 = "propoor"; 12 = "antipoor")					
Mean	**1.40**	**1.91**	**1.87**	**1.51**	**6.65**
Protestants (All)					6.71
White Protestant					7.21
Black Protestant					5.72
Catholics					6.50

late in the views of Protestants—in this area anyway—is the difference between African American and white Protestants rather than differences between denominations.

How much of the index variable is explained by religion? The answer is not as great as some people might have expected: About 10 percent of the variance in ALLDEVAR is explained by the religion of the respondent.

Variables other than attitudes toward helping and welfare policies reveal other differences between Catholics and Protestants. The GSS data consider a variety of variables, as follows:

1. POLIVIEWS: (think of self as liberal or conservative: 1 = extremely liberal; 7= extremely conservative)
2. EDUCATION (highest year in school completed: 1, 2, 3 = low, medium, high)

3. REGION (New England = 1; Pacific = 9)[23]
4. SEX (1 = male; 2 = female)
5. AGE (age of respondent)
6. RACE (race of respondent:1 = white; 2 = black; 3 = other)
7. RINCOME (income of respondent: 1 = low; 2 = medium; 3 = high)
8. PRESTIGE (respondent's occupational PRESTIGE score: 1 = low; 2 = medium; 3 = high)
9. CATHPROT (Catholic = 1; Protestant = 2)

Other religious codes include the following:

10. JEW (0 = no; 1 = yes)
11. WHITEPROT (0 = no; 1 = yes)
12. BLACKPROT (0 = no; 1 = yes)
13. CATHOLIC (0 = no; 1 = yes)
14. NONE (no religion) (1, 1−)

Regression analysis results are displayed in Table 11.8. These data are Bs, betas (β), and level of significance for seven of these independent variables.

Table 11.8 is interesting for several reasons. First, the overall equation is significant, in that none of the predictors (the independent variables) derive their importance through chance. Within this overall picture, however, there are important differences for separate variables. For example, the *Cathprot* score is important, but not as important as other variables. It shares last place with *Age* and *Prestige* as predictors of the helping index. In this respect, the results are in the appropriate direction but not as strong as might be expected to show the existence of a Catholic ethic tradition. Which variables are strongest? Education, race, and political views are in the top spots; *Poliviews* is highest, with a β of .24. Race is a strong second, with a β of −.22.

These results are similar to those in a 1987 analysis of policy opinion data in 17 different areas of public concern with questions on the trustworthiness of the government, the rights of accused criminals, and women's rights (Tropman 1987). Data were from the National Election Survey (NES), conducted every other year (coinciding with congressional elections) since 1952 by the Institute of Social Research at the University of Michigan. For this analysis, data gathered between 1952 and 1978 were considered in a huge matrix involving multiple questions and multiple years. There, as here, several independent variables were considered as explanations for the patterns of the data. In the NES data, race was statistically significant the greatest proportion of times (mean

TABLE 11.8   *Multiple Regression Results Predicting Helping Index (ALLDEVAR):
Race and Policy Opinion Are Strong; National Opinion Research Center General Social
Survey, 1983–1988 Combined*

Variable	B	β	Significance
1. Cathprot	0.37	0.08	0.03
2. Education	0.48	0.17	0.00
3. Poliviews	0.35	0.24	0.00
4. Rincome	0.26	0.10	0.01
5. Race	−0.86	−0.22	0.00
6. Age	0.01	0.09	0.03
7. Prestige	0.19	0.08	0.05

Multiple $r = 0.47$
$r^2 = 0.22$
ALLDEVAR scored with 4 = propoor; 12 = antipoor.

number of times = 72 percent); a variable similar to the GSS's *Poliviews*, *Party Identification*, was second (mean number of times = 69 percent). Catholic identification was important (mean number of times = 44 percent) and ran in the middle of the predictor pack. In the NES data, as in the GSS findings, income was of low importance in predicting attitudes (Tropman 1987, especially tables 3 and 4).

These similar results from separate surveys confirm the robust relationships between similar types of variables. Apparently, thinking of oneself as a liberal or conservative is an "ethic" also.

Looking at the combination of race and religion is important. Developing an equation in which Whiteprot as a variable in its own right enables us to see whether this idea holds up. These data are presented in Table 11.9a and 11.9b.

These numbers are similar to those in the previous table. The r^2 are quite the same, even though the specific variables are a little different. What is critical here is that in the data in Table 11.9a, Catholic identification is unimportant in predicting the negative helping index ALLDEVAR, while Whiteprot is in third place, just behind the negative value of Race.

If one adds other religions to white and black (African American) Protestants in the same equation (predicting ALLDEVAR, our helping index), then Catholic has a β of .046, black Protestants have a β of −.002, and white Protestants have a β of .163! Not only may the Catholic ethic be more supportive of helping and poor people in general; the Protestant ethic may be slightly negative.

TABLE 11.9a   *Multiple Regression Results Predicting Helping Index (ALLDEVAR): White Protestant, Race and Policy Opinion Are Strong; National Opinion Research Center General Social Survey, 1983–1988 Combined*

Variable	B	β	Significance
1. Whiteprot	**0.55**	**0.14**	**0.019**
2. Education	0.35	0.12	0.001
3. Rincome	0.26	0.10	0.007
4. Poliviews	0.35	0.24	0.000
5. Prestige	0.19	0.08	0.047
6. Catholic	**0.03**	**0.00**	**0.888**
7. Race	−0.62	−0.15	0.004

Multiple r = 0.459
r^2 = 0.211
ALLDEVAR scored with 4 = propoor; 12 = antipoor.

Given these results, one is encouraged to look further, perhaps at class/income divisions as well as race. For this purpose, a variable called RELCON was constructed, involving high, low, and middle positions on three variables: income, education, and *Prestige*. The results are presented in Table 11.10. The most astonishing difference in this social class

TABLE 11.9b   *Multiple Regression Results Predicting Helping Index (ALLDEVAR): Policy Opinion, White Protestant, Education and Race Are Strong; National Opinion Research Center General Social Survey, 1983–1988 Combined*

Variable	B	β	Significance
1. Poliviews	0.34	0.24	0.000
11. Whiteprot	0.64	0.16	0.214
2. Educ	0.39	0.14	0.000
6. Race	−0.49	−0.12	0.061
8. Prestige	0.19	0.08	0.055
7. Rincome	0.20	0.07	0.064
5. Age	0.01	0.06	0.076
3. Region	0.04	0.05	0.150
13. Catholic	0.20	0.04	0.687
4. Sex	−0.11	−0.03	0.444
10. Jew	0.53	0.03	0.487
19. None	0.18	0.02	0.745
12. Blackprot	0.00	0.00	0.985

Multiple r = 0.470
r^2 = 0.221
ALLDEVAR scored with 4 = propoor; 12 = antipoor.

TABLE 11.10   *Helping Variables, by Catholic/Protestant Religious Identification and Social Class (High Social Economic Status [HISES] Featured); National Opinion Research Center General Social Survey, 1983–1988 Combined*

Helping Variable	Catholic			White Protestant		
	LoSES	AveSES	HiSES	LoSES	AveSES	HiSES
Assistance to the poor						
% Too Little	72	72	**69**	73	62	**49**
Should government improve standard of living?						
% Favor	38	33	**30**	35	24	**15**
Government spend less on poor						
% Disagree	70	64	**57**	75	54	**41**
Government reduce income differences						
% Agree	57	51	**45**	57	46	**31**
Responsibility of government to meet needs						
% Agree	67	65	**54**	63	45	**39**
Social welfare benefits are a disincentive						
% Agree	**45**	47	32	**60**	48	38

Note: Bold type emphasizes text discussion of interaction of religion and class.

index over a range of variables is the extent of the disparity, in all but one of the reports, between the Catholic group of high socioeconomic status (SES) and the white Protestant high-SES group, ranging in magnitude from 14 percent to 20 percent. These differences are substantial and statistically significant in every case. In a sense, then, there is greater diversity of attitudes within the white Protestant community, with an important element of concern about poor people and programs for them coming from the high-SES group.

This distinction could mean that Catholics have more "communal consciousness" across class lines. Although money is one indicator of class, it may have differential effects depending on the variables with which it is combined. This point is worth stressing because income alone, as measured in the foregoing regressions, is not a reliable indicator of attitudes toward helping.

This argument suggests a new twist on the old concept of class consciousness. Perhaps one cause of the objections to that term has been its supposed universal application. In these data, however, we see a tension between the "class consciousness" of white Protestants and the "communal consciousness" of Catholics. This idea of communal consciousness articulates well with the descriptions of Catholic communities Greeley shares in his scholarly and fictional works; it reflects a communalism in which a sense of family and community is important.

Let me speculate further about this distinction before I go on to the final section of data analysis. Communal and class consciousness may have more than one axis of differentiation—more than one way of looking at the axis of differentiation. Both orientations require a "precipitate" (an activator or starter). For community consciousness, the precipitate may be a sense of "we" or "us." Conceptions of "them" or "the other(s)" are present; these "others" represent people who are outside the clan, but they are amorphous and undifferentiated and lack centrality and focus.

For class consciousness, on the other hand, the precipitate may be—and may be defined by—"the other." "The other" is highly differentiated and focalized and perhaps very threatening and specific. "We-ness," the beginning point in communal consciousness, is a residual in class consciousness. Hence, individuals might act not out of class consciousness "for" themselves as much as "against" others.

Concepts of poor people and of poverty, as well as the thoughts and actions involved in helping disadvantaged people, may be important precipitates for class consciousness and a central "other" to it, rather than a product of it. It may be for this reason that in Catholic helping there is no distinction between the worthy poor and the unworthy poor. Indeed, as Gregory Baum points out in Appendix A, there is no theological position that would justify such a distinction.[24]

I have argued that the very issue of poverty and how it was viewed was one of the growing, unbridgeable tensions in Christianity that caused the Reformation—a value chasm too large to span. Perhaps I can put some meat on the bones of that argument here. The additional flesh involves this very point: the developing difference between community-centered and class-centered thinking and identification, between categorical (similar, parallel) forms of membership and corporate (interdependent) forms of identification, between what Durkheim (1960b) called mechanical and organic solidarity. If class consciousness is corporate and organic, a question about understanding the importance of the "other" emerges: In the most general case, *a person's status is defined in relationship to the other.* More specifically, the position of poor people is now much more clear; for those at the top of the ladder, position is determined by relation to those at the bottom; *simply—indeed simplistically—stated, if there is no bottom, there is no top.* Hence in the Protestant ethic, the position of poor people, the certainty that they have their own deserved status and that prosperous people should not help them too much, is essential to maintaining social position. Indeed, in this organic/corporate formulation, helping poor people destroys one's own position, actually and/or psychologically.

Here, perhaps, we can speculate about two crucial mistakes Marx (and others) may have made about class consciousness. One error was to assume that class consciousness operated equally across horizontal strata in society. Apparently, if the foregoing observations and data are valid, different processes operate in different parts of society, and some, including class consciousness, crystallize in social layers; other processes, including those that support a communal nature, crystallize along society's columns.

The second error, which is even more interesting, is that those thinkers assumed that the primary driver of class consciousness was deprivation. The foregoing data indicate, however, that affluence may be the prime indicator of class consciousness instead; well-to-do people are more conscious of class distinctions than less well-off people.

The Catholic Ethic and Welfare State in International Perspective

One additional point about the Catholic ethic and the welfare state must be considered from an empirical point of view. In considering the role of the Catholic ethic in the development of the welfare state, it is necessary to consider the history of European states, especially Sweden, that are Protestant and have substantial welfare programs.

First, it is necessary to look at the historical connections between Protestantism, Catholicism, and economic achievement—the effort that roused Weber's interest initially. Data from one of the most recent works in this field, Inglehart's 1990 book *Culture Shift*, are displayed in Table 11.11.

These results show the power and the decline of the Protestant ethic. Around the turn of the twentieth century—the time Weber was writing— the economic growth rate of Protestant countries was 152 percent of the economic growth rate of Catholic countries. The economies of Protestant countries were growing much faster than the economies of Catholic countries. By 1984, however, the Protestant growth rate had dropped to 72 percent of the Catholic growth rate. Inglehart comments, "The system that linked Protestantism with wealth and democracy seems to be becoming less distinctively Protestant because it is permeating other regions of the world" (1990, 60–61).

Thus, the Protestant ethic may be losing some power and was more temporally specific. What of a Catholic ethic? Inglehart reviews Durkheim's study of the link between Catholicism and lower suicide rates:

Cultural differences in reported subjective well-being may be somewhat similar to cultural differences in suicide rates. Over ninety years ago, Durkheim (1897 [1951]) observed that suicide rates are mark-

TABLE 11.11   *Economic Growth Rates in Protestant Countries (P), Compared with Catholic Countries (C) and Japan (B), 1870–1984*

Rank	1870–1913	1913–1938	1949–1965	1965–1984
1.	U.S. (P)	Japan (B)	Japan (B)	Japan (B)
2.	Canada (P)	Norway (P)	W. Germany (P)	Norway (P)
3.	Denmark (P)	Netherlands (P)	Italy (C)	France (C)
4.	Sweden (P)	U.S. (P)	France (C)	Belgium (C)
5.	Germany (P)	Switzerland (P)	Switzerland (P)	Italy (C)
6.	Belgium (C)	Denmark (P)	Netherlands (P)	W. Germany (P)
7.	Switzerland (P)	Sweden (P)	Canada (P)	Canada (P)
8.	Japan (B)	Italy (C)	Denmark (P)	Netherlands (P)
9.	Norway (P)	Canada (P)	Norway (P)	Denmark (P)
10.	Gt. Britain (P)	Germany (P)	Sweden (P)	Sweden (P)
11.	Netherlands (P)	Gt. Britain (P)	U.S. (P)	U.S. (P)
12.	France (C)	France (C)	Belgium (C)	Gt. Britain (P)
13.	Italy (C)	Belgium (C)	Gt. Britain (P)	Switzerland (P)

Mean economic growth rate in Protestant countries, as a percentage of mean economic growth rate in Catholic countries:

152	120	98	72

Source: Inglehart (1990, 60).

edly higher in Protestant or nonpracticing Catholic countries than in predominantly Catholic countries. Despite immense socioeconomic changes and a widespread decline in religiosity (especially in Northern Europe), the national suicide rates indicate that Durkheim's finding is still valid to a considerable extent. Though suicide rates fluctuate with economic conditions and other events, a substantial difference persists between the suicide rates of countries in which the public consists primarily of practicing Catholics (such as Ireland, Spain, and Italy) and those of Protestant countries and countries where attachment to the church is weak (Inglehart 1990, 205).

More of Inglehart's data are displayed in Table 11.12. Inglehart adds a caveat to these figures, however:

Clearly, the situation is more complex than a simple Catholic versus Protestant or nonpracticing dichotomy would suggest, for by this standard, the Greeks are more Catholic than the practicing Roman Catholics, and Northern Ireland, though mainly Protestant, shows a suicide rate almost identical with that of the Catholic Republic of Ireland. Nevertheless, there is evidence of considerable continuity in cultural attitudes toward suicide (Inglehart 1990, 205).

TABLE 11.12   *Suicide Rates in Western Nations,*
1976–1978

Country	Reported Suicides per 100,000 Inhabitants
Hungary	40.3
Finland	25.0
Denmark	23.9
Switzerland	23.8
Austria	22.7
West Germany	21.7
Sweden	19.4
Japan	17.7
Belgium	16.6
France	15.4
Canada	12.8
United States	12.5
Norway	11.4
Netherlands	9.2
Portugal	8.5
Great Britain	7.9
Italy	5.8
Ireland	4.7
Northern Ireland	4.6
Spain	3.9
Greece	2.8

Source: U.N. Demographic Yearbook, 1979. See Inglehart (1990, 244).

All the same, Inglehart's (1990) data and analysis show that attitudes that reflect a Catholic ethic tradition were thriving, in effect, when Weber described the Protestant ethic and when Durkheim looked at suicide data for various religions; furthermore, data indicate that the Catholic ethic tradition continues to be influential to this day.

To measure the social impact of the Catholic ethic tradition, we must assess whether the Catholic orientation can be observed working through political channels to influence government policy. Such a study would involve assessing the predominantly Catholic political parties found in Europe and examining whether community helping legislation prospered when Catholic political power was in a position to move governmental policy and action.

In his study of "Leftism, Catholicism, and Democratic Corporatism," Wilensky (1981) addresses some of the concerns posed by this question.

This paper attempts to (go) . . . beyond both old versus young party systems and crude measures of working class strength to consider the ideological stance and power of two mass-based political parties—Left and Catholic. . . . What counts is the strength of the collective push for equality (1981, 348).

Wilensky devised measures for left party dominance and Catholic party dominance.[25] "In general, Catholic power (wherever Catholic parties exist) shapes welfare state development much more than left power" (1981, 347–48). Wilensky points out that Catholic power is an important variable in European states, even controlling for other variables.

Catholic power holds up as a direct and indirect determinant of big spending. For instance, when they are in the same equation, Catholic power is even more important than the proportion of aged as a predictor of welfare effort in 1966 (1981, 356).

In the particular equation, Wilensky (1981) predicts social security spending as a percentage of gross national product in 1966. The variable of Catholic party power between 1919 and 1976 had a β (predicting weight) of .55 (p = .01). The proportion of persons age 65 and over in the population (an important variable in explaining social security spending in almost all countries) had a β of .51 (p = .01). This result is amazing, especially considering the relative strength and political organization of elderly populations (see Wilensky 1981, 356). These results indicate that there is a Catholic ethic at work, acting powerfully in many countries and over time.

Wilensky makes two additional points that are relevant to the argument here. First, the Catholic party works through and energizes the institutional church. "Catholic parties, once formed, can and do build upon the ancillary institutions of the Catholic Church, which are much older than the Centralized State" (Wilensky 1981, 362).

Second, it is not just Catholic political power being examined but a Catholic ethic that comprises several important dimensions. One of these dimensions (which I discuss in chapter 10) is the structural organization of the Catholic Church. The argument was that one of the reasons for welfare state support among Catholics was that the church itself is a bureaucracy—and a bureaucracy that is devoted to the cause of helping people: The Catholic Church is organized like a welfare state, and this historical experience makes the transition from sacred bureaucracy to secular bureaucracy easier.

Thus, the Catholic ethic directly supports welfare state activities, and it does so indirectly, through supporting what Wilensky (1981) calls

Catholic Party Power   Corporate   Welfare Effort
1919–1976 $\longrightarrow$ Technocratic Linkages $\longrightarrow$ Social Security/GNP

FIGURE 11.1. *Evolution of the Welfare State from the Catholic Ethic: Wilensky's Hypothesized Path*

corporatist democratic structures. Wilensky defines corporatism as follows: "By democratic corporatism, I mean the capacity of strongly organized centralized economic interest groups interacting under government auspices within a quasipublic framework to produce peak bargains involving social policy" (1981, 345). His model looks like Figure 11.1 (Wilensky 1981, 362). Thus, there is some support for the importance of the structure of the Catholic Church itself as contributing to, and extending, the Catholic ethic.

Catholicism and leftism work in similar directions, according to Wilensky (1981). Although they are not identical, they have a common interest in poor people: "What contemporary socialists and Catholics have in common, aside from their desire to attain and maintain power, is a traditional humanistic concern with the lower strata" (1981, 364).[26]

This affinity can help answer—or at least provide perspective on—a question regarding the development of welfare state activity in predominantly Protestant countries. There are two answers: The first anwer, which is correct but not awfully strong, is that the Protestant countries were Catholic first and have those Catholic traditions as a part of their cultural heritage. The Catholic ethic is present and practiced still.

The second answer depends on that heritage but uses some of Wilensky's observations: "There remain at least three clear exceptions: Sweden, Norway, and Finland. . . . [The] pattern . . . suggests the functional equivalence of Catholicism and leftism. . . . Where Catholicism cannot leave its mark, leftism can" (1981, 366).

In short, where Catholicism was replaced or rejected, the concerns represented by the Catholic ethic remained, and they emerged in leftist politics. Something like the model in Figure 11.2 might be a useful rendering.

In short, where Catholicism became limited, for whatever reason, concerns for poor and disadvantaged people that were a part of its tradition became transmuted into another form—a form that was acceptable within the culture and structure of the time. In many locations, that meant leftist political orientations. Doubtless there were other reasons for the formation of leftist politics. Secular humanists have always existed. Individuals who felt they could not support Catholic doctrines, for

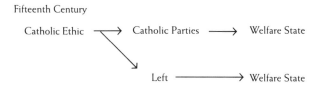

FIGURE 11.2.   *Evolution of the Welfare State from the Catholic Ethic: Tropman's Hypothesized Path*

historical (the Inquisition, for example) or contemporary reasons might have found a home within the left.[27]

Conclusion

In this chapter I have attempted to show that the Catholic ethic has support in the empirical realm. An examination of relevant data reveals support for the general idea of a Catholic ethic, support for a helping emphasis within the Catholic ethic, and support for an international (or at least European) version of the Catholic ethic.

Some caveats are in order, however. Support for these notions has been documented within a range of controls. However, differences between views held by different religious groups are not huge. Anyone who expected to see Catholics on one side of a big fence and Protestants on the other will be disappointed. Indeed, as I discuss in chapter 12, there probably is some trace of a "Catholic ethic" and something of a "Protestant ethic" within each individual.

A second caveat is that there is an important difference within Protestantism (at least in the United States) between white and African American believers. African Americans seem to be, if anything, more "liberal" than Catholics on certain "welfare state" measures. This finding suggests that although the Protestant ethic is important, it has some powerful limitations.

White Protestants considered as a group, however, were somewhat negatively oriented to welfare activities. This finding suggests the importance of exploring the "other side" of an ethic that celebrates work and achievement.

Finally, the Catholic ethic seems to exist in an international, or at least European, context. This finding was encouraging, documenting that the Catholic ethic endures across national boundaries.

This chapter does not, of course, provide exhaustive empirical support for the Catholic ethic concept. Many questions remain. Could we, for example, develop a Catholic ethic "scale" (as has been done with the Protestant ethic)—using, perhaps, relevant elements from Greeley's "GRACE" scale? How much are these "tilts" really put into practice? Can we look at actual behaviors (as the Catholic Hospital Association was looking at budget fractions)? How do we explain "inverted" Catholics (those for whom subdominant elements of an ethic have become dominant or prominent, although they remain nominally, at least, identified with the ethic anyway) who look more like Protestants on public opinion measures? What about "inverted Protestants" (Quakers, African Americans, Salvation Army, among others) who have a helping orientation that looks like the Catholic ethic? More detailed study of empirical data is yet to be done. We can show statistically significant differences between Catholics and Protestants, however—certainly significant enough to give credence to the concept of the Catholic ethic. An exciting agenda lies ahead.

PART V

The Long View: Past, Present, and Future

What is the meaning of the Catholic ethic and the spirit of community in the larger picture? What is the importance of the fact that Catholics tend to be more inclusive of community? Would the Catholic ethic make a "better world" for people than the Protestant ethic? No, because in the real world all drinks are mixed drinks. Cultures are a mixture of ethics.

Thus, there are no "orthodox" cultures. One of the great causes of wars is the search for the one "shining path" and the insistence that everyone live according to it. For most true believers, the right way is pretty much the same as "my current way" or, perhaps, "the way I grew up with." Yet the search for cultural and ideological purity apparently is never-ending. Humans—many of us anyway—are uncomfortable in fuzzy reality.

Each of the ethics I have been looking at here is itself a mixed bag. Within the Catholic ethic itself, diversity rather than uniformity is the rule.

Problems don't stop there, either. Even in a fuzzy state, ethics still have force. Although Benedict's (1934) shame orientation and guilt orientation (as thumbnails of Eastern and Western cultures) have a lot of ambiguity within them, they still have a driving orientation, a thrust, something that requires an "other." There is, it seems, a search for complementarity. The bad news is that no ethic is sufficient unto itself. Community calls out for individualism; the reverse is true as well. Hence, from the perspective of your culture, other cultures may meet many of your needs that your own does not. For this reason, there is a process of incorporation going on all the time, a process in which elements of "foreign" cultures are brought into your own and claimed, after one fashion or another, as your own. Blending occurs not only within but between.

Then, of course, there is the attitude/behavior problem. Social psychologists have long been aware of the fact that what people believe they should do is not always what they actually do. Sometimes this gap is for the worse: People are supposed to love their neighbor—and say they do—but act to drive their neighbor away. They fail, as it were, to "walk the talk." At other times, our enemy saves our lives. In the current analysis, "Catholics" and "Protestants" act in ways that are different from the core value system. We see Catholics who are not community or helping oriented and Protestants who are community helpers.

Sects break off; become, over time, churches; in turn cause other sects to form; and so on. According to Winston Churchill, the future is "just one damned thing after the other." Yet it seems to have a repeating pattern. Yogi Berra put it well: "It's like déjà vu all over again." Hegel put it more philosophically: thesis, antithesis, thesis. . . .

Chapters 12 and 13 explore some of these issues. In chapter 12, I explore the value of "ideal typology" as a way to present the Catholic and Protestant ethic perspectives and extend this analysis into a dualistic theory of values. I also use the Catholic ethic perspective to review the history of the American "welfare" state and explore why we Americans find helping so difficult.

In chapter 13, I consider things that might bother one about the Catholic ethic concept—or any religious-based culture, for that matter. For example, can someone be *both* Protestant and Catholic? The answer, at the cultural level, is "of course," but that answer perturbs Catholics and Protestants alike. What happens if one is "trapped" in one's religion? By this I mean that one commits to some, but not all, of the religious elements of the religion of origin. One can leave, of course, but then *trapped* would not apply. Some people prefer "schism," in which the old religion is replaced by a legitimized new one; others prefer "sects" in which the main commitment is retained but a different— sometimes substantially different—practice is expressed. Trying to work out competing commitments is a constant in the human condition.

CHAPTER 12

Applications of the Catholic Ethic Concept: Schematics and Prismatics

Schematics

This work has described the Catholic ethic as an ancient tradition—older than the Protestant ethic, but still vital today. The Catholic ethic has been, and is, oriented toward community, helping, and sharing. The Protestant ethic—which arose partly in responsive adjustment to over-emphasis in the Catholic ethic—was and is oriented toward achievement, gain, and individualism. The Catholic ethic culture has strong supports for prosocial activities; the Protestant ethic has strong supports for proindividual actions. The Catholic ethic fosters a communal class consciousness, whereas the Protestant ethic engenders a personal status consciousness. The Catholic ethic has a fair-share orientation, whereas the Protestant ethic has a fair-play orientation; the Catholic ethic considers concern for others to be central, whereas the Protestant ethic considers concern for individual achievement central.

The shape and influence of these different cultures can be measured and observed in many ways—from ethno-Catholic nation-cultures such as France, South America, Quebec, Italy, Ireland, Poland, Mexico, and Spain to the ethno-Catholic community cultures of Irish, Polish, German, Hispanic, and so forth in the United States; from the early hospitality structures for pilgrims trudging to the Middle East holy lands to Catholic Charities USA. Empirically, in American society at least, there are clear and significant, albeit not massive, differences between attitudes held by Catholics and those held by Protestants.[1] How should we think about these differences?

An Archetypal Paradigm

One way to look at the two ethics is to see them sharply etched—as archetypal or ideal typical paradigms. Naturally, such an approach pushes the differences further apart. It is a way to look at the differences overall, however. Table 12.1 illustrates the differences in polar form. It is expanded from a shorter list in my earlier book (Tropman 1996). There I called the types Alpha and Omega; hence, here they are Alpha 2 and Omega 2. This list establishes a set of defining terms that represent the "essential" ethic. No one would really be totally one or the other—a point I stress below. Ideal types do provide a useful point of departure, however.

In the left-hand column of Table 12.1 are dimensions of culture. These dimensions are vectors on which all cultures usually take a position. One is the self. How is the self constructed? One approach is the "Frank Sinatra approach": I did it my way, and alone. The self is regarded as me, myself, and I. Alternatively, the self can be regarded as entwined in a community of identification. In this approach, an individual, though still an individual, cannot imagine oneself within thinking of oneself as a Jew, a Japanese, an Italian, a whatever.

In looking at others, cultures develop perspectives on what to expect. One expectation can be of fundamental cooperation: People will help. Another perspective regards competition as the fundamental element: The game of life is tough, and the winner takes all.

Cultures have norms for being "out and about." One set of rules is called "fair play." Everyone starts at the same starting line, and differential finishes are allowed and expected. Another is called "fair share," in which it is important to see that everyone has basic resources and every kid has a turn.

Status can have two aspects as well. One is a fixed status—sort of a caste system; the other is a mobile system. Alpha 2 has mobility in this life, caste in the next (saved or not); Omega 2 has more of a fixed system in this life (your place!) but a lot of mobility with respect to salvation status.

When trouble comes, one ethic asks, "Whose fault was it?" and then, "Can I help?" The other ethic asks, "Can I help?" and then, "Whose fault was it?" In the former, as often as not, trouble is regarded as the victim's fault.

In terms of helping, there are differences (remember the Buffalo, New York, example) regarding whom we should help. One ethic emphasizes people who are worthy of help; the other emphasizes those who are in need of help. In particular, "worthy" often is defined as chipping in as opposed to copping out. If God helps those who helps themselves, then they are worthy of my help as well.

The ethics also take different perspectives on the nature and availability of resources. Alpha 2 regards resources as scarce; stockpiling is

TABLE 12.1 *Two Basic Value Packages*

Value Dimensions	Alpha 2 Attitude	Omega 2 Attitude
1. Religious connect	Protestant ethic	Catholic ethic
2. Self	Solo self	Ensemble self
3. Others	Competitive	Cooperative
4. Major process norm	Fair play	Fair share
5. Status	Either/or	Up and down
6. Responsibility	Cause/fault Blame the victim	Condition Help the victim
7. Bases of help	Worthy	Needy
8. View of resources availability	Draining pond	Refilling spring
9. Key metaphor	Each tub on its own bottom	A rising tide lifts all boats
10. Property	I "own" my personal property	I am a "trustee" of my personal property
11. Approach to conflict	Responsibility	Remorse
12. Approach to resolution	Justice	Recompense
13. Approach to offenders/ perpetrators	Punishment	Treatment
14. Approach to personal anger	Retribution	Forgiveness
15. Approach to situations	Rules over results	Results over rules
16. Capturing phrase	Mountain man	Wagon train
17. Other ethics	Tokugawa ethic (Japan)	Jewish ethic
18. Salvation view	A few slots—the chosen; zero-sum game	Many slots—my Father's house has many mansions; non–zero-sum game
19. Conceptualization of God	Angry Father	Holy Trinity
20. Intercessor to God	In Jesus' Name	Mary; all the saints; the church
21. Decision processes	Optimizing	Satisficing[a]
22. Rewards	Winner take all; die with the most toys	Winner take enough; die poor
23. Hero	Patton	Gandhi; Mother Teresa
24. Signature value	Achievement	Equality
25. Deming connect[b]	Unique causes of variation	Common causes of variation

[a]Satisficing means "good enough," looking for *a* needle in the haystack not *the* needle.
[b]"Deming connect" refers to W. Edwards Deming, the guru of the quality movement. Until recently Deming was not well accepted in America because he emphasized the collective elements of the organization, rather than the individual, as responsible for quality. On the other hand, Deming's work was widely accepted in Japan; that country's most prestigious award for quality is named after him.

okay. Omega 2 regards resources as plentiful—there is more than enough for all—so there is no need to acquire. The draining pond perspective and the refilling spring perspective capture these differences exactly. In the draining pond, each tub is on its own bottom: Everyone is on his own. In the refilling spring, the added resources lift us all.

With respect to orientation toward property, in the Alpha 2 perspective, my property is *mine*. I own it. It does not matter if I am using it, or even if I need it; The fact that it is mine is enough. There is no stricture or suggestion, therefore, that I should do any particular thing with it. Whatever I want to do is okay. On the other hand, the Omega 2 trustee perspective says that although I *have* the property, I also am a *caretaker* of it for others around it/me and for my children and the future. Hence, I have a responsibility to at least be prudent. (There also is the sense that I should not have "too much.")

The human condition seems to entail continuous conflict. How should one respond and manage one's own anger when offenses occur? In Alpha 2, responsibility, rules, retribution, and punishment are key concepts. In Omega 2, remorse, recompense, rehabilitation, and forgiveness are key words.

Looking to American history for examples, one ethic emphasizes the Mountain Man (or the Marlboro Man, or the Lone Ranger) as key to the development of the West. The other ethic emphasizes the wagon train.

There may be other ethics based around religious ideas that fit in here as well. Robert Bellah (1957) argues that Tokugawa values in Japan (from the sixteenth century to the latter part of the nineteenth century) were very much like Protestant ethic values. On the other hand, if there were a "Jewish ethic," it would be similar to an Omega 2 ethic.

Religiously, there is a difference in the approach to the afterlife and to God. One ethic regards salvation as a scarce good, with few available slots operating on a zero-sum basis. God is an angry judgmental father, who can be approached through Jesus. The other ethic regards salvation as having ample slots and being run on a non–zero-sum basis. In lieu of the angry father there is the Holy Trinity, and God can be approached through Mary and the many saints (especially St. Peter—who actually has the keys!).

In terms of this world, an Alpha 2 approach takes achievement as its signature value, regards General George S. Patton as its hero, and supports a winner-take-all mindset.[2] Optimizing is the name of the game: Get the biggest score, the most dollars. As the bumper sticker phrase has it, "He who dies with the most toys wins!" The other ethic stresses equality, satisficing (die poor—that means you have spread the wealth), and a winner-take-enough mindset.

Finally, the two ethics provide a way to look at the work of W. Edwards Deming, the quality guru. Deming argued that there are two kinds of forces that cause quality problems in industry: common causes of variation and unique causes of variation. Common causes are structural causes, collective causes. To fix them, you must fix the community of production. Unique causes are individualistic in nature. To fix them, you fire "Joe" (if he is on the negative side) or reward him (if he is on the positive side.) Both types of problem, of course, are always present, but Alpha 2 focuses on the unique causes, whereas Omega 2 focuses on the common causes.

Obviously I can push this analysis too far. The point is not to do that but to show that the two "ethics" not only address issues of religion but that religious issues themselves code into larger typologies. Table 12-1 is illustrative and, by design, looks at things from an either/or perspective. It is obvious that each of us, in this large list, has both of these elements. This point, which I consider in chapter 13 ("duality of identification"), pushes us to think in practical terms of dominant and subdominant rather than either/or.

The Dualistic Theory of Values

This bivariate, dualistic approach itself has wider implications. In my view, a dualistic approach to values orientation is the most sensible, most integrating, most interesting approach. Such an approach begins by observing that "ethics" and "values" are simply ideas with certain features assembled into cultural packages. Individuals always have seemed to require such value packages to help them understand the world. Intellectual historians have tracked the connections, evolutions, interconnections, and interpretations of these ideas; philosophers have examined the bases and presuppositions (metaphysics) they require and offer.

In this view, values are ideas to which commitment has been attached. Values begin as ideas, but they differ from other ideas in that they have *affect* attached.[3] The difference between an idea and a value is the differences between "just words" and "fighting words."

Religious-based ethics are value packages of several interrelated and supporting values. Most of the values that are commonly understood and discussed as elements of these ethics (achievement, equality, independence, interdependence, personal, family, performance judgments, quality judgements) are value bits that, when wrapped together in certain combinations, become—or can become—an "ethic" or, more broadly, a "culture."

Most societies have a dictionary of values—that is, a list of values to which members of the society subscribe. What is only recently emerging, however, is that there is a grammar of values a well: a way that values are packaged. The dualistic theory of values is an initial foray into understanding the grammar of values.

This grammar may have many features. One of them—the dualistic feature—suggests that values are linked in pairs or juxtaposed sets, meaning that individuals cannot think of, deal with, or act on one element of the pair without invoking the other, at least mentally: Thoughts of personal achievement invoke concerns for family; thoughts of achievement spur thoughts of equality; issues of punishment lead to thoughts of compassion. One reason this structure may function as it does in society is to prevent individuals from going too far in pursuit of any one value. In social life, an individual's identity is forged through such pairs (mother/father, father/son, husband/wife), and each person plays multiple roles in any role pair, with opposing roles providing some guidance and definition of any individual's performance.

Juxtaposition is important too, however. One typical value structure may be illustrated as follows:

Achievement	Equality
Individualistic/Personal	Collective/Communal

An oppositional structure such as this means that an increment in commitment to one value is a decrement in commitment to another value. A juxtaposition of values, however, suggests that an individual may be committed, unequally, to two values at the same time: In this model, acting on one diminishes the influence of the other, over time.

The threat one value presents to another also depends on the degrees of commitment a person has to the two values in the pair. If an individual is highly committed to both values (as represented by the upper-right quadrant of the illustration in Figure 12.1), that would suggest a high level of conflict between values. Those whose commitments to neither of these particular values is very strong, represented by the lower-left corner of the illustration, have a low level of conflict between opposing values. Some individuals who are highly committed to one value over another are described by the "off-diagonal" cells of the table. Over time, balances and rebalances develop in a dynamic equilibrium. In the foregoing example, the values of achievement and equality are in tension but not as completely opposed; hence the idea of juxtaposed values.

The dualistic theory suggests that individuals are expected to maintain a balance between the values in the set, although "balance" is

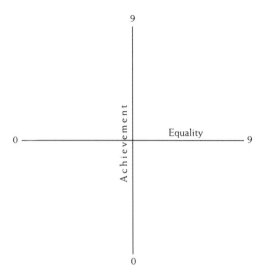

FIGURE 12.1   *Achievement and Equality*

broadly defined and includes high and low positions on the value vectors. A high position on one vector, however, is not presumed to remain high always, and a low position is not permanent. Thus, individuals are considered to be attending to two sets of values, including those that are routinely preferred, or dominant values, as well as those that are attended to but are less-preferred or subdominant values.

One can think of the Catholic ethic and the Protestant ethic, especially in their more "secularized" forms (optimizing and satisficing approaches), as fitting exactly into this framework. This is why the idea that we may all be a little "Protestant" and a little "Catholic" makes so much sense, odd as it may seem at first blush. Especially in a pluralistic culture, each person can be expected to absorb some elements of the values that are current in that society. Such adoption is especially likely if those value dimensions represent more fundamental orientations to the world—orientations that I call the Protestant ethic and the Catholic ethic here but are found under other guises in other cultures.

Prismatics

If "schematics" provide "schemes" through which one can organize the Protestant and Catholic ethics, "prismatics" use those schemes to examine other facets of social life. Because helping has been such a theme of this book, it seems useful to look at American "welfare history" through the prism of the Catholic and Protestant ethics.

Implications for Helping

Each of these points has particular implications for community welfare. I need not go through all of them to illustrate this point; a few will do.

Solo self means that the individual is more or less responsible for her or his own condition, which makes providing aid more difficult. Optimizing orientations create a condition in which either one is acceptable or one is not. If one is not acceptable, provision of aid is difficult. Competition creates a situation in which aid is regarded as either making the giver's role in the competition more difficult or actually and in some way inappropriately (because of optimizing orientations) doing something that is wrong. Arguments that say that aid to disadvantaged people actually hurts them fall into this category. Thus, the Protestant ethic makes provision of social aid more difficult. The Catholic ethic, in its most general form, makes social aid easier. Ensemble self recognizes human interdependency and interconnection and allows more of a bond between haves and have-nots than might otherwise be the case. The satisficing orientation creates more of a recognition that "have" and "have-not" status is temporary and might change from one to the other. Furthermore, in a satisficing orientation, one is more willing to share than to accumulate. Hence, if one has enough resources, surplus resources can be used for others. There is no such thing as surplus resources in an optimizing orientation, however. Cooperative orientation again supports giving aid. The Alpha 2 orientation in American society (and perhaps elsewhere) made/makes it harder for us to help than it might otherwise be.

The Big Picture

Helping poor people has always been a tension point in American society. We want to do the right thing, yet we are constantly afraid (more than people in other countries, it seems) of helping too much. In many senses, we are more generous to other countries than we are toward "our own" (although we are among the least generous in comparison to other countries). Cries for "American leadership" seem to resonate "offshore" but do not ring many bells inland. Other countries have moved ahead of us in child care (recall the French example), health care (Canada), and children's allowances and other public programs. Many of these programs establish eligibility through citizenship of the country rather than "employeeship" in a firm or company (recall the discussion in chapter 11). One might wonder—at least I wonder—why, especially in a wealthy country, there is such great tension over providing help to people. Why should it be that supermarkets have several rows of pet food when many people in our land go hungry? Why do many Americans have second and third homes (and second homes, at least, are supported through tax expenditures) when many do not have any home?[4] Poor people, it seems, "bug" us. Why? And do the concepts of the Protestant ethic and the Catholic ethic shed any light on this question? Perhaps the first step involves figuring out who, exactly, poor people *are*.

A Reluctant Welfare State

The history of helping—of welfare—in American society can be divided into six periods: communal, voluntaristic/private, mixed public/private, public/private conflict, public/private partnership, and public devolution (Tropman and Tropman 1987, vol. 2, 827). The communal period emphasized informal and ah hoc modes of helping; it lasted from 1620 until the Civil War—approximately 250 years. The voluntaristic period extended from the Civil War to the passage of the Social Security Act (August 14, 1935). This was the heyday of the development of the "social agency" and the "middle class mission to the poor." The mixed period lasted from 1935 until about the beginning of the 1960s, when the period of conflict began. Conflict lasted until about 1970, when a period of partnership between public and private agencies began. That lasted until the 1990s, when devolution began and public responsibility began to be transferred to local public, voluntary, and for-profit organizations.

This whole history shouts "reluctance." Two-hundred-fifty years of local neighborly helping is enough to make the point, I think. To emphasize it, however, we need only note that attempts at establishing public, communal responsibility were defeated.

The most popular example involves the work of Dorothea Dix and her very important efforts to secure funding for indigent insane people. Dix had had success in the states, and she convinced Congress to provide 10 million acres of land for the care of these folks (which would have established land-grant mental hospitals). President Pierce vetoed the bill providing this land:

> [I]f Congress has the power to make provision for the indigent insane without the limits of this District, it has the same power to provide for the indigent who are not insane and thus to transfer to the federal government the charge of all the poor in all the states . . . the

whole field of public beneficence is thrown open to the care and culture of the federal government. Generous impulses no longer encounter the limitations and control of our imperious fundamental
law (Pumphrey and Pumphrey 1961, 132).

Mr. Pierce was reluctant.

After the Civil War, two organizations of public responsibility were
set up: the Freedman's Bureau, to aid freed slaves, and a federal organization to provide Civil War pensions. Both, or either, of these organizations could have emerged into an early infrastructure for the welfare
state, but both were disbanded. Federal responsibility would not come
until 1935.

We were reluctant.

During this time, social work began and grew. Charity organization
societies developed in England and came to the United States through
Buffalo, New York. Settlement houses arose to aid working poor people
and women in the cities. It was still very much each tub on its own bottom, with a little extra help if you needed it.

There were counterforces. The Quakers, the Salvation Army, the
Mormons, and the Prohibition movement, for example, each represent
"prosocial" elements within the Protestant tradition. Of course, there is
the social gospel as well.

The emphasis on the social gospel—which talked about the concept
of "social sin" and pointed to collective, as opposed to individual, causes
of need—is an explicitly religious-based movement that sprang up
around the turn of the twentieth century (see White and Hopkins 1976).
Mainstream Protestantism was not all that receptive. Social gospel represented something very different from traditional Protestant approaches.
White and Hopkins quote historian Carl Degler: "[A]cceptance of the social gospel spelled a transformation of American Protestantism" (White
and Hopkins 1976, xi). White and Hopkins add:

> Always more than a traditional religious movement, the social gos-
> pel stepped outside the churches to intersect the political, social and
> economic sources changing America. . . . Toward the end of the pro-
> gressive era the social gospel was defined by one of its adherents as
> "the application of the teaching of Jesus in the total message of the
> Christian salvation to society, the economic life and social institu-
> tions . . . as well as individuals" (White and Hopkins 1976, xi).

The social gospel was important in several ways. It took account of
collective forces—in terms of responsibility for social conditions and for

their amelioration—as well as individual forces. It provided fuel for municipal reformers and others who were seeking to improve the social order. Its emphasis on "social sin" was a counterpoint to the individualism that was exemplified in the "solo self." Although the social gospel was not the dominant element of American Protestantism, it represented the expression of subdominant elements within that ethic.

Other examples of social concern within the Protestant ethic tradition might be considered as well. The social settlements—such as Hull House—arose in part from that tradition. Similarly, the Bull Moose party's elements of social reform also had links in Protestantism. Prohibition, particularly with its emphasis on the relationship of drinking to poverty, is an important movement as well (Tropman 1986). The question of whether Prohibition was an honest attempt to control substance abuse or an attempt on the part of native Protestants to establish a position of moral superiority over immigrant Catholics (Gusfield 1963) and Jews is an open question, but it still is worth attention.

Social work itself can be seen as arising from this subdominant tradition in American Protestantism. The middle-class mission to poor people had mixed bases for concern, conflicting directions for "friendly visiting" behavior, and ambivalent attitudes toward provision of cash assistance. Early social work, characterized by "friendly visiting," provided material help in the form of cash but also in the form of directions for how to avoid poverty in the future. Its identification as a women's profession underscored this subdominant element within mainstream culture (Tropman 1987). Furthermore, the help offered to poor people was suffused with suspicion. Individuals who received grants of cash and food often were suspected of going from agency to agency, taking as much as possible from each.[5] This suspicion remains to this day. "Welfare cheats" often are front-page news.

An overall point is that these elements, though always present, were subdominant. They were defeated politically, as with Dorothea Dix and the Bull Moose Party. They were of limited duration, as with the social gospel. Continuation of programs such as the Freedman's Bureau and Civil War veterans' benefits was rejected.

Looking at the sweep of American history, then, one can begin to see the nineteenth century as a time of developing social change that contained the potential for welfare state development. With the development of industrialization and urbanization, Protestant ethic culture—with its lack of sympathy toward social aid—came under increasing pressure even from within, where subdominant themes were stimulated and arose. From the middle of the nineteenth century and the work of Dorothea Dix through Civil War pensions, the Freedman's Bureau, and the Bull Moose Party, conditions were present for major social welfare steps to occur. Dominant culture, however, rejected these opportunities; not until 1935, with the passage of the Social Security Act (SSA), was a hallmark piece of social legislation developed for the country as a whole. The Protestant ethic during that time was changing, of course, and we have seen evidence of this change; the SSA was a kind of bookend. On the other hand, the Catholic ethic was becoming more prominent. Increasing numbers of Catholics were moving to America. Their orientations, dispositions, and points of view were becoming more powerful. The balances between the Catholic ethic and the Protestant ethic and between elements within the Protestant ethic were changing. The welfare state developed in the United States as a result of the changes in balance among all of these forces.

Nonetheless, American society was slower in developing community helping programs. It also has had a seemingly continuous and easily roused hostility toward disadvantaged people. In 1984, John Kenneth Galbraith wrote an important piece for the *New York Times Magazine* called "The Heartless Society." A few years ago I wrote a book asking, *Do Americans Hate the Poor?* (Tropman 1998). American society still seems reluctant. Why should this be so?

Recent sociological research has tended to focus on structural features—state structures especially—in describing community helping development in the United States. What has been less popular but perhaps ultimately will be no less central is to look at cultural explanations, sets of commitments, and convictions held by groups within the populace that may facilitate or retard a certain set of activities or actions.

Clearly the Protestant ethic deserves close inspection with respect to its potential for welfare hostility and social negativism, as it does for its possible support of capitalism. The Protestant ethic concept is a hardy perennial in the context of thinking about capitalism and has been a vigorous contender in the field of cultural explanations for establishment of a capitalist state. Its impact on the welfare state has not been examined as closely. It could be important because in all of the discussion of what the Protestant ethic might promote, there is little discussion about what it might *hinder.*

My view is that the Protestant ethic actually discouraged the development of helping activities and the welfare state in the United States for several reasons linked to the very definition of community helping.[6] First, the Protestant ethic focused on the *advantaged* or the *elect* rather than the disadvantaged or excluded. Second, its ethos of individualism discouraged provision of aid. Third, whatever aid was available focused on the personal rather than the programmatic and dealt extensively with the value or worth of the individual receiving it rather than the nature and extensiveness of the need that generated it. Fourth, political means were discouraged—at least at the federal level. An example appears in the aforementioned statement by President Pierce. Even today, "devolution" is moving helping programs into the voluntary sector once again (e.g., "Seniors helping Seniors").

We have moved toward a more helping posture, however. Given our negativism, how can this movement be explained?

For one thing, the Protestant ethic, as I have argued repeatedly, is not all of a piece. There is a subdominant stream of helping within it. In addition, there is the increasing presence of a more propoor ethic that supports generally and specifically, directly and indirectly the development of welfare state activity. Such an ethic is the Catholic ethic. As time passed, the ratio of Catholics to Protestants in the United States increased. The dominance of Protestantism decreased and, because of a set of beliefs and structures, Catholicism became more powerful and influential on the local and national scenes.

Even so, we had to find ways to make help okay. Categorization of needy people was a way to do this, and dividing people into the worthy and unworthy poor was one approach. The history of poverty relief shows many attempts to place poor people into categories that made poverty tolerable. As De Schweinitz ([1943] 1961) points out, some people were regarded as "casualty poor." These people were poor because of a casualty—such as fire, flood, or death of a spouse or parent. On the other hand, there were the "shiftless poor in their own homes"—people who presumably could work but did not, or did not work hard enough. This distinction was one of the bases of the categorical approach to poor relief in which the casualty poor were supported (for a while) and others were not.

This categorization continues in the United States, as exemplified by programs to help mothers and children and newer programs for families in need: Aid to Dependent Children (ADC), Aid to Families with Dependent Children (AFDC), and Aid to Families with Dependent Children—Unemployed (AFDC-U) and now Temporary Assistance to Needy Families (TANF). Other categorical programs were developed under the Social Security Act of 1935 and its revisions, including Aid to the Blind, Old Age Assistance, and (in 1950) Aid to the Permanently and Totally Disabled, which were reorganized in the 1970s into Supplementary Security Income (SSI). Needy families or needy adults were still not "deserving" of federal aid. They were handled by a state-based program called general assistance, which was largely phased out in the late 1980s and 1990s.

To some extent, the "worthy poor" concept—on whatever bases worthy was argued—is a part of the Protestant ethic worldview. In the Catholic ethic worldview (as Gregory Baum argues in Appendix A), that kind of separation does not exist.

The current period (at the turn of the twenty-first century) raises the same issues that have always plagued us in America in terms of helping. We still feel that individuals should be responsible for themselves. We moved to "end welfare as we know it," and AFDC was cancelled, replaced by "workfare" programs—now called (since "welfare reform") TANF—under the Personal Responsibility and Work Opportunity Reconciliation Act.[7] Help is okay if the time for which it is provided is short and if it aims to assist you in taking personal responsibility and to get ahead (opportunity). Once again, work has surfaced as a litmus test of self-help, proper motivation, and good intentions—and another basis through which money could be provided.

Work and Welfare in American Society

Work and welfare have a long history of attachment in the welfare policy and program field. Workhouses were places—institutions really—where people could go to receive help and work. Work programs have been popular in prisons, and they were an important feature of Franklin Roosevelt's New Deal. The Works Progress Administration (WPA) tried to find or create public service jobs for recipients. Often, apparently, the workers did not have much to do, however—hence the humorous renaming of WPA to "We Poke Along." The controversy has to do with whether it is appropriate and necessary for work to be enunciated and required as a value. This issue continues to this day. George Will comments:

> [T]hree years ago a task force of Democratic congressmen was debating a new social agenda, *and many members wanted it to declare that the work ethic is the core value of society*. Rep. A. Hawkins, then the senior black member of Congress, strenuously objected, saying the declaration would be seen by welfare recipients as a slap in the face. The statement was dropped (Will 1992, 68; emphasis added).

Work, then, seems to be "it" in American society. This is a legacy of the Protestant ethic—a legacy all of us share. We love work. We overwork. Work is the excuse that lets many of us out of any obligation. We even are supposed to work when we are sick. I love the story of a bar that was called The Office; thus, someone could call home and say,

"Honey, I am running late at The Office." No doubt the ruse would be discovered in time, but the fact that work rose to the level of excusatory humor is telling in and of itself. Work is the pipe through which we run our social programs; fringe benefits, for example, are simply a combination of private and public social insurance of several kinds (health, pension, and so on). If you don't work, the state has had to give you money; of course, this is a Catch 22 because if you are working you usually do not need money. Americans are more willing, however, to give money to people who already are working. The very definitions of "welfare" change. "Welfare" is reserved for people who are not working; for those who are, and are still getting help, who is to complain about "a little help from the government (farmers, veterans, homeowners, corporations, and others)" (Tropman 1998, x).

If some people are poor because they are unworthy, perhaps it is because they do not work hard or well enough. In that case it is, perhaps, somewhat sacrilegious to provide them cash aid. If money can be provided *through work,* however, it legitimizes access to money and makes the giver feel all right about it because there has been a sort of exchange. The early workhouse—where poor people were fed and forced to work— was an early version of this philosophy. For people who seemed to be lazy and did not appreciate the nature of work and its benefits, houses of correction were established. As time went on, public employment programs of various sorts developed, especially in the United States.

Nonwork—The Stigma of Unemployment

The sacred nature of work in the Protestant ethic culture means that "nonwork" takes on special significance. Nonwork, of course, is unemployment. Since the work of Bakke in 1934, there has been a sharp awareness of the psychological stress of unemployment—of losing one's job. Naturally the loss of income is a shock, but that is not the point here. It is the sense of loss of meaning and value that is important in this context. Karl Marx thought that the job itself could be a theft of meaning—that piece work and the industrial system robbed people of the total task; he probably was right. What Marx did not sense, however, is that *some meaning* may be better than *no meaning.* Having no job creates a sort of vacuum, but only if one believes that one has been excluded from the sacred liturgy, the special rites that, in a particular culture, make meaning. In the Broadway play *Aspects of Love,* the words in the title song, "Love Changes Everything," capture part of this sense: "Days are longer, words mean more; . . . nothing in the world will ever be the same." Being excluded from love (divorce, rejection) is like being excluded from work (being laid off or fired). We all suffer rejections, however, so what makes this one different?

What makes this rejection different is the work ethos to which one is committed.[8] If one believes, and is committed to, the idea that being excluded from work is being excluded from friends, association, and meaning, as well as money, then the loss is more painful, more acute. Within a tradition that assigns high meaning to a liturgy, exclusion from that liturgy has special—and especially negative—meaning. If, in addition, the explanation is that "it's your fault," remediation is more difficult.

This special nature of unemployment in Protestant ethic culture is almost completely captured in the title of Katherine Newman's (1988) book on unemployment, *Falling from Grace*. This apt title completely captures the sacred meaning of work! Newman cites several parallels between Protestant work ethic ideas and the experience of older unemployed former executives who are members of a support group known as "Forty Plus":

> As the months pass, as hundreds of applications go unanswered and the number of interviews shrinks from a trickle to none, the unemployed managers begin to realize with horror *the stigma of having lost their jobs,* and the fact that they are applying for new ones as "unemployed persons" outweighs their many years of experience, formal credentials, and specialized expertise. Instead of being treated as experienced applicants, ready to work, they are treated as *"spoiled goods"* (Newman 1988, 56; emphasis added).[9]

The foregoing passage suggests that exclusion from the sacred liturgy of work not only affects the unemployed person and her or his actions toward others, as well as that person's impressions about what others think, it affects others and their actions toward the unemployed person. Hence, she or he feels that treatment is different. In part, it is different. Both alter and ego are involved!

In *Declining Fortunes: The Withering of the American Dream* (1993), Newman observes:

> American culture is allergic to the idea that impersonal forces control individual destiny. Rather, we prefer to think of our lives as products of our own efforts. Through hard work, innate ability and competition, the good prosper and the weak fall by the wayside. Accordingly, the end results in people's lives—their occupations, material possessions and the recognition accorded by friends and associates—are proof of the underlying stuff of which they are made.

When these domains of our lives do not pass muster, the tendency is to assume that this fate is deserved: the unemployed are dead wood (Newman 1993, 89).

Naturally, this view—an important one (though not the only one) in the kaleidoscope of American culture—makes helping harder. After all, you can't resurrect dead wood. Indeed, effort spent there is doubly wasted: It does no good, and it uses up energy that could do good elsewhere (for the "worthy poor," perhaps). If one is out of work, then one is out of the safety net of benefits that work provides, especially retirement and medical insurance support. Indeed, if one is out of work, even social security eligibility for that period is lost (you have no covered quarters).

Overwork—The Bleary-Eyed Badge of Courage

This emphasis on work as the magic portal to meaning, resources, and benefits may stimulate folks—Americans at least—to work harder. Americans do tend to work hard, which makes it all the more difficult to help those who are not working. Indeed, Juliet B. Schor, in *The Overworked American* (1993), argues that we are working (those of us who *are* still employed) harder then ever. On the downside, overwork makes—or can make—citizens a bit heartless. I was walking with a professor friend of mine who also has a job as a lecturer at another university. His wife works as well, and he is putting two kids through college. We passed a homeless person asking for money (the homeless guy had the bad luck to sit under a "help wanted" sign in a drug store). My friend said, "I work two jobs; why should I give him anything when he is working no job?"

The professor's kids go to elite schools. He lives "high end." He is not just "keeping up with the Joneses," he is keeping ahead of the Joneses. He feels everyone is running fast behind him. He is in the earn/spend cycle Schor talks about. She calls it the "squirrel cage" (Schor 1993, chapter 6). We may have moved beyond the work ethic into the "overwork" ethic.

Conclusion

This chapter considers some ways in which the Catholic ethic and Protestant ethic concepts can be used. One application ("schematics") proposed a dualistic way of looking at this idea—archetypal or ideal-typical, if you will—which puts the differences into sharp relief. As long as these distinctions are not reified, they have a utility.

In the section on "prismatics" I use these concepts as a lens to look at the history of helping in the United States. I argue that, to some extent, our unique welfare history can be regarded as a contest between Protestant and Catholic conceptions of the public good and how that good is to be achieved.

Two final observations should be stressed. Neither conception of the public good is better than another; each has upsides and downsides. Certainly no one would object to the need for personal responsibility; pushed too far, however, that concept can be a problem. Certainly no one would object to the appropriateness of helping; too much help is a problem as well, however. Ideally, it is better to teach someone how to fish than to give them a fish. Someone without arms will never be able to fish, however—and so it goes.

American helping history—and, I suspect, many parts of other histories—can be better understood within an evolving dynamic of tensions between Catholic and Protestant ethic conceptions of the public good and the means to achieve it.

CHAPTER 13

The Catholic Ethic:
Questions and Conclusions

In any set of ideas there are things that bother, disturb, and cause concern. As I talk about religious-based ethics with scholars and citizens, they ask lots of questions. Some of the most common are questions such as the following: "Are people really that different?" and "Are the ethics really so unitary? Aren't there differences within each one?" The question of "Where might my faith fit on a cultural/ethic grid?" intrigues many people. Others ask, "Is work *really* that important?" and "Is our view of work changing?" Another question is, "Are there political differences between the faith groups?"—a concern stimulated, I think, by the 2000 presidential race. Then there is the question of whether *other* religious-based value systems might be operative. There is speculation that the Catholic and Protestant ethics are "simply" manifestations of larger, even more fundamental dualisms in our world. Finally there are the questions, "What do you conclude from all this?" "Where are we now?" and, more important, "Where are we going?"

Are People Really that Different? The Enmeshment and Entanglement of Ethics

The answer, of course, is no. The Protestant ethic and the Catholic ethic are not two completely independent "personalities" in Catholics and Protestants. Instead, there seems to be some Catholic ethic and some Protestant ethic in most people. In chapter 12, I argue—based on earlier work (Tropman 1989)—that values come in dialectally juxtaposed pairs. From this dualistic perspective, it only makes sense to believe that there should be a Catholic ethic where there was a Protestant ethic—an ethic that would emphasize other themes, some of them contradictory to those

175

found in the Protestant ethic. It is not likely that any one value system would meet all human needs: for individuation and linkage, for independence and membership, for self and for family, for competition and cooperation, for comfort in the certainty of status and the excitement of the mobility of status, for fair play and fair share. These religious ethics themselves might be expressions of the underlying duality of life itself, in which no faith, value, or idea is completely sufficient.[1] Greeley makes the same point, but not right away. He has to work up to it:

> Therefore, I concluded, the fundamental differences between Catholicism and Protestantism are not doctrinal or ethical. The different propositional codes of the two heritages are but manifestations, tips of the iceberg, of more fundamentally differing sets of symbols. The Catholic ethic is "communitarian" and the Protestant "individualistic" because the preconscious "organizing" pictures of the two traditions that shape meaning and response to life for members of the respective heritages are different (Greeley 1990, 44).

Greeley summarizes the essence of these difficult constructs, based on work by David Tracy (1989):

> On the basis of his [Tracy's] study, he suggested that the Catholic imagination is "analogical" and the Protestant imagination is "dialectical." The Catholic "classics" assume a God who is present in the world, disclosing Himself in and through creation. The world, and all its events, objects, and people tend to be somewhat like God. The Protestant classics, on the other hand, assume a God who is radically absent from the world, and who discloses himself only on rare occasions (especially in Jesus Christ and Him crucified). The world and all its events, objects, and people tend to be radically different from God (Greeley 1990, 45).[2]

The crucial point comes next, however:

> The word "tend" in the previous is used advisedly. Zero-sum relationships do not exist in the world of the preconscious. The analogical and dialectical imaginations exist side by side in the personalities of the authors of the classics, opposing, but also complementing each other (Greeley 1990, 45).

Catholicism and Protestantism are religions, of course, and we usually think about religious commitment as exclusive: Believing in more than one religion is like being a citizen of two countries. Yet just as there are many countries that allow dual citizenship, there is no reason dual religious identification could not be practiced. Such dualism would be especially likely if religious identification itself arose from functional pressures of the human condition and if any specific creed is unable to meet the needs that follow from that condition.

Whether we can accept bireligiosity as we accept binationalty is open to question. The idea of "dual" religions as opposed to "dueling religions" is really made much easier, however, if we think of religions themselves as the tip of the values iceberg. Greeley himself could not get to the duality point until he had "transcended" religion-as-dogma through his own work and the work of David Tracy. Dual imaginations are easier to accept than dual religions. No doubt we all have a ways to go here.

Are the Ethics Really All of a Piece? Counterforces within Each Ethic

Balance *between* ethics is one issue; balancing *within ethics* is another. Even if the overall dispositions or overall orientations discussed here represent dominant attitudes with respect to the cultures in question, that is not the whole story. As readers may be thinking already, there are counterforces ("minority perspectives") within each trend that are important to take into account as well.

Here Sampson's (1985) idea about indigenous psychologies is very helpful. One may look at dominant and subdominant elements within indigenous psychologies. Looking at the Catholic ethic and Protestant ethic as indigenous psychologies, one can see conflicting dimensions within each; dissident subdominant elements point in the other direction.

With respect to the Catholic ethic, Hennesey's (1981) work is instructive. He quotes Novak as follows:

> Catholics *do* tend to differ (from others) in their sense of reality, in their particular passion for justice, in their sense of the meaning of family and children, in facing death, in their approach to education, and to personal relationships (Hennesey 1981, 331).

It is in this specific area that one may want to note a difference between a "liberal" orientation and a "helping" orientation (which often are lumped together in contemporary political dialogue). The Catholic ethic, for example, may support aid to people who are in distress and need and in that sense be "liberal." Catholics have been far from open over the years, however, with respect to freedom of the press, freedom to see any movie one chooses, and so on.

Hennesey (1981) also points to some of the "less helping" orientations within Catholicism. For example, the Catholic community was not in the forefront on issues such as emancipation of slaves (as the Quakers were), child welfare legislation, and birth control. In short, there are several areas—only a few of which are suggested here—in which the Catholic ethic might be thought of as uncommunal, unhelping, and (even!) individualistic.

Similarly, there are communal and helping orientations within the Protestant ethic. This is exemplified by the fact that since the colonization of America, social aid was provided on a local and village basis. The aid may not have been more than "quid pro quo," but it was helping nonetheless.

There also are the Protestant religions and ministries that make helping a central part of their presentation. The Quakers have been mentioned; the Mormons, the Salvation Army, and social agencies— Methodist, Lutheran, and so on—all are dedicated to helping at home and abroad.[3]

Of course, as the survey results reported in chapter 11 suggest, race matters with respect to helping orientation. Black Protestants are simply different from white Protestants. One can understand the history a bit even if one is not African American: They are coming from a different place.

There also have been Protestant communal elements standing the individualism of American Protestantism on its head.[4] Communes have not lasted well in the hardscrabble soil of American individualism. They did not last well in the nineteenth century, and they did not last well in the 1960s. The commune idea is one of those things that "seemed like a good idea at the time." Nevertheless, emphases breed their opposites.

The differences, of course, are that in Protestantism these emphases tend to be expressed as "sects," whereas in Catholicism they tend to be expressed as variation. Hence, Protestantism looks more different than Catholicism does, initially. Each has much diversity within it, however.

Where Might I Fit?

If we look at the Catholic/Protestant ethic differences as a grid, various locations might be possible for any specific person. Consider the array in Figure 13.1.

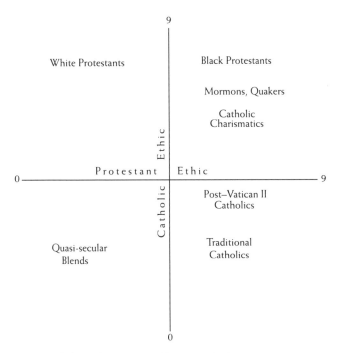

FIGURE 13.1 *Catholic and Protestant Ethics as a Grid*

Using the dualism perspective model, we can see a Protestant/Catholic "space" of competing values. In this model, traditional Catholics, in the lower-right quadrant, are low on the Protestant ethic dimension and high on the Catholic ethic dimension. White Protestants, in the upper-left quadrant, are high on the Protestant ethic scale and low on the Catholic ethic scale. Black (African American) Protestants are somewhat high in both scales, placing them in the upper-right quadrant.

This chart is offered for demonstration purposes only; if a Catholic ethic scale were developed and run against a Protestant ethic scale, an actual array of respondents could be displayed, and these hypothetical distributions could be tested. This effort would be most exciting. A series of empirical assays by gender, race, religious denomination, and so on would be a first step in answering questions about the distribution and relationship of these ethics among various groups.

In addition, such scales would be helpful in examining differences within religious groups—between Catholics of different ethnic backgrounds, for example. Although much is made of differences between various Protestant denominations, people often assume that Catholics are a single group, without "denominational" difference among Irish

Catholics, Italian Catholics, Polish Catholics, American Catholics, Spanish Catholics, and so on. Anecdotal evidence suggests that, indeed, there are differences between strains of Catholicism that may be as significant as those between denominations within the Protestant compass.

How Important Is Work, Anyway?

I have discussed "work" as a quintessential American value. At first blush, many workers (many Americans) would be inclined to agree. Then there comes the question, however, "Really, how important *is* work?" How many people really fall into this category of work as being so very important? The answer is, "a lot!" One set of numbers from Yankelovich and Immerwahr (1983) is presented in Table 13.1.

Table 13.1 suggests several interesting features about work. Yankelovich and Immerwahr asked about perspectives on work.

1. **Unpleasant necessity view**—Work is one of life's unpleasant necessities; I wouldn't work if I didn't have to.
2. **Morally neutral/exchange view**—Work is a business transaction; the more I get paid, the more I do.
3. **Interesting but limited claims view**—I find work interesting . . . but I wouldn't let it interfere with the rest of my life [Catholic ethic perspective].
4. **Intrinsic moral value view**—I have an inner need to do the very best job possible, regardless of pay [Protestant ethic perspective].

One may disagree with the measures, but at least Yankelovich and Immerwahr (1983) have laid out the views. One result is that the "Protestant work ethic" view (number 4) is held by a majority—52 percent. There are other, competing, views, however. The view that work is interesting but has limited claims (number 3) is the one I would place close to the Catholic ethic perspective, and it is held by 21 percent of respondents. (Unfortunately, data here are not available by religious identification.) The other perspectives—the unpleasant necessity view and the morally neutral/exchange view—also are important to consider. How do these views fit into religious identification? This question needs more exploration, but it is important to stress here—as I have mentioned elsewhere—that religious identification is not the only source of

TABLE 13.1   *Attitudes toward Work: United States, 1983*

Statement	Agree (%)
UNPLEASANT NECESSITY VIEW Work is one of life's unpleasant necessities; I wouldn't work if I didn't have to	17
MORALLY NEUTRAL/EXCHANGE VIEW Work is a business transaction; the more I get paid, the more I do	9
INTERESTING BUT LIMITED CLAIMS VIEW I find work interesting, but I wouldn't let it interfere with the rest of my life	21
INTRINSIC MORAL VALUE VIEW I have an inner need to do the very best job possible, regardless of pay	52

Source: Yankelovich and Immerwahr (1983, 20–21).

values, by any means. Other perspectives and commitments may generate work-related belief systems. The Protestant ethic and the Catholic ethic are two important systems, to be sure, but other ethoses are almost surely involved as well.

Most Americans seem to subscribe to the Protestant work ethic, with an important minority subscribing to what I call the Catholic work ethic. Another important minority subscribe to other postures. Hence, the focus on work is a good place to begin the discussion of the differences in perspective. One last question remains, however: Are things changing? With so much talk of the "new narcissism," might not the traditional ethic of work here in this country be on the wane?

Is the View of Work Changing?

Greenberg reports that "High PE scorers [respondents who score high on the Mirels-Garrett (1971) Protestant Ethic Scale] have been differentiated from low scorers on the basis of their greater ambition and self control, *higher values placed on hard work and their condemnation of laxity and laziness*" (Greenberg 1977, 682; emphasis added). That was in 1977. Yankelovich and Immerwahr (1984) indicate, however, that things are not as one might expect. They suggest that a "problem in America's workplace" is that workers do not seem to be working as hard as their belief in the work ethic might suggest.

Is the Protestant ethic on the decline? Are attitudes toward work changing? The answer to that question is complex. Four points can be stressed here. One is methodological; the second involves the presence of competing values; the third involves the ascendancy of family values; and the last involves the locus of work.

Methodology

First it must be said that at least with respect to opinion polls, work ethic responses are highly responsive to question wording (Ladd 1981, 25). This picture, in which respondents are highly sensitive to nuance, suggests some unsettlement and concern on the part of the public with respect to the question area. On one hand, 64 percent of respondents in Ladd's sample agreed that "people should place more emphasis on working hard and doing a good job than on what gives them satisfaction"; on the other hand, 49 percent also agreed that it is "most important to do things that give you personal satisfaction and pleasure" (Ladd, 1981, 25). These mixed responses may well not *prove* change; they may, however, *presage* change and serve as a kind of evidence of the "mixed ethic" posture I describe above. As Ladd (1981) says, "[T]here is so much ambivalence surrounding work—which looms so large in our lives and values—that one cannot . . . arrive at a neatly defined and unambiguous set of opinion survey answers" (Ladd 1981, 21).

Competing Values

The second point is that there are competing values. Some of these values relate to views of work itself. Elsewhere I have pointed to conflicts between work and leisure (Tropman 1987), and Ladd specifically notes that "work is a very important value but still only one of a number of competing values" (Ladd 1981, 20).

What might these values be? One set of competing values involves the way we think about "family." The same *Los Angeles Times* poll asked the following question:

What's the most important thing in your life? (Code as work or work-related, family or family-related, or anything else.)

Of those responding, 61 percent answered that family was the most important thing in life; 29 percent indicated other things, and only 9 percent indicated that work and work-related elements were the most important! That response pattern certainly looks like change.

That was 1981. Ten years later, Rosabeth Moss Kanter, writing in the *Harvard Business Review*, reported on a survey of 12,000 managers worldwide. She observed one group of countries emerging that she called "cultural allies"—Australia, Canada, Great Britain, New Zealand, Singapore, and the United States. Its dominating feature: a preference for family over work (Kanter 1991)! With two-income families the popular stereotype and latchkey kids a cultural icon, however, one wonders exactly what "the most important thing in life" really means.

As we move into the twenty-first century, a better work-family balance seems to be the hallmark. Contemporary employees are demanding that employers be more flexible with time, understand the demands of home and family, and provide a workplace that is consistent with the quality of whole life, not just work life (Tropman 2001). This "new voice" comes from several sources. Important among them is the increasing proportion of women in the labor force, for one thing. Moreover, younger workers are not willing to spend the huge amount of "face time" that had characterized previous work life.

Locus of Work

One more point suggests—echoes really—the caution Ladd suggests. This has to do with work behavior as opposed to work values. Yankelovich and Immerwahr (1983) point out that most Americans believe that the setting for work is not conducive to working harder—that even if they do work harder, there will not be any reward for it. Their respondents cite poor management, lack of differential rewards, and decline of workplace authority, among other reasons, for lack of investment in work behavior. So it may be workplaces, rather than the work ethic, that are changing. The old "giving-getting compact" (I give you my work life; you give me a lifetime of work) is not out the window. Hence, it is hard to tell what, in fact, may be changing.

Protestant and Catholic Work Orientations

Pyle comments, "Most researchers have looked at Catholic-Protestant differences in status achievement and mobility" (Pyle 1991, 1). Although the consensus seems to be that Catholics and Protestants are close or equal in economic achievement, Pyle adds, "Several studies argue that Protestantism disproportionately encourages a work ethic" (e.g., Johnson 1961; Dearman 1974). One might think, then, that the Protestant work ethic is alive and well.

With respect to change, however, the story might be different. The crossover of belief systems and the counterforces within each ethic add complications. This clearly is a situation for further research. My conclusion is that people who are committed to either ethic seek a bit of tempering from the other.

Let's consider an example. Yankelovich and Immerwahr (1983, 1984) define two broad work value groups: one in which people work to improve their standard of living and one in which people work for self-development. For purposes of a thought experiment, I call these two value groups Protestant and Catholic "work ethic packages."

For the first package, basic job requirements include "1) high pay; 2) some relationship between pay and performance; 3) a chance for career advancement and promotion; 4) some degree of fairness in the rules governing promotions." For the second package, employees require "1) a job that enables a person to develop abilities and potentials; 2) an interesting job; 3) a creative job; 4) a job with say in important decisions" (Yankelovich and Immerwahr 1983, 28). A considerable number of Americans (49 percent) have a mismatch on two or more of these characteristics.

Perhaps is is not so much that the work ethic is "changing" but that there is more than one work ethic, with different goals and desires in the mix. We could well be in the process of rebalancing the ethic mix.

Are There Political Differences between the Faith Groups?

A discussion of this question, of course, is a book in itself. Because of the interest in the presidential race of 2000, participants in seminars and presentations would almost always ask, "How do the religious groups line up? Does religious affiliation matter?" And so on and so on. Marjorie Connelly (2000), writing in the *New York Times*, assembled exit poll data for the period 1976 to 2000. The results are displayed in Table 13.2.

The results clearly show that religious affiliation—or religious culture, from my perspective—does matter. In seven elections, Catholics preferred the Democratic candidate (a proxy for more collective, people-based policies) four times. The exceptions: Catholics voted twice for Reagan and once for Bush. Reagan was extremely popular, and Bush was running against the widely unappealing Michael Dukakis. Even in those three cases, however, Protestants *strongly* preferred Reagan and

TABLE 13.2   *Who Voted: A Portrait of American Presidential Politics, 1976–2000*

	Religious Affiliation	% of 2000 Total Vote
	White Protestant	41
	Catholic	54
	Jewish	4
	Black	10

1976 Carter	1976 Ford	1980 Reagan	1980 Carter	1980 Anderson	1984 Reagan	1984 Mondale	1988 Bush	1988 Dukakis
41	53	68	31	6	72	27	66	33
54	44	50	42	7	54	45	52	47
64	34	39	45	15	31	67	35	64
83	16	11	85	3	9	90	12	86

1992 Clinton	1992 Bush	1992 Perot	1996 Clinton	1996 Dole	1996 Perot	2000 Gore	2000 Bush	2000 Nader
33	47	21	36	53	10	34	63	2
44	35	20	53	37	9	49	47	2
80	11	9	78	16	3	79	19	1
83	10	7	84	12	4	90	8	1

Source: Connelly (2000).

Bush (68 percent to 50 percent in 1980; 72 percent to 54 percent in 1984; 66 percent to 52 percent in 1988).

Religious culture does show differences—and they are differences that make a difference. Race obviously played a role as well. I include results for African Americans for two reasons. One, of course, is because the numbers for Protestants are "white Protestants." One might be interested in how African Americans voted, and the large majority of African Americans are Protestant. Second, the numbers for African Americans are truly astonishing. They vote "Democrat" in the 80–90 percent range. These numbers suggest how alienated this group feels from "mainstream" politics of a Republican variety. In a sense, African Americans are trapped in the "wrong" religion for their culture, and black churches have had to reinvent their religion (like Quakers and Mormons) to meet their social needs. Are there other variables of importance? Certainly: Income, education, all the usual suspects still matter. Religious culture matters as well, however—not overwhelmingly, but I have not claimed that. The fact that it is not overwhelming suggests the "dueling cultures" idea that I have mentioned between groups, within groups, and within ourselves.

Other Religious-Based Ethics

If there is a Protestant ethic and a Catholic ethic, a question that immediately comes to mind is whether there are any *other* religiously centered ethics. That seems likely. Why should there not be a Muslim ethic, a Hindu ethic, a Shinto ethic, a Zoroastrian ethic? No reason, it seems. Scholars would need to look carefully at the properties of the religion and its orientations and inquire about the effects and impacts, function and dysfunction of that particular belief system and mindset.

By way of illustration, a Jewish ethic is a handy candidate (Shapiro 1982, 1987). In many respects, the Jewish ethic seems to include the communal and helping elements of the Catholic ethic. In the Gallup and Castelli (1989) data, Jews exceeded white Protestants in three of the four categories and were even with them on "aid to the elderly." Jewish helping was well established before the common era and, like the Catholic ethic, continues to be a characteristic of Jewish community and social life to this day. In an article on "The Jewish Tradition of Helping," Shapiro comments:

> In particular, the obligation of the Jew to care for others is almost as old as the Jewish people. In this respect, it is revealing that there is no Hebrew word for "helping"; rather, "Tzedakah," the word for "righteousness," also serves for what other languages term "helping." The right of the poor to helping treatment and the *obligation* of every member of the Jewish community to those less fortunate is deeply rooted in our Biblical traditions. Just as God was thought to bestow helping upon man, so the individual Jew is obligated to behave charitably toward his or her fellow Jews (Shapiro 1982, 2).

I have chosen to speculate about two major points. One has to do with the possibility that the Catholic and Protestant ethics may be manifestations of two universal elements that are common everywhere and in every time to the human condition: individualism/achievement/me/I on one hand and community/spread-the-wealth/us on the other. As humans, we may need each of these perspectives. Religions may be just one way, one vehicle, through which we recognize and express these competing goods.

I also have suggested that other religions may embody similar important universal elements within their belief systems. They may be other ways of expressing the one stressed here. The Jewish ethic, for example, seems like a potential candidate and is supportive of community and helping. There may be important values conflicts on a world scale, however, other than the individualism/community conflict. Exploration is needed.

Other Forms

Besides applications and complications there are speculations. Although the line between any of these "-ations" admittedly is less than crisp, speculations turn our attentions to "what-ifs" and "perhaps-es" and "could-bes." Separating the ethics from their Western religious nomenclature leads one to conjecture about whether the ethics may be the precipitates—but not uniquely the precipitates—of two universal value systems. One of the ethics is an inner-directed, optimizing ethic that emphasizes work, production, anxiety, and scarcity. A second ethic is an other-directed, satisficing ethic that emphasizes good works, security, and sufficiency. Do these bundles or "core ethics" appear in other "cultures" as well? I think the answer has to be yes.

One example might be Japan. Robert Bellah (1957) points out that some elements of the Japanese value system of the Tokugawa period had characteristics that were similar to those of the Protestant ethic. By the same token, the more communal sharing orientation of some tribes of Native Americans might be considered to resemble the Catholic ethic.

Another example might be gender. I am not sure if there are "male" cultures and "female" cultures. The issue is hotly contested with regard to the "between gender" aspects and the "within gender" aspects, not to mention changes as each gender ages. What I can say, however, is that in many public presentations of these cultural archetypes that I have made, audience members ask about this connection. They universally have seen and asked about the Protestant ethic as a "male" culture and the Catholic ethic as having a more "female" aspect. Listeners have argued that I might look at male culture and female culture as examples of individualistic and collectivist models, broadly conceived. More than one seminar participant has argued that the "battle between the sexes" may be understood, in part, as a battle between these two mindsets. This idea is worth thinking about.

Over the course of history, at different times, one or the other ethic may have predominated. For example, in the settling of the American West, there is the individualistic "mountain man" mindset as well as the "wagon train" mindset. These are very similar, religious practices aside, to the ideas I am suggesting here. The "rugged individualistic," Lone

Ranger approach to understanding what happened is very different from the "prairie schooner" perspective. The latter view had individuals working together, each helping the other. Wagon trains really were small mobile communities, moving across space. Of course, even these examples reflect the tension within the ethics as well. In the Lone Ranger example—as in many hero examples—there is a "sidekick"—in this case, the Native American "Tonto." It is not a surprise, perhaps, that the subdominant "sidekick" also is a minority person. (This is true with other "heroes" as well; Superman, for example, has a woman— Lois Lane—as a sidekick; Lamont Cranston, "The Shadow," had Margo Lane.) On the other hand, even in wagon trains there was a powerful "wagon master."

Even within a single person there might be two "personas." Economist Thomas Schelling, in an engaging little piece called "Egonomics" (Schelling 1978), writes about a "here and now" self and a "then and there" self. One is more individualistic and action oriented; the other is more contemplative and future oriented. Similar thinking has been advanced by Thaler and Shefrin (1981) in their "doer/planner" model, which is almost identical to Schelling's idea. This "two self" approach, of course, could give us a perspective on ourselves as we look at the two ethics in terms of reference points for actions. One could, however, apply the dual personas at different times during the day. At work, for example, I might be Mr. Individualistic Achievement, arguing that "business is business." At home, however, I might be more family and collectively oriented and less seeking of personal gain—a veritable "Joe Family Man"!

The point here is not to say these hypotheses are true. It is to speculate about the possibility that what I have been referring to as the Protestant and Catholic ethics might be two manifestations of very universal tensions of panhistorical and pancultural application. One piece of evidence for this hypothesis is the fact that many non-Catholics and non-Protestants would identify with the core elements of the ethics.

It also is possible, of course, that there are value packages or ethics that are not necessarily based on religion or derive only indirectly from religious traditions. One very important value package that emerges in U.S. data is well established and has a great deal of empirical robustness: "party identification" (Tropman 1987). Party identification is a variable that allows respondents to locate themselves with the political party (Republican, Democrat, Conservative, Liberal)[5] that is closest to their belief system without actually asserting that they are members of, supporters of, or contributors to a particular party. Hence, questionnaires use the word *identification* rather than, for example, *membership*.

Party identification is amazingly stable over generations. It is a powerful variable (i.e., it has high predictive power) in organizing and predicting other attitudes and values and qualifies as an "ethic" in the sense that term is used here (as in Catholic ethic or Protestant ethic). It reminds me a lot of the individualistic/collectivistic orientations discussed here. Party identification may be powerful because it codes and expresses these two powerful value streams. Indeed, party identification is as powerful a variable as race in the data I analyzed—a truly amazing finding that speaks to the power of culture in shaping human affairs.

Where Are We Now? Where Are We Going?

This volume is a continuation of an exploration of the idea of a Catholic ethic as a parallel belief to the Protestant ethic. I first suggested this idea in "The 'Catholic Ethic' versus the 'Protestant Ethic': Catholic Social Service and the Welfare State" (Tropman 1986) and explored it in greater detail in *The Catholic Ethic in American Society* (Tropman 1996). This volume adds even greater historical and empirical detail.[6] Several points introduced in earlier writings (Tropman 1986, 1996) emerge more strongly here. The first is that there *is* a Catholic ethic. Based on my work of the past twelve years and the work of Novak (*The Catholic Ethic and the Spirit of Capitalism* [1993]), as well as the many scholarly and popular writings of Andrew Greeley, this conclusion seems clear. As Americans often define themselves by their associations, the Catholic ethic concept further reinforces the notion that one's identify is bound together with a specific community of participants and believers.

Second, these "ethics" really are best regarded as cultures with a religious center. One can think of cultural Catholics and cultural Protestants as well as cultural Jews. Religiously based or informed cultures have core ideas, values, beliefs, and attitudes that have panhistorical and pannational application, although there obviously will be unique adaptations in specific historical periods and national settings. In the specific case of the Catholic ethic, more research is needed into ethno-Catholic forms of the Catholic ethic.

Third, these "ethics" are archetypes. Actual people are more of a mix and a muddle. Tensions exist between groups, within groups, and within each of us. Specifically, more research is needed into "counterphobic forms"—black Protestants, "conservative Catholics" and so on.

Fourth, the Catholic ethic is community based. Community based means not only doing things within the context of community but also seeing community membership as a part of one's very identity—the ensemble self. Organizational requirements of the church—requiring attendance at Mass at certain times, for example—reinforce the notion that certain religious activities must be done *in community and through community.*

Fifth, the Catholic ethic is a helping ethic. Organizationally, it is impressive. "By the 1990s the umbrella organization, Catholic Charities U.S.A. represented the largest system of provate social welfare in the nation" (Brown and McKeown 1997, 1). Individual priests often were exemplars of caring. Blantz's (1982) biography of Father Francis J. Haas, *A Priest in Public Service* is an outstanding example of this point. There were others, of course—lay leaders such as Dorothy Day and the Catholic Worker Movement. Rosalie Troester's *Voices from the Catholic Worker* demonstrates these concerns admirably.

Community and helping are often conjoined. The community aspect is keenly important, particularly in a society that increasingly "bowls alone." The Catholic ethic suggests an alternative to the highly individualistic American culture. As Mary Jo Bane puts it in "Bowling Alone, Praying Together," the parish is one reservoir of social capital:

> Social Capital is developed through the pot luck suppers, bingo games and small groups that most parishes sponsor. It certainly grows through worship and celebration of the Eucharist in the diverse, inclusive community that is our church. It can perhaps be most successfully developed through caring and service to one another both church members and the wider community . . . (Bane 2000, 6).

As historical and vital as I believe the Catholic ethic to be, its community and helping emphases are being tested in the crucible of American society and social change. This bastion of individualism is becoming even more so. Putnam's (2000) work, *Bowling Alone* suggests that there is a decrease in the social capital that informal, voluntary associations brought to American society. Although Protestants are numerically decreasing and Catholics increasing, the individualism of the Protestant ethic seems to be vitally alive. How the Catholic ethic responds—is responding—to this upsurge of individualism will be an interesting chapter in its history.

Perhaps corresponding to individualism-in-ascendance is an increase in materialism. It may be that the increase in personal capital—wealth—on the part of many Americans has led to a decrease in "social capital" of the kind Putnam describes. Prosperity has created some issues for us "haves": How can we feel "okay" about doing really well in the face of wide-scale poverty and suffering? How can we rationalize the "have-nots"? At the same time that many of us are feeling a lot less economic pain, the rich/poor gap is widening, not only within the United States but between the United States and much of the rest of the world. Writing before Christmas 2000, Cynthia Crossen of the *Wall Street Journal* points out that in the twentieth century, Christmas gift-giving has moved from the "necessity set" to the "luxury goods set." The title of her piece is "Last 100 Years Show Growth of Luxury, Greed." "'Want,'" she comments, "has supplanted 'need' as the prime gift-giving catalyst. . . . One hundred years ago a woman might long for a Bissell carpet sweeper. Today a holiday vacuum cleaner might be met by an icy stare" (Crossen 2000, B6). Robert Frank (1999) makes a similar point in *Luxury Fever*, as does Abby Ellin (2000) in "Money, Money, Money, Guilt, Guilt, Guilt." Frank points out that total U.S. spending on luxury goods increased 21 percent between 1995 and 1996—a typical figure in recent years. Having more extra cash can create moral problems; if we believe that we deserve it as a result of our hard work, however, it eases some of whatever sting we have. Robert Frank also addressed these issues (this time with Phillip Cook) in *The Winner Take All Society* (1995).

Conclusion

Max Weber ([1906] 1956), in *The Protestant Ethic and the Spirit of Capitalism*, was fundamentally correct, I think, though perhaps not exactly in the way he intended. For one thing, he was looking at the German context, where the Protestant ethic had developed as a second ethic, *in competition with and as a correction to* the Catholic ethic (which he did not mention.) Though he visited the United States, I believe that he did not recognize what could happen—what had happened—when the Protestant ethic became the first, and essentially only, ethic. Its power as a culture increased exponentially. Whether it was necessary and/or sufficient to get "capitalism" going (I am referring to causal order here), it certainly was instrumental in keeping it going and fanning its flames here in the United States. Yet any good thing, pushed too far, becomes a bad thing. The "dark side" of the Protestant ethic is that it can emphasize money too much, emphasize work too much, stress individualism too much, recognize the role of fate in our success and failure too little, perhaps be too suspicious of folks who need help, and stress the distinction between the "poor" and the "worthy poor " too much. The Catholic ethic provides another perspective. Its presence, in its many specific versions, helps American society really work better than either ethic could alone. It is sort of like a thermostat: Iron and copper bonded together make the thing work. One metal alone would not work. Bonded with each other, these two cultures drive achievement and sustain equality.

APPENDIX A

Theological Reflections on the Catholic Ethic

Gregory Baum

Max Weber's famous *The Protestant Ethic and the Spirit of Capitalism*, published in 1906, tried to demonstrate that the spirit of capitalism, the rational dedication to the accumulation of wealth, was able to spread so rapidly from the sixteenth century forward because this spirit had a certain affinity with a religious ethos—the this-worldly asceticism of Protestantism—that prompted believers to practice self-discipline, work hard in their trade, and overcome the religious prejudice against wealth accumulation entertained in traditional, Catholic society. Weber never made a systematic study of the Catholic economic ethic in medieval times or in later periods. Is there such a phenomenon as the Catholic ethic?

Bernhard Groethuysen has argued that eighteenth-century French Jansenism—with its emphasis on duty, seriousness, and the avoidance of pleasure—produced the Catholic equivalent of Weber's Protestant ethic. Weber himself thought that in industrial society the work ethic was communicated through secular education and suggested, by implication, that in industrial society people, whatever their religious background, were likely to share in the same work ethic. Relying on his empirical research among Protestants and Catholics in the United States, Andrew Greeley concluded that there was no difference between them with regard to their industry and enterprise.

John Tropman takes a new look at people's economic ethics, this time focusing not on the dedication to hard work but on the implications of this ethic for the community. Does an ethic foster the spirit of self-reliance, or does it create an awareness of interdependence? Tropman tries to demonstrate that once the question is posed in this way, an identifiable Catholic ethic does exist and that it favors not self-reliance but common welfare.

In this essay I inquire whether there is a basis in the Catholic doctrinal tradition—especially its teaching on charity and justice—for what Tropman has called the Catholic ethic. To do this I must return to some of the old debates between Catholics and Protestants and clarify the differences between their theological positions. Before I get to that, however, to avoid misunderstanding I wish to make a few remarks about Weber's thesis on the Protestant ethic.

It is important to realize that Weber did not suggest that the thought of the Reformers or subsequent Protestant theology favored the accumulation of wealth. To propose such an idea would have been absurd—and insulting. Weber realized that the central affirmations of Protestantism were justification by faith and divine predestination and that Protestant ethical teaching recommended selflessness, simplicity, modesty, love of neighbor, and concern for the community. The original Calvinist teaching urged Christians to create a just and holy society. When Weber spoke of the Protestant ethic, he referred not to Protestant teaching but to the religious practice adopted in due time by Puritans and later by all Protestants. Their religious faith made them self-responsible, hard-working people. What they discovered was that by living a life marked by seriousness, responsibility, simplicity, modesty, sobriety, and the avoidance of pleasure, they actually accumulated wealth without intending it. Weber called this asceticism "this-worldly" because it prompted self-denying behavior aimed at acting more effectively in the world, in contrast with "other-worldly" asceticism that was present, for instance, in traditional Catholicism that prompted self-denying actions—works of penance— aimed at results belonging to the spiritual order. Personal experience, not Protestant teaching, made Protestants realize that their religious ethos had a certain affinity with the rational dedication to individual enterprise, characteristic of capitalist society.

What, then, is the link between classical Protestant doctrine and the so-called Protestant ethic? The central doctrines of the Reformers (justification by faith and divine predestination) moved personal salvation into the center of believers' attention. Whereas traditional Catholic teaching, following the ancient creeds, began with God's cosmic plan of creation, redemption, and consummation and located the life of the individual in this context, the Reformers—reflecting the emerging sense of personhood—began their teaching with the liberation of the anguished individual through the forgiveness of sin and justification by faith. The self-responsible person was no longer embedded in a sacramental community that mediated divine grace to its members but stood alone before God in Jesus Christ, addressed by the divine summons and responding to it with total surrender. In Catholicism, Weber reminds us, the term "vocation" referred to the call to the priesthood or religious life, whereas in Protestantism "vocation" defined the life of every single Christian. The religious seriousness that at one time was proper to monasteries was now extended to every member of the Church. What counted above all for the Protestant Christian was trusting faith, personal decision, unmediated self-responsibility, and dedication to service of God and the community. This asceticism constitutes the narrow link between Protestant doctrine and Weber's Protestant ethic.

Weber went further. He offered an argument—which, I believe, he never proved—that the ambition of the later Puritans to become successful and acquire wealth was related to the Calvinist doctrine of divine predestination. Deeply troubled by the question of whether they belonged to the divinely predestined, the Puritans eagerly looked for signs assuring them of God's good pleasure and concluded that their earthly success was a divine signal that their name was on the list of the chosen. Thus, they worked, saved, and invested to be reassured by their wealth. This is only a slight step from believing that poor people are sinners deserted by God.

Even without Weber's controversial theory, it is plausible that Christians who define ethical commitment in terms of seriousness, self-responsibility, and perseverance easily think of poor people as lazy, lacking in good will, or even debilitated by vice. The worthy among the poor are those who struggle to extricate themselves from their predicament.

After this remark on Protestant asceticism, I turn to the main question of this essay: Are there significant differences between Catholic and Protestant teaching on charity and justice?

It is well known that at the time of the Reformation the important doctrinal debate between Protestants and Catholics had to do with the justification (salvation) of the sinner. Protestants affirmed justification "by faith alone," and Catholics spoke of justification "by faith and works."

Protestants believed that the anguished sinner is justified (or saved) by his or her trusting faith in God's gratuitous mercy promised in Jesus Christ. Justification by faith here means God's forgiveness of sin and the loving extension of Christ's own justice to the believer. The Christian is justified not by his or her own justice but by *justitia aliena*, the justice of another—the justice of Christ. Stressing the intimate union between Christ and the believer, some Reformers (especially Luther) held that the believer participated in this *justitia aliena* and hence became deeply transformed; other Reformers, uncomfortable with Luther's mysticism, taught that the merciful God pardoned the sins of the believer by extending or forensically attributing to him or her the justice of Christ, the *justitia aliena*—a justice that remained external to him or her. What counted primarily for all Protestants was the believer's trusting faith in God's promise.

Notice that this process of justification in and of itself does not include a changed relationship to the neighbor. Love follows justification. Protestants believed that with justification comes the gift of the Holy Spirit, who stirs up Christians to love God and love their neighbor.

Catholic preaching reminded the faithful that salvation came to them through faith and works. Faith was not enough to be saved: Sacramental practice and good works also were required. Catholic preaching of this kind easily creates the impression among the listeners that they are saved by their good will and their own moral effort, even if this notion contradicts the official Catholic doctrine passionately defended by St. Augustine and defined by the Council of Orange (A.D. 529) against the Pelagians and Semi-Pelagians. According to Catholic doctrine, faith and salvation are gifts of God freely given, and even our good works are initiated, sustained, and perfected by divine grace. Following this doctrine, the medieval theologians (particularly St. Thomas Aquinas) presented the justification by faith and works—or, better, by faith and love—in a way that maintained the gratuity of the divine gift.

Responding to the Reformation and drawing on the medieval theologians, the Council of Trent defined that justification was indeed by faith—or more precisely, by *a* faith, freely given by God, that was alive with hope and love. Faith here did not signify, as it did for Protestants, trust in the divine promise. In the Catholic understanding, faith was free assent to the gospel message of salvation. If this faith did not expand to include love of God and God's creatures, it was a "dead faith"—that is, a faith that, though divinely granted, did not yet mediate forgiveness and salvation. Only as the surrender of faith is spirited by hope and love does faith become salvific. Christians are justified by *fides caritate formata*: faith enlivened and shaped by love of God and love of neighbor. In this sense, faith and works are intimately joined as Christians enter their salvation.

Notice that in contrast with Protestant teaching, the process of justification in and of itself does include a changed relationship to the neighbor. According to the Catholic understanding, saving faith implies a loving turn to others.

During the polemical age that followed the Reformation, Protestant theologians accused Catholics of holding the heretical view that sinners were saved and sanctified by God as a result of their own efforts, and Catholic theologians accused Protestants of heresy for holding a doctrine of justification that emptied the biblical message of its ethical content.

These virulent debates had destructive effects. They were self-destructive, in fact, because Catholics and Protestants dangerously narrowed their own perspectives. Only with the coming of the ecumenical age in the twentieth century did Christian theologians listen to one another, try to understand other points of view, and beyond that were eager to bring their own confessional positions into greater conformity with the biblical testimonies. Protestant theologians began to put greater emphasis on the bond between faith and love, and Catholic theologians articulated more clearly the gratuitous divine initiative in the good works performed by Christian believers. The studies of scholars such as Hans Küng, Herman Pesch, and Harry McSorley have demonstrated that there was no essential difference—only a difference of emphasis—between the Protestant and Catholic theologies of justification; this finding has since been confirmed by Protestant-Catholic ecumenical study commissions, established by their respective churches, and in documents such as the Malta Report of 1972.

I have lived in this new ecumenical climate most of my academic life. In my work as a theologian and churchperson, I have stressed the common ground between Catholics and Protestants; more than that, I have tried, through dialogue and critical reflection, to broaden this common ground. In this essay, for analytical purposes, I wish to do the opposite. I want to clarify the difference between Catholic and Reformation teaching on charity and justice. To allow the reader to check my interpretations, I follow the articles on faith, love, justice, and justification in two highly respected, multivolume theological encyclopedias: the Catholic *Kirchenlexikon fur Theologie und Kirche* and the Protestant *Evangelisches Kirchenlexikon*—the latter being known for its faithful presentation of classical Reformation teaching.

In the Christian tradition going back to patristic times, we find two distinct understandings of love: one often called *ecstatic* and the other *ontological*—both echoing certain New Testament themes and both reflecting the impact of Hellenistic culture. According to the ecstatic concept of love, the Christian is called to love God without measure, prefer God to all of God's creatures, and sacrifice for God's sake all attachment to this world, including especially all love of oneself. Love of God is here the very opposite of self-love. The more the Christian loves God, the more he or she enters total self-forgetfulness. The Christian, standing alone before God, allows himself or herself to be graciously lifted out of the prison of self-concern, even including the desire for salvation.

Because, according to some biblical texts (especially the Pauline epistles), God has loved us when we were still sinners—loved us not out of need but gratuitously and mercifully—we must love God, not out of need, not for the sake of benefits to be obtained, but freely and with total selflessness. The divine *kenosis* (self-emptying), echoed in the self-emptying of Jesus on the cross, was to be imitated by the Christian believer. At the same time, this ecstatic concept of love (sometimes called *amor purgans*) also reflected the Gnostic longing for total purification from worldly attachment so that the soul becomes open to the knowledge of God. The ecstatic concept of love—a minority position in the Catholic tradition—was taken up in an original way by the Reformers.

More common in the Catholic tradition was a notion of love that reflected the experience of Christians loving one another in their ecclesial community. Here the love of God prompted a whole-hearted "yes" to God and to all that was loved by God. Loving God—creator, redeemer, and consummator—comprised the love of God's creation, especially God's human creatures, including even the love of oneself. This concept of love is called "*ontic*" because it embraces uncreated and created being.

Here the love of God and the love of neighbor are formally identical. Why? Because the neighbor is loved for God's sake. This does not mean that the neighbor is loved as a means to a higher end and therefore not loved truly for herself. Because the neighbor is created in God's image, to love her simply as a means to an end would demean and dishonor her. Because the neighbor is loved for God's sake, the neighbor must be loved for what she is in herself. Although this is a metaphysical argument, there also is biblical evidence for the unity of the love of God and love of neighbor: They constitute a single divine commandment. We are to love God and community. Here the Christian's salvific experience is not standing alone before God but being surrounded by brothers and sisters.

According to the ontic concept, love of God also includes love of self. Christians are summoned to love themselves for God's sake—again never simply as means to a higher end, however, but as images of God and therefore as end in itself. Included in the love of God is the yearning of the self for salvation and beatitude. Self-love is sinful only when it becomes exaggerated and disordered. The concept of Christian love (*agape* in Greek, *caritas* in Latin) here integrates in modified form the classical Platonic concept of *eros*: the spirit's yearning for the true, the good, and the beautiful and the spirit's love of beings to the extent that they embody truth, goodness, and beauty. According to the ontic concept, love of God includes the yearning of the human spirit for personal fulfillment. Catholic theologians even recognized in all human beings a natural desire for God—a desire that could only be satisfied in the Church, the community of believers.

The ontic concept of love also integrates the call for self-sacrifice. The divine gift of love indeed has a kenotic dimension. Love of God and community summons the believer to be selfless and self-sacrificing, forgetting oneself in the worship of God and service of the neighbor, yet hoping that in this very love one will find one's own fulfillment, joy, and happiness. According to the paradoxical biblical counsel, whoever who loses his or her life shall find it.

We find both concepts of love in St. Augustine. Sometimes he speaks of *gratis amare* and *amor castus*. He proposes that because love means total self-forgetfulness, Christian ethics transcends the obligations of the law. He writes, "Love and do what you will!" Most of the time, however, he regards love of God as the way of human fulfillment: "God, our hearts are restless until they rest in thee." Here Christian *caritas* includes the longing of *eros*. As we shall see, the Reformers regarded this latter aspect of Augustine's teaching as a corruption of the biblical message.

St. Thomas developed the ontic conception of love. Following Aristotelian psychology, he understood love (as well as faith and hope) as abiding dispositions or virtues perfecting the human faculties, yet divinely given and wholly gratuitous. Divine love became the integrating principle of personal human life—purging and perfecting the natural human dispositions—and of social human life, purging and perfecting people's communal interconnections, including their attitudes and their institutions. The gift of divine love made a just and peaceful community possible. For Thomas, love of God has social consequences, among which he mentions in particular compassion with people who suffer. Love of God prompts us to identify with the poor and downtrodden people who are closest to God's heart and to experience their suffering as our own. Love of God expresses itself in almsgiving and other forms of help extended to people in need—"the preferential option for the poor," to use a contemporary ecclesiastical expression. These actions can be called the works of salvation if we remember that the love they express is the *forma fidei*: the vital principle that nourishes and strengthens Christian faith.

How do the Protestant Reformers understand the love of God? At the center of their attention, as we have seen, was justification of the sinner by faith in the divine promises. From the human point of view, justification involved repentance and trust. With and after justification, God freely grants Christians the power to love their God and their neighbor without self-regard. Because the love commanded by the gospel transcends the limitations of the human's sinful nature, this love remains forever a surprising and unmerited gift; in its exercise it is forever blunted by human selfishness. The Reformers deny that love (or even faith) can become an abiding disposition of virtue. Uncomfortable with Aristotelian psychology, they do not believe that the divine gifts can be seamlessly assimilated by human nature, however elevated by grace.

The commandment to love God and the neighbor points to the limits of what is humanly possible. Only Jesus loved wholeheartedly and without reserve. In the Church there are no saints; there are only forgiven sinners. Because Christian believers remain fragile vessels even after justification, they continue to rejoice every day in justification by faith and forgiveness of their sins. Protestant preaching summons believers to repentance and humility and at the same time prepares them for the intervention of the Holy Spirit that will prompt them to transcend their brokenness, love and honor God as they should, and selflessly serve their neighbor.

Developing the ecstatic concept of love, the Reformers insisted that the love of the New Testament was not self-regarding. These theologians had no sympathy for the mystical dimension of ecstatic love, understood as a way of purgation preparing the soul for union with God. All-important for the Reformers was the kenotic message of the Pauline epistles. As God loved us when we were still his enemies and saved us by sending his only-begotten Son to take upon himself the ignominy of the cross, so in response must we offer a love that is wholly self-denying, without thought for our own benefit. The Reformers purged the Christian *agape* of the *eros* Catholics had deceptively joined to it.

For the Reformation theologians, the love commandment of the New Testament was extravagant, scandalized human reason, unmasked the selfish kernel in the quest for personal fulfillment, and went beyond the inclination of human nature—especially as this commandment included the love of one's enemies. The love commandment can be grasped, they argued, only by those who have first have been loved by God.

Because the divine summons to love exceeds what is humanly possible most of the time, the believer always has reason to feel guilty. According to Weber, this Protestant anxiety was a contributing factor to the asceticism of disciplined and conscientious application to duty. Weber thought that after every sacramental confession, Catholics were at peace with God and the world: They relaxed, took it easy, and assumed a moderate pace in their work and actions. Who knows whether this is true? I mentioned the Jansenist movement; in industrial society, secular educational institutions communicate the work ethic to all members, whatever their religion.

The concept of love preached by the Reformers summoned Christians simultaneously to repentant modesty and leaps of greatest selflessness. Protestant inwardness, open to the surprising acts of the Spirit, reveals an inner dynamic that is quite different from Catholic spirituality, which relies on God's grace and seeks an abiding orientation of ordered love. For Protestants, love was an explosive principle that lifted humans out of their regular course; for Catholics, love was an integrating principle that elevated humans and their institutions to constitute a just and peaceful community. Catholics regarded love as a society-shaping power and hence developed a tradition of "Catholic social teaching." Protestants did not generate an equivalent tradition. In classical Protestantism, love prompts individual believers to the impossible possibility of acting with perfect selflessness, but love is not a principle of social ethics. This observation inevitably brings us to the topic of justice.

Reformation theology, as I have noted, returned to biblical teaching in an effort to leave behind the Greek philosophical ideas that were present in Catholic theology. Justice in the Bible had two principle meanings, both of which acquired central importance in Protestant thought. First was God's justice. God was just—following the deepest meaning of this word—when God intervened in history to protect people who were unjustly treated, poor, and oppressed. God's justice rescued Israel from the land of bondage. God's justice was revealed not so much in the divine judgment pronounced on the wicked as in the divine mercy extended to the crushed and the needy. In time, God was called just precisely because God pardoned the sinner. This teaching reached its high point in the Pauline epistles, in which God's justice is revealed in the gratuitous, unmerited justification of the sinner. Reflecting on justice, therefore, leads the Reformers to the principal topic of their proclamation: justification by faith alone.

Another biblical meaning of justice, which is not easily reconciled with the first, emerges in the distinction found in the Old Testament— later taken up by Jesus himself—between the just and the sinners. In English Bibles, the word *just* usually has been rendered as *righteous*. Who are the just or the righteous in the Bible? They are people who walk humbly before God, follow the commandments, do good, speak the truth, and avoid bloodshed—or, in general terms, those who practice their religion and follow its ethical teaching. Jesus seems to adopt this distinction, which was current in the Judaism of his day, between "the righteous" who practice their religion and follow the Law (including almsgiving, prayer and fasting) and "the sinners," the great mass who are indifferent to religious practice and carelessly break the commandments. Because this understanding of the just reveals a tension running through the New Testament between faith and works, I offer the pertinent references: Mark 2:17; Matthew 5:45; and Luke 5:35, 15:7 (*cf.* Romans 5:7; Matthew 23:28; and Luke 14:14, 20:20).

Following this biblical teaching, Reformation theology insisted that the Christian, the repentant and the justified sinner, live righteously. Although remaining a sinner in need of forgiveness, the Christian practiced justice, in Luther's famous dictum, *simul justus et peccator*. Christians were righteous when they practiced their faith; were selfless, humble, and modest in their comportment; did good; and dealt honestly with their neighbor.

The emphasis on righteous living, especially in the Calvinist tradition, eventually produced the modern ethic of democratic citizenship: self-responsibility, honesty, respect for legislation, suspicion of hierarchies, preference for egalitarian values, social voluntarism, responsibility for society, and so forth. James Luther Adams rightly has complained that Weber confined his study of the Protestant ethic to its impact on economic life and paid little attention to its impact on political voluntarism or the making of modern democracy.

The Protestant understanding of justice in the two foregoing senses, drawn from the Bible, left largely unattended the issues that today are called social and economic justice. This changed in the nineteenth century when Protestant Christians were confronted by the social consequences of industrial capitalism. Minority movements such as Christian Socialism in Britain and on the continent and the Social Gospel in North America were no longer based on classical Reformation theology. The religious dedication to social justice was defended by these Protestants in terms drawn from some forms of liberal Protestantism; or, especially in Britain, from a conservative natural law tradition, close to Catholic social teaching; or, in some cases, directly from the biblical prophetic tradition. Only after World War I did Protestant theologians faithful to the classical Reformation elaborate a social ethics for modern society, beginning with Karl Barth and Emil Brunner in Europe and Reinhold Niebuhr in the United States.

The Catholic theological tradition was different. Here the concept of justice was largely taken from classical Greek thought, even though the theologians integrated this concept into a biblical understanding of human life, threatened by human sin and saved and sanctified by divine grace.

Following Aristotle, Catholic theology defined justice as a virtue or abiding disposition thanks to which one firmly acknowledges to all and each what is due to them. Justice is *ad alterum:* It is oriented toward the other. Because the other cannot be reached by mental acts alone, justice demands material action on the other's behalf. It is possible to fulfill the external obligation of justice without the appropriate inner attitude—for instance, when we act justly because we are afraid of getting caught. Although such action is not worthless, justice exists in the full sense only when the inner intention corresponds to the outward deed. In the Aristotelian scheme taken up into Catholic theology, justice is the highest of the moral virtues because it alone is *ad alterum;* consequently, sins against justice are the gravest.

Note again that whatever area of Catholic theology we examine, we find that the human being is regarded not as self-responsible alone but as other directed, interdependent.

From Aristotle, Catholic theology accepted the threefold division of justice: "commutative justice," which concerns just dealings among people—such as respect for property, fidelity to contracts, honest information, just prices and just wages; "distributive justice," which concerns just governance, people's needs, and allowing the participation of all in the community's spiritual goods; and "legal justice," which concerns the obligations of people toward public authorities that are responsible for the common good, such as obedience to laws, paying taxes, and military service. Of these three, the most startling and subversive is distributive justice.

At the end of nineteenth century, when Pope Leo XIII—in his encyclical *Rerum novarum*—began to articulate the Catholic concept of justice in public and apply it to the conditions of industrial society, he criticized liberal capitalism because it exploited the workers and thus violated distributive justice. Leo XIII attributed to public authority the strict duty of protecting the workers and providing for their welfare. A hundred years later, in his encyclical *Centesimus annus*, Pope John Paul II has recalled the teaching of his predecessor, noting that it was daring at the time. Because Leo XIII's encyclical is well known for its ardent defense of private property against the error of socialism, John Paul II finds it necessary to point out that Leo XIII "was well aware that private property is not an absolute value" and that "he did not fail to mention the necessary complementary principles, such as the universal destination of the earth's goods." In the Catholic theological tradition, even personal property is *ad alterum*: Its ownership is private, but its use is common.

How does Catholic theology relate this secular concept of justice to divine revelation in the Scriptures? It would have been possible to graft this theory of social justice onto the biblical prophetic tradition—which announced, in the words of the Magnificat, that "the powerful [will be] pushed from their thrones and those of low degree exalted: the poor [will be] filled with good things and the rich sent away empty" (Luke 1:52, 53). This is the biblical basis invoked by the radical preachers of the Protestant Social Gospel and invoked today by Protestant and Catholic liberation theologians.

Yet classical Catholic theology followed a different path. It argued that the natural virtue of justice—including its three forms of commutative, distributive, and legal—was not sufficient to assure an equitable, peaceful, friendly society. Why not? Because justice had to be tempered by mercy. Sinful humanity cannot become a harmonious society by natural virtue alone, without forgiveness, without going beyond strict obligation. In other words, without Christian *caritas*, the virtue of justice reveals itself as imperfect and often damaging and destructive. Faith, hope, and love, divinely given, purge and lift up what is left of natural virtue in a sinful world. In this context, faith makes Christians aware of the gratuity or gift-character of the human achievement; hope generates fervor for the common project, tempered by patience; and love—as we have seen—is the integrating principle, healing and elevating, of personal and social human existence.

In this essay I look only at what Catholic theologians taught. I pay no attention whatever to what Catholics—including their priests, bishops, and popes—actually have done. In no sense have I tried to answer the question of whether or to what extent Catholics allowed themselves to be affected by their theological tradition. The question I have asked is simply whether there is a peculiar ethos; a characteristic ethical stance; a special, possibly largely implicit understanding of the human vocation present in classical Catholic teaching.

My brief analysis has shown that there is such a Catholic ethic and that it is different from the Protestant ethic. In Catholic teaching the process of justification, including the forgiveness of sins, is not the trusting response of the alone to the Alone; it includes a turn to the other, to the community. According to Catholic teaching, faith is not salvific unless it is spirited by hope and love. In their faith, believers experience themselves as interdependent beings and not so much as self-responsible ones. Catholics hold that all good things, including divine grace, come to them mediated by others.

According to Catholic teaching, love of God—which is both divine gift and abiding disposition—includes the love of neighbor. Loving God implies love of the community. The effects of this love include especially identification with and compassion for people who are poor and downtrodden, a religio-ethical stance that today often is called the preferential option for the poor. *Caritas,* or the love of God, even includes loving oneself and affirming unashamedly *eros*—that is, the deep desire of the human spirit for beatitude and fulfillment. According to Catholic teaching, only disordered self-love is sinful. The theological virtue of love, in which God is graciously present to the Christian, is regarded as capable of integrating service to the community with just concern for each person's own fulfillment. This integration is deemed possible because, according to Catholic teaching, the human being is essentially other-oriented, oriented toward God and neighbor; hence, by moving toward one's fulfillment, one is liberated from self-centeredness and increasingly longs to serve and be present to the other. Divine *caritas* is the principle of integration that is destined to heal the human family from its sins, its wars, and all of its oppressive operations.

In Protestant teaching, *justice* referred mainly to God's justice (equals mercy), by which the sinner was justified, and to the justice (equals righteousness) the forgiven sinner exercised in his or her religious practice and ethical engagement. In Catholic teaching, *justice* referred principally to the virtue of justice, thanks to which people are committed to render to all and each what is due to them. Distributive justice, in particular, demands that citizens help their neighbors in need—here almsgiving is understood as acts of justice—and that public authorities serve the material and spiritual welfare of all. According to Catholic teaching, divine revelation promises that the natural virtue of justice, fragile because of the sinful human condition, is lifted up and perfected by the gift of God's love. The impetus to social justice and public welfare is built into Catholic *caritas*.

If the foregoing analysis is correct, the comparison between Catholic and classical Protestant teaching on justification, love, and justice reveals that Catholic teaching includes a conception of the human being as other-oriented, interdependent, embedded in community, bonded especially to poor people and responsible for the welfare of all. This orientation *ad alterum*—this Catholic ethic—is presented as the fulfillment of each person's *telos*, not as radical self-forgetfulness.

The Practice of Charity: The Example of Catholic Charities USA[1]

Thomas J. Harvey[2]

I. Catholic Charities: Radical Roots in Biblical Experience

From a theological point of view, the Catholic Church traces its mission and ministry to Jesus. Indeed, in its official writings, the Church has described itself as the very Body of Christ. This incarnational self-consciousness demands that the Church be the continuing sacrament of God's immeasurable love for the human family.

Yet from a very human and practical point of view, the Catholic Church is a product of history. The Church, from its institutional stirrings in Jerusalem, has enjoyed and suffered an almost symbiotic relationship to society and culture. One can see this in virtually every century. This relationship surfaced in the importance given to martyrdom in the first centuries as the Church endured the persecution of the pre-Constantinian Roman Empire. During the fifth, sixth, and seventh centuries, authority schisms divided the Eastern and Western Churches. These divisions were highly influenced by the secular—that is, by the political struggles and rivalries of the Byzantine and Roman seats of imperial government.

Even the shift in the Church's moral vision introduced by the 1891 labor encyclical of Pope Leo XIII cannot be divorced from the nineteenth-century political, economic, and social realities of Western society. This shift moved the Church from an almost exclusive accent on preparing the individual for eternal life to a growing consciousness for responsibility in establishing God's reign on earth. Such a major transition reflected the irreversible impact of the Industrial Revolution, which created longevity and leisure as well as the social evils so graphically described in that period's poetry and prose. When the majority of people could live a long life, it was inevitable that the Church would need to place greater emphasis on life on this earth.

Actually, the Church always had a theology that focused on the demands of community. Unfortunately, until the upheaval and new experiences brought on by the Industrial Revolution, even solving societal problems and enhancing the quality of community life were put in the context of assuring one's eternal destiny.

Nonetheless, the theology did exist. Community is a core concept in the Judeo-Christian tradition. It can be traced to the earliest pages of the Bible. During the exodus from Pharaoh's Egypt, the ancient Hebrews came to a new consciousness of who they were. A perception that God played a role in their deliverance from slavery was at the center of their new consciousness. They even felt that God had entered into a covenant with them. From this covenant arose a set of expected behaviors. We have come to refer to these behaviors as the Ten Commandments.

These commandments were not only normative guides to appropriate moral behavior. They also served as guidelines for individuals to use in measuring their commitment to the covenant and thus to their God. One overriding measure for the people as a whole to use in assessing their fidelity to the covenant was concern for those with the greatest needs. The strength of the people was to be assessed by their commitment to and concern for the weakest, who often were symbolized in that nomadic society by the orphan, the widow, and the stranger.[3] Thus, the earliest biblical concept of community has, as an essential characteristic, concern for everyone—especially those whose level of need puts them at risk.

The Christian Bible picks up this theme in a variety of ways. In the parable of the Good Samaritan, Jesus describes one's neighbor not in terms of the extended family—of shared religion or a common ethnicity—but in terms of compassionate behavior.[4] One visiting foreigner who cared for the victim of a street crime was held up as the epitome of what the neighbor should be.

In another text, Jesus depicts the great scene of the final judgment.[5] Those who are rewarded are those who gave him food when he was hungry or clothed him when he was naked. When challenged by his disciples to reveal when anyone saw him hungry or naked, Jesus totally identifies with every hungry and homeless person. "When you did it to one of these, the least of my brothers [and sisters], you did it to me!" The followers of Jesus were put on notice that the poorest and weakest were those with whom Jesus most identified. To ignore them or their needs was to disregard Jesus himself.

Another passage brings home the message even more pointedly. After John the Baptist is arrested, he calls together his discouraged disciples. From his prison cell he sends them to his cousin, Jesus, with a question: "Are you the one who is to come, or are we to wait for another?"[6] The question is so direct and so filled with frustration that one can conclude that the gospel writers wanted to prepare readers for a powerful insight. Jesus does not disappoint. Instead of using the question to give a detailed analysis of his person and identity, Jesus prefers to appeal to the deep-seated concern of his people for those with the greatest needs. He invites John's followers to look around: "Go tell John what you have seen and heard: The blind receive their sight, the lame walk, lepers are cleansed, the deaf hear, the poor have good news brought to them."

Organized religions that claim this heritage have a biblical imperative to be concerned about how to proclaim good news to poor and disenfranchised people. There is great diversity among religions, however—and even within some—with regard to how to live out this mandate. At one end of the continuum, one finds religious and religiously affiliated organizations that tie service of any kind to a benefit of membership. Such religious bodies fulfill the biblical mandate by making special resources available to people within the congregation who have the greatest need. Such groups tend to limit their activities to those supported by private donations given by the congregation.

At the other extreme of the continuum are those religious organizations that give various services for the mutual benefit of members but also are willing to collaborate with the government in meeting a public objective. To assure the integrity of the religious organization and accountability for any public money involved, such collaborations generally are guided by grant agreements or purchase-of-service contracts. Catholic Charities USA lies at this end of the continuum: Nearly 60 percent of its overall services are tied to government grants and contracts. Religious organizations in this category fulfill the biblical imperative to be concerned for the poorest and weakest, without regard to membership. Between the two extremes are various religious organizations that limit service primarily to members, except in special circumstances such as natural disasters, which affect the entire community. In light of recent political initiatives to promote more faith-based solutions to social problems, the diversity of religiously organized services is sufficiently broad to warn against any analysis that presumes a uniformity of behavior or philosophy in so-called faith-based organizations.

"Faith-based" is a recent term of art that has arisen in public policy debates at the national level. These debates center around possible and actual roles played by religiously identified human service organizations in meeting public objectives. The debate relies on assumptions that require careful analysis and, in some cases, challenge.

II. Catholic Charities: Recent Roots in the Experience of the Industrial Revolution

The Industrial Revolution caused perhaps the most extreme axial shift in human history. It affected virtually every institutional expression of life, from family and government to work and education.

For nearly 5,000 years of recorded history, land was the basis of wealth. Control of land caused wars, bestowed rights, and created a ruling class. Except for a few professions, family and work were associated with the land. An apprentice model of education passed on the skills of living on the land through hundreds of generations over a score of centuries.

Enter the mine and the mill: industrialization. Everything changes. Capital replaces land as the basis of wealth. Work is separated from the family. Education moves from the apprentice model to specialization. With specialization comes deferral of mate selection and marriage.

Industrialization fashioned a New World—a world that had little history on which to draw. The guideposts of order—religion and government—were experiencing their own challenges of adaptation to change.

Officials of the Catholic Church throughout Europe at the time of industrialization themselves were drawn mostly from the landed classes. As such, they were little prepared to view the new experiences through the prism of the Gospel. Instead, they tended to withdraw inward to accent missionary activity, private spirituality, and moral discipline and to urge caution about all things new.

Across the mosaic of the Catholic societies in Europe, however, arose charismatic individuals who immersed themselves in the new realities. They often were patricians who recognized that humanity was being put at risk in the extremes emerging from industrialization. A pattern evolved. They would immerse themselves in the fabric of life of those put most at risk in the unfolding industrialization. In turn, they would rally other caring individuals to join them in activist communities of concern.

These leaders organized specific services to meet identified needs. In doing so, their lives and services challenged many of the assumptions of their day and called for a change in the conditions of work, the distribution of rights, and the role of government as the guardian of the public good.

In a 1982 essay published by the Catholic Health Association, Joseph Holland succinctly describes this new ecclesial reality:

> Before the Industrial Revolution, modern social apostolates such as ministries in health, education and other charitable works were lim-

ited phenomena for church or society. . . . [T]he social dislocation of the Industrial Revolution led to the birth of many new religious congregations. Heroic women and men (more often women) were moved by great compassion at the sight of a disrupted peasantry cast from their rural roots into the heartless world of new urban industrial centers. They looked around, saw the suffering of the unemployed, orphaned, homeless, and ill and acted in spontaneous and direct ministries. . . . They did not act solely as individuals; in the midst of their ministries, they called others to join them.[7]

Thus, this group of charismatic believers from the seventeenth through the twentieth centuries created the modern religious orders and lay associations of the Catholic Church. They also created the modern, organized health and social welfare services offered under the aegis of Catholic health providers and of Catholic Charities.

The fascinating aspect of this organized development of services reveals two unique and interrelated realities. They developed in isolation from one another—whether in Dublin or Lisbon, Paris or Prague, Vienna or Venice. A common set of circumstances that put humanity at risk called forth a common response. The emergence of these organized charities was a movement within the Church and within society. Later, the Church's official documents—generally referred to as the social encyclicals—would authenticate these efforts with a powerfully challenging theology. That would not happen until 1891, however.

One example makes the point that the Catholic service system was never limited to specific services. In eighteenth-century France, the prevailing assumption was that poor people could not or would not be educated. John Baptist de La Salle, a priest, gathered a group of men around him who became known as the Brothers of Christian Schools. They opened schools for poor boys throughout France. In doing so, they challenged a prevailing assumption of the day. Eventually this initiative led to universal access to education in the western world. Hospitals, orphanages, other social services, parochial schools, and colleges and universities also served specific constituencies while empowering a broader-based participation in the benefits of the emerging world of opportunity created by industrialization.

The effect of this social praxis did not go unnoticed by commentators of the time. In the United States, public attitudes toward poor people during the colonial (eighteenth century) and laissez faire (nineteenth century) periods were anything but sympathetic. In their study of the Colonial period, Axinn and Levin point out, "[Concern] about poverty was not to be construed as sympathy for the poor, who were viewed as having to be coerced to work and deterred from pauperism."[8]

Benjamin Franklin was not untypical of this prevailing attitude when he challenged public provision for poor people in a 1753 letter:

> I have sometimes doubted whether the laws peculiar to England, which compel the rich to maintain the poor, have not given the latter a dependence that very much lessens the care of providing against the wants of old age. I have heard it remarked that the poor in Protestant countries, on the continent of Europe, are generally more industrious than those of the Popish countries. May not the more numerous foundations in the latter, for relief of the poor have some effect towards rendering them less provident? To relieve the misfortunes of our fellow creatures is concurring with the deity; it is godlike; but if we provide encouragement for laziness and supports for folly, may we not be fighting against the order of God and nature, which perhaps has appointed want and misery as the proper punishments for, and cautions against, as well as the necessary consequences of, idleness and extravagance.[9]

Franklin's narrow view of the nation's responsibility for the general welfare lives on in the attitudes of many citizens of the United States today. In contrast, Catholic Charities USA, in the 1972 foundational modern statement of its identity, states:[10]

> The good news of the Gospel and the scandal of human suffering together situate the paradoxical mandate of Catholic Charities. Our understanding of both the good news and human suffering has been restricted by our tendency to dichotomize the two. . . . We can neither serve others . . . except as we recognize the church of Christ as a witness of the solidarity of all persons. That is to say that all bear within them the riches and dignity of human nature so that as each discovers and gives expression to his/her need, all find in that person a mirror of themselves. Thus, instead of fostering a division between those who help and those who are helped, Catholic Charities must foster the compassion reflected in the Gospel wherein all experience themselves in each other rather than making each other other.[11]

III. Catholic Charities: The Embodiment of the Catholic Ethic

From 1982 until 1992, I served as the president and chief executive officer of Catholic Charities USA, a voluntary association of 1,200 health and welfare organizations developed under the auspices of the Catholic Church.

The oldest individual Catholic Charities organizations in the United States developed mostly within the ethnic enclaves of the large industrial cities of the mid- to late 1800s. These organizations reflected patterns of life in the lands of origin and primarily served people from those lands. They were administered and staffed primarily by religious congregations from those nations. The steel city of industrialized Pittsburgh tells the story of the period: Between 1842 and 1920, thirteen orphanages opened. Each was founded to respond to the needs of wave after wave of new immigrants from various Catholic countries in Europe.

This formed the infrastructure. Over the years, especially as need patterns changed, organizations began to enter into federations of social services under Catholic auspices. Although many names were used in different localities, Catholic Charities became the most common.

In 1910, the Catholic Charities movement reached a new level of institutionalization. The various organizations formed a membership association in Washington, D.C.: the National Conference of Catholic Charities. In 1985, on its seventy-fifth anniversary, the organization changed its name to Catholic Charities USA.

The organizing meeting in 1910 was convened on the campus of Catholic University. Three distinct groups were influential in the organization's development. Religious congregations of men and women who were heavily involved with a variety of social services but with a heavy concentration of residential services to children at risk were at the heart of the gathering. It might be appropriate to note here that this conference preceded the child labor laws. Until then, children were too frequently the collateral damage of the rapid and unregulated expansion of industry. Thus, people who managed the orphanages of the time had concerns that went far beyond the limits of the children who actually were in their care.

A second, large constituency that helped to form the conference was the St. Vincent de Paul Society, a lay association of Catholic men originally founded by Frederic Ozanam in 1833 at the University of Paris. The society spread quickly throughout the Catholic Church. The first unit in the United States grew in St. Louis, Missouri; the movement quickly spread to other large cities. This group of volunteers had a radical commitment to improve the lot of the poorest people. They often were successful children and grandchildren of immigrants. Beyond their volunteer activities, they formed many organized charities. One typical service involved the development of camps to give children trapped in urban blight the chance to experience nature.

The third leadership cadre that helped to form the National Conference of Catholic Charities was smaller but critically influential. It included a group of Catholic clergy who taught at Catholic University, as well as other priests who pioneered in giving a vision to the developing movement. These priests and their successors acted as key advisers to the Bishops of the United States and indeed to the New Deal administration of Franklin Delano Roosevelt. (Some of the best-known include William J. Kerby, John Ryan, John O'Grady, and Francis Haas.)

The Catholic Charities movement has a history that reflects the changing nature of the Catholic population and patterns of need in the United States. Its consistent ethic, however, has been to confront through service whatever puts humanity at risk—whether that cause is hunger or homelessness, abuse or abandonment, lack of skills or lack of opportunity.

Originally, Catholic-sponsored social services were organized within and through local congregations. As I have noted, these services often were ethnically focused. In 1935, when the federal government enacted the Social Security Act, it placed a safety net under some of the most vulnerable populations in the United States. This legislation relieved much of the poverty reduction relief efforts of Catholic Charities. In the wake of the Social Security Act, Catholic agencies began to incorporate separately. They moved away from their congregational base. In turn, they began to serve, in a professional way, the new Catholic middle class that emerged from the Great Depression and World War II. In many localities, they changed their names to Catholic Social Services or Catholic Family and Community Services. They offered services ranging from adoption to counseling. In residential settings, child care continued, as did long-term care facilities for frail elderly people. During this era—from 1935 to 1959—Catholic Charities joined Community Chests and United Funds. Their workforces also began to shift from primarily religious to laity.

In 1959, the federal government initiated an effort to address the nation's social ills by purchasing services from nonprofit social service providers. This effort expanded in the 1960s under the banner of the War on Poverty. With its large and well-distributed organizational infrastructure, the Catholic Charities movement became a major partner with the government in health care, child care, elder care, and economic development. The new experience unfolded incrementally. It took many years before leaders recognized the need to revisit the Catholic Charities identity and mission.

Government partnerships empowered Catholic social service organizations to work with constituencies that were not historically identified with the Catholic Church. This led to more pluralistic and inclusive employment patterns. Boards of directors in many cases were ecumenical. This development has had a positive effect on the quality and stability of services. There was a new and urgent incentive, however, to revisit the fundamental meaning of the movement.

IV. Cadre Study Establishes Philosophical Framework for Catholic Charities in the Modern World

From 1968 through 1972, the National Conference of Catholic Charities sponsored a strategic planning process to address the new reality and challenges. The result was exceptionally poetic and prophetic. The plan was published with the title *Cadre Study toward a Renewed Catholic Charities Movement.* Because it was the product of a cadre of the fifteen leaders of the Catholic Charities movement, it became known to those within the system simply as the Cadre Study. Clearly the document charts a course for Catholic Charities to maintain a consistent identity, rooted in the Gospel and in the spirit of its charismatic founders yet able to adapt to the changing environment of need.

To appreciate the power and practicality of the Cadre Study, one should consider the main principles it developed in its preamble to help Catholic Charities organizations state and understand their identity in a very pluralistic environment. The principles have been embedded in Catholic Charities for nearly thirty years and continue to guide that dynamic movement. The study also served as a strategic planning instrument for the National Conference of Catholic Charities in itself. The programmatic sections are more tied to the organizational challenges of the 1970s and have been adapted in later planning processes.

As I note in section III, religious congregations to serve at-risk Catholics from a particular part of the world had founded many of the specific programs of local charities. Thus, they often were as ethnic as they were Catholic. When staff and clients shared the same ethnic and religious heritage, questions of identity did not seem very important. By 1972, the majority of these clients were not Catholic. This change, coupled with pluralistic workforces and ecumenical governance structures, made such questions critically important.

The Cadre Study's preamble sets the context of a renewed Catholic Charities movement in five principles of faith and their corollary implications for Catholic Charities as a provider of social services. As the study builds on that principled base, it establishes three guidelines, through which a Catholic Charities entity could root itself within the framework of its faith tradition while functioning in a multicultural society.

The first guideline called for a commitment to offer quality service to anyone who was in need. Moreover, the first concern should always be for those *most* in need. This imperative gives Catholic Charities the mandate to be ready when human need surfaces, regardless of the faith of the person or persons whose humanity has been put out at risk. This service should be sacramental—that is, it should not only solve a problem; it must engender hope. Thus, this guideline was not a call to solve everyone's problems. It was, however, an appeal to offer such quality service that there would be a reason to regard all problems as solvable and all persons as endowed with a shared human dignity.

The miracles of Christ touched only a few individuals and communities in a very qualitative way during a very limited period of history. Yet their meaning was always transcendent. They revealed a power greater than leprosy, hunger, disabilities, and even death itself. The service base of Catholic Charities was to be sacramental in this transcendent sense. The role identified for Catholic Charities in the modern world called for it to humanize and transform the social order. In this priority, the Cadre Study saw that people who had hands-on experience in dealing with those who were oppressed by pain or poverty, depravation or discrimination, abuse or abandonment, or any other dehumanizing reality had a moral obligation to confront the cause of such maladies. This perspective reminded the service community that it always must avoid the temptation to be co-opted and become an instrument that perpetuates dependence. Thus, the Cadre Study recognized the need for social analysis and a commitment to public education and political activism.

The final role that prioritized Catholic Charities to be true to the theology and values of the Cadre Study involved convening the Christian community and other concerned people. Such convening did not refer simply to an openness to new partnerships and collaborations, although it certainly supported any linkage that would enhance the quality of the community's life. More specifically, the Cadre Study valued convening as a source of empowerment. "We do not give to people what is theirs by right. Nor do we give to or do for the needy and oppressed; rather; we enable them to become aware of their need and oppression and to search out the means to improve their condition of life. This dawning awareness, this self-searching is described by the Latin American term *conscientizacion*."

The process that takes place—or should take place—when "concerned" people are "convened" begins with dialogue. The dialogue must take place between equals, however. There must be no imposition of concepts and values, but an exchange and a sharing."[12]

The value of the Cadre Study's framework for understanding the meaning and purpose of Catholic Charities in the modern world has proved itself again and again. Perhaps a few personal reflections on my tenure as president and chief executive of Catholic Charities USA will make the point.

In 1982, when I became the president of what was then still called the National Conference of Catholic Charities, I managed an association of more than 1,000 religiously affiliated social service organizations. Their services touched the lives of more than 3.5 million individuals, of whom 23 percent needed survival support such as food and shelter. By 1992, this service network served nearly 13 million clients, of whom more than 60 percent needed food or shelter.

This situation presented fundamental challenges to the Catholic Charities mission, which was to empower people to live freely in spite of a stressful environment. Yet our resources often did not permit our system to bring to its clients what they most needed—training, new jobs, and participation in the full opportunities of the American dream. Instead, as a partner with the government during that extreme period of economic dislocation, Catholic Charities (and, for that matter, most social service providers at the time) opened shelters and food pantries to help people survive.

Yet even in such a frustrating situation, the principles of the Cadre Study kept most Catholic Charities from being defined by their statistics rather than their mission. I remember visiting an industrial city in Pennsylvania that had been particularly affected by a radical out-migration of capital, with the consequent loss of industrial jobs. The ranks of hungry and homeless people swelled. When I stopped into a spotless and well-decorated hall where many homeless and near-homeless people could gather each day to eat, I was struck by the small vase on each table that held a cut flower. A Mercy sister directed that "kitchen." I commented on the flowers on every table. Her response showed that she understood the Cadre Study. She mentioned that the closing of so many plants has put so many unemployed people on the streets that they were not welcome in very many places. While they gathered to eat together, they should be reminded that they share our common humanity and dignity. The flower was a better reminder than a sterile table.

Eventually the real answers had to be found in the new economy. People who fell through the cracks of the transition period of the 1980s did not have the support of a generous national public policy. As the Catholic Charities personnel of the time became more immersed in the plight of the new poor, as well as the more chronically poor, they became more active in public education and political activism to "humanize and transform" the social order to be more just and inclusive of all peoples. Even in the year 2000, after nearly ten years of an expanding economy, there are continuing reminders that there is an unfinished agenda for Catholic Charities and other service providers who care about marginalized people. We still are a nation that permits 20 percent of its children to be raised in poverty, and the gap between the richest and poorest continues to widen.

The Cadre Study rightly notes that our society will not be whole until all of its people are "convened"—that is, given the chance to be heard, valued, and invited to full participation. As long as this important priority is delegated to organizations such as Catholic Charities, these very service providers must invest their resources in a balanced way among specific services, political activism, community education, and client empowerment. In the language of Christ, assuring the discouraged disciples of John the Baptist that there are signs that the one who was to come is present, "Go tell . . . what you have seen and heard: The blind receive their sight, the lame walk, lepers are cleansed, the deaf hear, the poor have good news brought to them."[13] Catholic Charities, in philosophy and practice, is determined to keep the message alive and fresh.

APPENDIX C

The Cadre Study

Note: The Cadre Study was commissioned by Catholic Charities USA to help chart a course for the future. (Thomas J. Harvey mentions it in Appendix B.) Following is a statement of core principles that, I think, embody Catholic ethic ideas.

Preamble

The good news of the Gospel and the scandal of human suffering together situate the paradoxical mandate of Catholic Charities. Our understanding of both the good news and human suffering have been restricted by our tendency to dichotomize the two.

As an integral expression of the Church of Christ we are charged not simply with attempts to meet human need, but with the further challenge of a reflective penetration of every expression of need as a revelation of the human condition that all share. Recognizing that such radical understanding of need and suffering cannot be achieved except through the people who most experience and express them, it is incumbent that we face the dynamics of baptism; namely, that of challenging and enabling those we serve to push their consciousness of their need and its causes to the deepest level possible. Only in this way can we be faithful to the good news of liberation which proclaims no superficial escape from the dilemma of humanity, but rather qualitative and substantive life flowing from a courageous death to myth and fantasy.

We can neither serve others in embracing this process nor participate in it ourselves except as we recognize the church of Christ as a witness of the solidarity of all persons. That is to say that all bear within them the riches and dignity of human nature so that as each discovers and gives expression to his/her need all find in that person a mirror of themselves. Thus, instead of fostering a division between those who help and those who are helped, Catholic Charities must foster the compassion reflected in the Gospel wherein all experience themselves in each other rather than making each other other.

In addressing itself to its paradoxical challenge, Catholic Charities can lean heavily on the dynamic values and principles of the Church which is the source of its challenge.

1. A deep respect for all reality as a medium through which a loving God becomes available to all persons.
2. A consequent awareness of the need to bring wonder and reflection to the examination of every experience.
3. A deep respect for the capacity of every person to face up to the challenge of human existence in his/her own unique way which is nonetheless educative of everyone else.
4. A struggle away from defensiveness toward an understanding of recognized sin as a moment of hope in which a person can, in the context of love, come to grips with his/her inhumanity.
5. A sensitivity to our individual and corporate need to create vehicles of celebration which enable us to digest every kind of experience and the discovery of self that the Lord makes possible for us in and through the fabric of our lives.

Implications:

1. Services provided by the Catholic Charities movement should be evidently sacramental, that is, transparencies of the mercy and love of Christ.
2. Catholic Charities must be grounded in the participation of the Christian community in the works of charity. In its services it must provide the forum for growth and learning of all. It must draw from all hearts the love and concern that is there.
3. In order to foster individual freedom and liberty, the spirit and programs which Catholic Charities sponsor should be of such a nature as to discern, to call attention to, and to prevent the causes of bondage and oppression. Catholic Charities then must stop wishing to resolve the poverty, the misery, of the oppressed by individual acts of charity alone.
4. Catholic Charities, like the church of which it is a part, is in constant need of reform. Although reform would take many forms, emphasis should be focused an the "foolishness" of the Gospel in the public forum. The truth of Christ cannot impose itself except by virtue of its own truth as it makes its entrance at once quietly

and with power in the hearts of all persons. When Charities replaces inspiration and love with coercion under and form, it assumes a secular character.

5. Programs benefit people only when they contribute to the individual's freedom and independence. Catholic Charities must
commit itself boldly to the complete liberation of persons so that
they can be the real artisans of their destinies, the shapers of history, the free active builders of their futures.

Theology of Catholic Charities

Explication of Preamble

I. The preamble attempts in a philosophical, theological way, to lay
a groundwork for renewal that is not looking to something detached, removed, and new, but is seeking organically to build upon the principles
and premises that have been not only those of Charities but also of the
total Church for a very long time, trying, however, to see these principles and premises in a new and fresh way.

The first and fundamental premise is the fact that Catholic Charities
is an integral part of the Church, responsible not only for delivering services, or taking care of the poor, or doing the job for the rest of the
Church, but responsible primarily for contributing to and shaping the
thinking and life and lifestyle of the Church. This is so because the fundamental responsibility of the Church is to look at God and to try to see God
revealed in the fabric of human and social events, objects, and issues, to
look at God in a way that recognizes that, at God's hands through this medium of reality, we're going to grow organically, and change, and constantly come to be. Once that is stated, it should also be stated that both
scripture and tradition seem to indicate that God is most graphically revealed in the poor and in the oppressed.

If we look back to the time of Moses, we find that, rather than just
binding up the wounds, so to speak, of the Jews who were faced with the
problems and sufferings of bondage and slavery, he pushed them to a
real confrontation with the dimensions and causes of their problems,
and thus brought into being a major part of the revelation of Jewish theology and also the liturgy and ritual that went along with it.

The whole Gospel is replete with examples of Christ's good news
coming from His encounters with people who were subject to oppression, encounters that did not simply, in a superficial way, help the people
adjust to whatever the problem was, but challenged them to confront
that problem to the point where they got some sense of the cause of it.

In our own time, there have been Sojourner Truth, Martin Luther King, and Malcolm X with black people, or Cesar Chavez with farm workers, or Gloria Steinem with women, or the Welfare Rights Organizations, or the National Federation of Priests. They have not simply bound the wounds of their people, but have really pressed them and challenged them and goaded them to a deeper and deeper confrontation with their needs and the cause of those needs, and have thereby brought about the birth of a people, the birth of new organizations, new actions, new thrusts, new insights about the whole society, as well as about the people themselves.

It also has to be pointed out that no one comes to this vision of God and to the dynamic growth that can occur at God's hand simply by looking for God or looking at God superficially. There is a whole process of what we could call prayer or reflection that is absolutely necessary if a person is going to really penetrate his/her own sense of contradiction, problem, need, and come to some sense of the cause of that need, and come to some kind of new life.

We, as Catholic Charities, and we, as a Church, are responsible not so much for praying for the oppressed and the poor that we serve, but rather praying with the people that we serve in an effort to get them to reflect to the point where they plunge into a deeper confrontation with themselves and their problems. We have to recognize that it is the oppressed, and not those who serve the oppressed, who have the greatest possibility of coming to this in-depth vision of God revealed in and through their oppression. Such a posture would expose us to an even greater challenge, because to help a person engage in dialogue which leads to greater confrontation with frustration, worry, pain and anger is not an easy thing to do. It is not easy because it increases the suffering of the people who are oppressed and it also involves one who is praying with those people in greater suffering and death to himself.

Another value of the Church that comes to mind immediately, and that has been there since the beginning, is the whole notion of baptism. If we are to be ministers of baptism, we are charged with the responsibility of stimulating and encouraging people to face their own deaths; to enter into burial in the waters of their own problems and needs with some faith, so that, even as we see them suffering and dying, in a certain sense, we believe that a new life will come from this real penetration of and confrontation with the problems and needs that they face. And this in turn will involve us in a kind of death, a death, perhaps, to some of the staid ways of experiencing ourselves and seeing ourselves as the Church, or as a Charities movement, a death to some of the time-honored ways we have of doing things, to some of the security that we find in the present ways of fumbling and living out our existence. And yet, if we are truly ministers of baptism and are really looking to the Church and the Gospel through the dynamics of growth and development, we have to face up to this responsibility to stand for baptism in the sense of getting ourselves and the people we serve to really be willing to face death, in the sense of loss to self, in the sense of contemplating, anticipating, and even welcoming the loss of our present self-image.

This ministry of baptism also challenges us to recognize, affirm, celebrate, and stand for new forms of life that are, perhaps, threatening, because they don't conform to professional standards, or governmental standards, or even our own sense of what true responses to problems and needs should be, Welfare Rights Organizations, for instance, or groups of tenants that get together in rent strikes, or groups of people (and maybe this is the most threatening of all), who, confronting their own problems, come up with fresh and creative responses that are by no means sophisticated and are by no means immediately recognizable as a new, valid, vital thrust of men facing their problems and coming up with solutions for themselves or society. This is what is meant by discernment: the need to be on our toes, with our eyes wide open, contemplating God, and seeing God's new life appear through human beings who are willing to face this death of confronting their problems and coming up with fresh responses to them.

The other challenge that this process asks of us is also something that is deeply rooted in our tradition and in our life and in the revelation that the Gospel offers us, and that is the need for us to be ministers of penance, not simply the one-to-one relationship of the confessional, but a recognition that if we are to embark on this deep confrontation with the problems and needs that face people, we are going to be involving ourselves in a lot of failure, we are going to identify with people in life-thrusts that will necessarily entail mistakes and wrong directions. This process also asks of us a willingness to abandon our defensiveness when certain aspects of the life of the Church, or the life of a social movement, or the life of the Charities movement are challenged because of their deficiencies. Being a minister of penance is being a person who can be utopian in outlook, not in the sense of looking forward to some false utopia or some fantasy of the future but utopian in the sense of being willing and able to denounce that which we discover as dead in ourselves at the same time that we proclaim support for tentative, new, fresh, unsophisticated forms of life that are evolving.

This is obviously not easy. It is not easy to recognize sin as a moment of hope in which growth becomes possible, especially in this society which is so defensive, and so intolerant of sin. It's a kind of winners' society where whole people belong. And if those who recognize a contradiction in themselves give expression to it, they go through the whole identity crisis of struggling to believe in themselves, even as they discover, taste, and proclaim a sense of lack of contradiction in themselves. It would seem that the Gospel that is rooted in a God of love, in a God who invited us to be human, to seek the truth, peace, new forms of confronting problems, and fresh responses, is saying, in a certain sense, that it's all right to sin. It's all right to recognize the contradictions in us precisely because God invites us to grow rather than to engage in the stale pursuit of professional or other kinds of images that we can use to cover up and hide the fact that we have contradictions within us.

There is still another role which our position seems to set up for us, and that is to be agents of compassion in the Church and in society, agents of compassion in the sense of recognizing that if a person—black, white, narcotic addict, policeman, prostitute, artist, a person suffering economically—no matter what person in the whole human race, dares, really, at deep levels, to confront his/her problem and need and comes up with some live sense of its cause both inside and outside their person, then that person is revealing not simply a personal problem and an insight that applies only to that person, but something that applies to all of us. It's such a mistake to think of drug addicts as "cases" or "problems," and of ourselves as being apart from them, as trying to help them with their problems—because the addicts are simply mirrors of our whole society. They use syrup to coat their nerve endings to make themselves numb to what's going on around them. But what are the people in the corporations, and the media, and the Congress, and even the Church, and the suburbs, and the slums doing, who don't have to use dope, but who nonetheless numb themselves and restrict their vision of what's going on around them so that they can achieve the same goal that the addict is achieving when he's putting the syrup in his arm?

The major issue facing us now is that of abortion and the lack of respect for life that is seemingly expressed there. We think of it as a problem of the people that are practicing abortion, or the legislation that is supporting it, and speak of the lack of respect for life that they reflect. And yet, if it is really confronted at deep levels, it becomes very clear that the whole abortion syndrome and the lack of respect for life inherent therein is simply a mirror of the extent to which life is not respected in our whole society. It is illustrated by the degree to which people slash and cut each other in competition in business, in universities, in the Church, in Charities movements, everywhere you go; the extent to which people are willing to destroy others to make 7 percent instead of 5 percent, or 10 percent instead of 6 percent; and the extent of our involvement in Vietnam and the way in which it so clearly reveals lack of sensitivity to the wonder of life and the wonder of the human being. It is all very much connected to the abortion issue.

We make such a mistake when we look at black people, who, with great leadership, have come to confront some of the existential problems that are theirs, and sometimes we say that it's not our problems, that we can not be involved with them and perhaps even that we can not learn anything from them. And yet, if we really push for a reading and understanding and compassionate interpretation of what black people are saying, we find that it is very much our problem because they are the ones who had the courage to get up in society and say they had some questions about whether they were human, some questions about whether they belong.

And what individual in our whole society does not, on a daily basis, have the problem of coming to grips with his/her own identity and his own experience of their own person? And yet, because we have degrees, or because we have collars, or because we are white, Irish, or Italian, because we seem to unite within ourselves all the criteria that prove to the world that we belong, we seem not to have that problem. Yet our whole tradition in baptism is suggesting that every person has the problem of identity crisis, of putting up with and identifying with their own coming to life on a continuous basis. Therefore, the building of bridges between those who are helped and the helpers, between those who seem to be oppressed and those who seem not to be oppressed, is another fundamental role which is ours precisely because of the position that we stand in. And it's an opportunity for us to give witness to the solidarity of the Church, which suggests that everyone has deeply within their being all the riches and dignity and all the contradictions and problems of the whole human race. If we could recognize and live up to this concept of building bridges, we would enable people to understand one another, each through the other's experience. And that is yet another aspect of renewal.

II. The preamble begins with a statement of the human condition in the light of faith in the resurrected Lord and places the mandate of Charities squarely in the mainstream of theological renewal: to overcome the dichotomy between the good news of the Gospel and the scandal of human suffering, for only in their blending will the mature and integrated life expected of the Christian community be forthcoming. Many of the issues stirring the religious roots of contemporary culture are implied in this attempted resolution: the value of the secular world, our understanding of human nature and the supernatural calling of human persons, our perception of God's presence in reality, the gratuity of God's elective love of human beings, the ambiguity of all human progress, the tension between the Christian's awaiting of the expected eschaton and his/her creative involvement in the construction of an evolving world.

The preamble attempts to weave a new pastoral mandate for Catholic Charities from two diverse strains of experience—Christian joy and the scandal of human suffering—by interpreting the scholastic understanding of reality and grace in a methodology that can be described as phenomenological, existential, and personalist.

This approach of the preamble has at least one advantage over the essentialist approach developed brilliantly by Father Richard P. McBrien at the 1971 annual meeting. As a Midwest lay director of Charities commented, Father McBrien's ecclesiology possibly contains the seed of a triumphalistic pitfall for Catholic Charities: the diakonia, or service interpretation of the role of the Church as the facilitator of God's Kingdom may offer the present Charities' personnel the excuse of not really confronting the need of renewal now. One could say comfortably: "Is not the Church, through existing Charities' programs and services, already offering its resources to enable the greater presence of the Kingdom?" Father McBrien gives Charities an apologetical look for justifying its services and even existence, something with which we can objectively identify. The preamble is a challenge to personal and organizational renewal or conversion.

The vital, experiential, and, if you wish, existential underpinnings of the preamble is best illustrated by an autobiographical anecdote told by Msgr. Robert Fox, a Cadre member. Msgr. Fox has been working and living in an area in New York City in which the lives of his neighbors reflect much of the anguish and deprivation of the American urban scene. During the garbage strike a few winters ago, the neighbors, seeing the buildup of debris in the street with the attendant rodent and insect danger were grumbling and complaining. Actually, by projecting their plight upon Mayor Lindsay at City Hall and Rockefeller in Albany, they were refusing to face the reality of their situation. The garbage continued to pile up as a menace to the health of their children and of the entire neighborhood. What Msgr. Fox succeeded in doing was to focus his neighbors' attention on their situation, and to provoke them to transcend it by posing various options. Despite the physical and psychological threats from the strikers, the people eventually decided that on a given day they would rent trucks to haul the garbage away themselves. While the women prepared food for the workers, the men went about the task of collecting the garbage and carting it away. That evening, reveling in their accomplishment together, they celebrated a neighborhood liturgy. Basically, they touched the garbage of their reality and ended up by transcending the situation through their work and celebration. This story can serve as a parable or a metaphor for the whole study and its process.

The preamble accurately reflects the balanced view of the social conditions of persons and nations developed in the Encyclicals of Pope John XXIII *Mater et Magistra,* and of Pope Paul VI, *Populorum Progressio,* wherein human progress is described as necessary but not the supreme good of persons and wherein religious persons in the world are exhorted not to be exclusively directed by a political theology which, by emphasizing the measurable progress of the technological, cultural, and social fields as its object does not demand the radical cost of discipleship: personal metanoia.

Pope Paul especially has called for more than just a political theology, a militant eschatology of action; he has called especially "for a new humanism which embraces the higher values of love and friendship of prayer and contemplation." The Pope explicitly states that "all growth is ambivalent," at the same time that he says that "development is the new name for peace."

As someone has said, "In the name of God we must denounce the idolatry of 'progress of people' and the polluting escalation of production"—a strong echo of Marcuse.

The preamble does not reflect a militant optimism by which it seeks to outbid by its optimism all forms of alienation or "the pain of finiteness." It rather recognizes and acknowledges those forms of human alienation which cannot be removed through any economic or social transformation, e.g. the experience of guilt, of evil, or of concupiscence.

The One Common Denominator: The Sacramentality of All Created Reality

The preamble considers all created reality (to the degree that it is personal) as sacramental, as the arena of our encounter with God who has gratuitously called us to this intimate life. "The world is charged with the grandeur of God." All created reality is radically incarnational since Christ has elevated it to the supernatural order. Consequently, secular reality shares a sacramental character by the will of Christ as really as the seven sacraments. This reveals the underpinnings of the preamble's understanding of the sacraments of baptism, penance, and the eucharist as climacterics, as peaks of explicitness in the continuum of supernatural encounter with God which constitutes a person's existence in the secular reality.

The preamble casts further light on the traditional distinction between nature and grace (and, by implication, the distinction between the secular and sacred) by adopting implicitly the theological insight of Karl Rahner—the supernatural existential in which, granting the gratuity of God's love for humankind, we live as persons in whom grace and nature are only theoretical distinctions and the sacred and secular are not separate and distinct experiential realities. Wherever genuine human love is realized, we have an instance of supernatural love of God and of neighbor, and wherever and to the degree that one promotes the genuinely human, he thereby fosters the supernatural.

The effects of this on our understanding of the relationship of the seven sacraments and of secular reality as a medium of God's revelation are drawn out brilliantly by the theologian John W. Glazer, S.J. "Therefore the prime analogate of God's self communication to man is the sacramental character (instituted by the incarnation) of created, personal reality (realized in love of neighbor). So the sacraments must be understood in terms of this fundamental sacramental encounter; the sacraments stand in the service of the sacramentality of the secular. This seems to me to be the implication behind Rahner's statement: We can definitely say that all prayer, all cult, all law of the Church, all the institutions of the Church are only auxiliary means to achieve one thing: to love God and our neighbor and we cannot love God except that we love Him in our neighbor; when we do this, we truly fulfill the law."

The preamble perceives all reality, then, as a medium of revelation of a good and merciful Being. By its very nature, reality should be experienced as inexhaustible and richly complex. In a kind of litany, we can speak of God being found not only in the obvious places and persons— sun, stars, trees, flowers, sand, children, but also in the tenement, slum, drug addict, pimps—yes, even in garbage. Philosophically, we are referring at least partially to the Thomistic principle of analogy of being; finite goodness, truth, beauty are considered patterns, inadequate yet real, of infinite goodness, beauty, and truth. Theologically, we are drawing out the implications of Jesus' death as most revelatory of God. As St. Paul stated in his epistle, He brought peace by His blood.

Since reality is a medium of revelation, the Christian may not attempt to manipulate or control it as its absolute master or allow himself to be manipulated by it. Two conclusions are drawn from this in the preamble: Charities should not impose itself through any form of coercive restraint or constraint in the politico-social forum or it will assume a basically non-biblical character. Conversely, by acknowledging the social and cultural causes of oppression, we stop attempting to resolve the poverty and misery of the oppressed by individual acts of charity alone.

Paradox of the Good News and Human Suffering: Death to Myth and Fantasy

In line with this, the preamble speaks of the paradox of the good news and human suffering. Many Christians claim, with Gospel support, that God is most revealed in Christ as He died upon the cross. The Godhead is most clearly transparent in the death of Christ. The valid theological insight of Luther, based on an improper translation of Isaiah—truly you are a hidden God—and the instincts of the Christian theologians of the Death of God school are appropriate here; the death of Jesus reveals most intuitively the God in Whom we give thanks—for love is most transparent in His death. The risen Lord is to be found in a prayerful reflection on the identification with the dynamics of discipleship of the cross, which is redemptive or liberating love. When the preamble says that in living the dynamics of baptism we experience in ourselves and proclaim to others the courageous death to myth and fantasy, we are responding to Pope Paul's call for a return to the tradition of contemplation. John of the Cross descriptively narrates in the Ascent of Mt. Carmel that the path to the summit is paved with the words nothing, nothing, five times nothing. "And even on the Mount—nothing—but only the honor and glory of God dwells on this Mount. Here there is no longer any way because for the just man there is no law, he is a law unto himself." St. John thus anticipates the challenge of the preamble to die to myth and fantasy.

A Call to Prayer and Contemplation

Since reality has this basic richness, we are called to a reflective wonder and respect for everyday experiences, especially those which involve other human beings. This reflective attitude may be referred to as prayer.

Renewal of Baptism

It is through this that we can realize the dynamics of baptism every day. The prototypical reality of the baptismal sign, life through death, is recurrently challenging us if we have the eyes to see it. "In challenging and enabling those we serve to push the consciousness of their need and its causes to the deepest level possible," we not only allow them by a kind of dialectic to create a new reality for themselves but also through their discovery and expression of need, we find in them a mirror of ourselves.

Thus, as we help the drug-dependent person individually or collectively to become conscious of his/her need and its causes, we can discover addictive adumbrations in ourselves: how many of us are not walking drug stores? More subtly, is there not a kinship between the drug dependent person and the compulsive addiction to work and power which cripples or kills so many of our young executives today? Or as Gary MacEoin has recently said: "too many revolutionaries are doing too many things, especially too many violent things. The cult of violence has spilled over from the Establishment that made Hiroshima and Vietnam 'respectable' and it is distorting many of the 'new men' in the 'new society' which the Revolution is bringing into being."

These insights may cause us to place less emphasis on the Augustinian "There but for the grace of God go I" to a more accurate, less well known, yet equally traditional in Christian asceticism "There go I."

Renewal of Penance

The preamble calls for a struggle away from defensiveness and implicit in this is a call for renewal of the sacrament of penance. Americans culturally deny failure. As David Wheeler writes about Eugene O'Neill's *A Touch of the Poet,* "O'Neill could veer his play toward his historical premise and locate a social rather than a psychic 'curse.' I'm going on the theory that the United States, instead of being the most successful country in the world, is the greatest failure . . . because it was given everything more than any other country. . . . Its main idea is that everlasting game of trying to possess your own soul by the possession of something outside it . . . we are the greatest example of 'for what shall it profit a man if he shall gain the whole world and lose his own soul?'"

The sacrament of penance tells us that personal failure and sin are not to be unexpected. In acknowledging our sinfulness (the matter of the sacrament) not only in the anonymity of the confessional or in the privacy of prayer but also in the situation of the sin itself, we create, as the preamble says, a moment of hope in which we can in the opening of ourselves to the forgiving love of others, come to face in another way the dialectical reality of our inhumanity and thus paradoxically become more human.

The public confession of Archbishop John Ireland of St. Paul in the late 19th century—"I have made mistakes, but I have done things," after the Connemara colonization failure—points out his greatness as a human being.

Despite this failure and the subsequent national embarrassment, his willingness to try to attempt to alleviate the economic and social tensions of the great eastern cities through colonization meant that he was responsible for Minnesota becoming and remaining "the center of Catholic culture in the Northwest." Defensiveness was not a characteristic of a man who said, "I have had many failures, but I have done things."

Renewal of the Eucharist

Besides the celebration-denouement in New York City, the Bread of Heaven theme of John's Gospel and of the Our Father assumes a deeper eucharistic theme in light of the preamble. We become more assimilated to the Body of Christ not only as we empathize with others in their need but also recognize that one person's suffering is educative of every person so that the communion between helper and helped is more and more experienced.

After we have heard the various minorities declaring themselves in bondage and oppression, the working out of the incarnational theology of the preamble leads to the logic of freedom. We have the option in returning to our dioceses and our parish communities to choose to penetrate through prayerful reflection every human situation, especially every incarnate being, and to see the revelation of Him who is our daily bread, who is the image of the invisible God, and by Whom all things were created.

APPENDIX D

Social Encyclicals of the Catholic Church

Gerhard J. Schwab

Since the early centuries of the Church, the term *encyclical* has been applied to circular letters written by popes, archbishops, and bishops that are directed to their own constituencies or other bishops and deal with matters of Church doctrine. Encyclicals condemn errors of interpretations of Christian faith, point out moral dangers, and provide directions for proper handling of expected or existing problems in society.

During the past three centuries, encyclicals gradually became used exclusively by popes—a development that goes hand-in-hand with other new roles popes have assumed in modern Church history. Strong tendencies toward a more centralized Church led to the First Vatican Council, which approved the notion of papal infallibility in 1870 despite strong opposition from several groups. Closer readings of that assembly's resolutions show, however, that this decision of about 700 bishops does not say that popes have the authority to be infallible in all matters at all times. Only under certain conditions are popes authorized to claim the status of infallibility. Subsequently, encyclicals become a prime instrument of popes to direct developments of Church doctrine. Encyclicals are not automatically final statements but expressions of the ongoing dialogue between "Zeitgeist and Holy Spirit." When a pope explicitly asserts infallibility, however, he can announce final judgments on controversial matters through the means of encyclicals.

Leo XIII (1878–1903) is sometimes called the "first encyclical pope." Politically very astute, he never used his infallible status, although he broke with several reactionary traditions of the Church and issued several progressive encyclicals. His circular letter on the living conditions of poor working classes (original Latin title, "*Rerum Novarum*"; title of English translation, "On the Conditions of Workers") is the classic social encyclical. Leo's advocacy for poor workers and his willingness to confront rich industrialists were so radical that the next two popes (Pius X and Benedict XV) and broad sections of the Church tried to silence his social message. In 1931, however, Pius XI commemorated *Rerum Novarum* by issuing a renewed protest against the living conditions of poor people. Since 1961, popes have revisited *Rerum Novarum* every 10 years, integrating new insights and learnings from most recent developments in society into the social teachings of the Church. No other document in the history of the Church has generated so many commemorative encyclicals. Table D.1 shows this sequence of social encyclicals.

Several other social encyclicals were issued during the twentieth century, making it difficult to decide which encyclicals should be included in this list. For the purpose of this appendix, four additional Vatican documents shed particularly valuable light on the proposition that a Catholic Ethic has been seminal in the development of the welfare state.

The Second Vatican Council not only changed the Catholic Church's liturgies and other surface features, it also restructured basic frameworks of the Church. The "Pastoral Constitution of the Church in the Modern World" (PC, 1965), drafted and approved by this assembly of 2,500 bishops, defined anew the role the Church should assume in modern society.

Only six years later, Pope Paul VI and the Synod of Bishops issued "Justice in the World" (JW). This document and Paul VI's social encyclical "A Call to Action," issued in the same year, complement each other and can be regarded as one entity.

The other significant encyclicals in Catholic social doctrine are Paul VI's "On the Development of Peoples" (DP, 1967) and the commemo-

TABLE D.1   *The "Social" Encyclicals*

Year	Pope	Original Name	English Name[1]
1891	Leo XIII	*Rerum Novarum*	On the Conditions of Workers (CW)
1931	Pius XI	*Quadragesimo Anno*	The Reconstruction of the Social Order (RSO)
1961	John XXIII	*Mater et Magistra*	Christianity and Social Progress (CSP)
1971	Paul VI	*Octogesima Adveniens*	A Call to Action (CA)
1981	John Paul II	*Laborem Exercens*	On Human Work (HW)
1991	John Paul II	*Centesimus Annus*	The 100th Year (HY)

[1]English names of encyclicals are not literal translations from the original Latin text, but refer to the main theme of the encyclical.

rative encyclical "On Social Concerns" (SC, 1987) by John Paul II. These two encyclicals look at the "social question" in its global dimensions. Given that the majority of Catholics today live in Third World countries, Catholic social thought cannot be fully understood unless it is seen in its global interplays.

Social encyclicals do not only reflect on the past century; they incorporate the accumulated collective social experience of Catholics. They contain the outcomes of discernment about the meanings and organization of social life of millions of people over thousands of years. The Church therefore claims to be an expert in humanity and offers this experience to anyone who wants to learn from it. Although the early social encyclicals were directed to "Patriarchs, Primates, Archbishops, Bishops, and other Ordinaries of Places" (CW, 1), recent encyclicals go beyond Catholic boundaries and address all people of "good will" (DP, 5).

The modern social encyclicals are by no means a complete catalog of Catholic social teaching, but it is fair to say that they constitute the core of Catholic social doctrine. They are the principle results of popes trying to "scrutinize the signs of the time and interpret them in the light of the gospel" (PC, 4).[2]

In recent decades, bishops' conferences on all continents have added important aspects to Catholic social teaching by issuing statements on social issues. Generally these statements are called "pastoral letters," and they are very much grounded in social encyclicals. For instance, the American bishops' major pastoral letters in modern times have focused on issues of war and peace, the unborn, the economy, racism, and Hispanics in the United States. Their pastoral letter "Economic Justice for All" has ninty-three footnotes referring to social encyclicals.

This brief overview of social encyclicals provides an impressive picture of a very institutionalized way of reaffirming "the continuity of the social doctrine as well as its constant renewal" (SC, 3). We also can see that this doctrine speaks to Catholics in a manner that is "at times imperative, at times optative, but never facultative."[3]

Social encyclicals "must not be considered a theory, but above all a basis and a motivation for action" (HY, 57). Although the popes resist calling Catholic social doctrine an "ideological alternative" to capitalism and communism, it undoubtedly does provide value orientations for a vision of society which evinces numerous and critical characteristics of what we call today the "welfare state."

Having outlined social encyclicals as major frames of Catholic social thought, we can now focus on some of their relevance for particular aspects of a Catholic ethic.

Charity and Social Justice

The human being as an image of God is the central belief of teachings in the social encyclicals, rooted in the first book of the Bible, Genesis. This affinity between the human person and God determines how people are viewed within Catholic value frames. Thus, poor and rich alike are images of God; charity is the medium to harmonize living among classes. When Pope Leo XIII in 1891 wrote what later became the foundations for Catholic social doctrine, he went so far as to say that only the Catholic Church would be able to successfully deal with class conflicts. He regarded the Catholic Church as the "common parent of rich and poor" (CW, 44) and felt obliged to treat labor relations thoroughly so "the conflict may thereby be brought to an end as required by truth and equity" (CW, 3). This, he thought, could be achieved when rich and poor "preserve in themselves and . . . arouse in others . . . the mistress and queen of virtues, Charity" (CW, 83). In 1991, Pope John Paul II wrote about the human being united with God: "This, and this alone, is the principle which inspires the church's social doctrine" (HY, 53).

This profound sense of common humanity among classes led Leo XIII to protest the conditions of the working classes and demand that "the poor must be speedily and fittingly cared for, since the great majority of them live undeservedly in miserable and wretched conditions" (CW, 5). Leo XIII's encyclical set in motion the Catholic Church's ongoing effort to seek better understanding of the societal dynamics of poverty. Subsequent encyclicals have gradually altered the way the Catholic Church sees the role of poor people within society and has enriched the concept of charity.

In 1891, Leo XIII stressed "the duty to give to the poor" (CW, 36) and asserted that "poverty is no disgrace" (CW, 37). In the effort "to bring together the rich and the poor" (CW, 29), Leo XIII allocates the larger share of responsibility to the powerful, who are expected to be the main agents in changing societal characteristics that are biased against poor people. At the same time, he affirms and encourages workers to form unions and to strive to better their situations. He also cautions poor people, however, not to demand too much and reminds them that "to suffer and endure is human" (CW, 27). In theological terms, he writes that "the favor of God Himself seems to incline more toward the unfortunate as a class" (CW, 37). This position may sound very conservative today, but it was radical 100 years ago.

Forty years had to pass before another pope built on the foundations established by Leo XIII. The English title of Pius XI's 1931 encyclical ("The Reconstruction of Social Order") indicates that he intended to go further in analyzing the causes of poverty and designing potential responses. One of the advances in this encyclical is the development of the notion of justice in a complementary function to charity. "Assuredly, charity cannot take the place of justice officially due and unfairly withheld" (RSO, 137), and "justice alone . . . can never bring about a union of hearts and minds" (RSO, 137). Pius XI regarded poor people as people "who, oppressed by dire poverty, struggled in vain to escape from the straits which encompassed them" (RSO, 4) and as victims of a "vast and unjust difference in the distribution of temporal goods" (RSO, 5). Pius XI stressed that this state of the world is not in accord with God's design, and he demands not only the betterment of moral conduct of individuals but a simultaneous reform of societal institutions.

Subsequent encyclicals ("Christianity and Social Progress," "Pastoral Constitution of the Church," "Development of Peoples") continued to put more emphasis on structural injustices within society. In general, they held that people are not poor because they are lazy, dumb, or of bad character but because of unjust societal dynamics.

This development climaxed with two major documents in 1971: the encyclical letter of Paul VI, "A Call to Action," and the Synod of Bishops' statement, "Justice in the World." These documents indicated a major shift in the Church's view of the role of poor people since Leo XIII's moral appeal to rich people. By now, the Church calls on poor people to "shake them(selves) out of any fatalistic resignation . . . and to liberate themselves . . . from whatever has become intolerable" (JW, 4). The collective body of the world's bishops, including Pope Paul VI, identifies an option for poor people and redefines their role:

> Action on behalf of justice and participation in the transformation of the world fully appear to us as a constitutive dimension of the preaching of the Gospel, or, in other words, of the Church's mission for the redemption of the human race and its liberation from every oppressive situation (JW, 6).

Albeit with a slightly different emphasis, the subsequent social encyclicals of John Paul II ("On Human Work," "On Social Concerns," "The 100th Year") continue to highlight the dignity of every human, with special attention to poor people. In the course of John Paul II's papacy, several new terms have been introduced and established in the vocabulary of Catholic social teachings, with notions of "structural sin," "liberation," and "solidarity" capturing significant dimensions of the most current understanding of charity within Catholic social thought. The concept of structural sin (SC, 36) acknowledges that certain economic, political, and social structures in society are the results of many individual sinful acts that over time have become institutionalized in society. Liberation (SC, 46) is the legitimate desire of the human person for freedom from oppressive and exploitative structures, and solidarity is the way to go about doing it:

> Solidarity is undoubtedly a Christian virtue. . . . [There are] many points of contact between solidarity and charity. . . . In light of faith, solidarity seeks to go beyond itself, to take on the specifically Christian dimension of total gratuity, forgiveness, and reconciliation. One's neighbor is then not only a human being with his or her own rights and a fundamental equality with everyone else, but becomes the living image of God (SC, 40).

In conclusion, we see that the concepts of charity and social justice are at the heart of all of the popes' social encyclical letters. Over the past century, charity has been penetrated and expanded with notions of justice and solidarity, assigning poor people higher social status and affirming their right for a more justly structured society.

Work

In 1891, Leo XIII claimed that "it gradually came about that the present age handed over the workers, each alone and defenseless, to the inhumanity of the employers and the unbridled greed of competitors" (CW, 5). He blamed the "very few and exceedingly rich men [to] have laid a yoke almost of slavery on the unnumbered masses of non-owning workers" (CW, 5). Regarding the nature of work, Leo XIII stated that "the fruits of labor belong precisely to those who performed the labor" (CW, 16) and therefore "among the most important duties of employers . . . is to give every worker what is justly due him" (CW, 32). "On the Conditions of Workers" illuminated the political dimensions of work and legitimated and encouraged workers' unions to enforce their rightful demands for just wages and better working conditions. Leo XIII used the terms "the poor" and "workers" interchangeably and conceptualized poverty as a consequence of the immoral behavior of rich people.

Work remained a main focus of succeeding social encyclicals. In 1967, Paul VI's encyclical "On the Development of Peoples" began, "Today the principle fact that we must all recognize is that the social question has become world-wide" (DP, 3). Although great sectors of working classes in industrialized nations have been able to get out of poverty and enjoy rapid economic development, growing numbers of people in the developing world are forced into "undeserved hardships" (DP, 9). In a way, Paul VI used the characteristics of employer-employee relations to analyze the relations between industrialized and developing countries. This step to globalize the issue of poor working classes is imprinted in all subsequent social encyclicals.

In 1981 John Paul II celebrated the ninetieth anniversary of "On the Conditions of Workers" by devoting an encyclical to the human person "in the vast context of the reality of work" (HW, 1). With this encyclical, "On Human Work," John Paul II synthesized developments that have occurred over the past nine decades and drew a comprehensive picture of Catholic social thought on work.

John Paul II wrote, "Work is a fundamental dimension of human existence on earth" (HW, 4)—another conviction rooted in the book of Genesis. Humankind, in the image of God, is called on to cultivate the earth by working according to God's plan. Thus, by working, "every human being reflects the very action of the Creator of the universe" (HW, 4). Work in an objective sense "finds expression in the various epochs of culture and civilization" (HW, 5) and accrues to the work of all generations before.

Work in a subjective sense explains the human person in the image of God as "being capable of acting in a planned and rational way, capable of deciding about himself, and with a tendency to self realization" (HW, 6). Human work therefore has many forms and an ethical value of its own. Work, sometimes accompanied with heavy toil, is intrinsically good for the human being. Not only does work produce the necessities for daily living; it is an important means to become "more human." Working builds human relations, integrates individuals into communities, and is important in developing individual and collective identities. This perspective implies that work cannot be treated solely as merchandise within an industrial production process. John Paul II warned of this reversal of order and described "exploitation in the field of wages, working conditions, and social security of workers . . . as a result of the violation of the dignity of human work" (HW, 8). He stressed the superiority of labor over capital and the need to look at capital and labor independently to design a proper relation of the two. In contrast with Leo XIII, John Paul II framed the labor question not as much in terms of moral obligations of employers but much more in terms of workers' rights (HW, 16–23). John Paul II reaffirms the general elements of previous encyclicals and pays additional attention to workers in disadvantaged sectors of society, disabled persons at work, and the situation of immigrant workers in affluent societies.

Only a few years later, in 1987, John Paul II issued another encyclical ("On Social Concerns") with a global focus on the social question. The letter drew attention to the "innumerable multitude of people . . . who are suffering under the intolerable burden of poverty" (SC, 13) and calls the widening gap between rich and poor a "manifestation of selfishness and a flaunting of wealth which is as disconcerting as it is scandalous" (SC, 14). John Paul II also noted that spreading unemployment and underemployment, especially in developing countries, show that "there is something wrong with the organization of work and employment, precisely at the most critical and socially most important points" (SC, 18).

Although the Church traditionally has fostered a particular spirituality of work, John Paul II actually seemed to consider work a form of prayer. He writes that "through work people come closer to God, . . . deepen their friendship with Christ, . . . share in the activity of the Creator" (HW, 24–25). He also indicates that this spirituality ought to permeate "the most ordinary everyday activities" (HW, 25) and should remind people not to work too much. As God rested after the creation, people are called to "imitate God . . . in resting" (HW, 25).

According to this evolving Catholic social thought, work is intended primarily to build community, to manifest the human dignity of each person, and to participate in God's ongoing creation. The activity of work has many forms and an ethical value of its own. Therefore its value cannot be assessed strictly in its material outcomes. The encyclicals dealing with these issues have formulated Catholic concerns about how regulations of work have been used in industrialized societies, as well as globally, to maintain a reservoir of working poor people to feed the selfish desires of rich minorities.

Money

The social encyclicals have analyzed money primarily through two perspectives: private property and the common good. These values are dimensions of Catholic social doctrine and can be understood only in their interdependence.

Over the past century, the societal conditions for acquiring and managing private property have undergone several fundamental changes. The social encyclicals have outlined these changes and established a

Catholic doctrine on private property according to perennial Christian values rooted in the Bible.

All of the social encyclicals have strongly defended the right of private property; in different degrees, they also have placed a social mortgage on it. In 1891, Leo XIII derived from the "natural" right for private property a claim that workers must be paid justly so they can make use of this right and "procure property for themselves" (CW, 9). Leo XIII was cautious about regulating the limits of private property but mentioned that private property never ceases "to serve the common interest of all" (CW, 14). After describing the situation of poor working classes, he noted that "wealth . . . originates . . . from the labor of workers" (CW, 51).

Forty years later, Pius XI elaborated on the obligations of ownership. While strongly defending private property, he also looked at private property according to the "requirements of social life" (RSO, 48). Pius XI not only appealed to the good will of the rich, he allocated responsibility to the state to regulate individuals in light of social consequences: "[T]he public authority, in view of the true necessity of the common good, may specify more accurately what is licit and what is illicit for property owners in the use of their possessions" (RSO, 49).

John XXIII's 1961 encyclical ("Christianity and Social Progress") added more weight on the side of social obligations of private property. John XXIII stated that changes in society make it necessary to look again at private property and newly define its proper use. In view of these changes, the encyclical called for a more effective distribution of "property to all classes of people" (CSP, 114) and called on "the body politic to modify economic and social life so that the way is made easier for widespread private possession of such things as durable goods, homes, gardens . . . " (CSP, 115). In instances in which the power of property may become "too great to be left in private hands" (CSP, 116), John XXIII expressed the importance of public oversight of private property. Accordingly, "the common good requires public authorities to exercise ever greater responsibilities" (CSP, 117).

The encyclicals of the 1960s and 1970s accelerated this trend, suggesting more and more restrictions on the use of private property and asserting the importance of considering the common good. A quote from Saint Ambrose, cited by Paul VI (DP, 23), reflects this direction:

You are not making a gift of your possessions to the poor person. You are handing over to him what is his. For what has been given in common for the use of all, you have arrogated to yourself. The world is given to all, and not only to the rich.[4]

In the words of Paul VI, "private property does not constitute for anyone an absolute and unconditional right. No one is justified in keeping for his exclusive use what he does not need, when others lack necessities" (DP, 23). An important boundary of private property is defined by the claim that the right of private property never "can be exercised to the detriment of the common good" (DP, 23).

In 1968, Catholic Latin American bishops issued the Medellin Documents, in which they outlined pastoral applications of the foregoing principles—placing the challenge of making a deliberate "option for the poor" before millions of practicing Catholics, especially poor Latin Americans. The Church then committed not only to taking part in the struggle for the liberation of poor people but also to liberating rich people from the burdens and restraints of being rich.

During the papacy of John Paul II (since 1978), this radical position has been moderated through several different strategies within the hierarchical Church. The major concern of Vatican officials seems to be that intimate participation in conflicts between rich and poor may lead to a kind of political involvement that is unwanted. Although these conflicts have slowed pastoral work in this area, they have not changed the general direction of Catholic social doctrine.

In 1987 John Paul II reiterated the core of Catholic doctrine on private property:

> The goods of this world are originally meant for all. The right to private property is valid and necessary, but it does not nullify the value of this principle. Private property, in fact, is under a "social mortgage," which means that it has an intrinsically social function, based upon and justified precisely by the principle of the universal destination of goods (SC, 42).

In 1991, John Paul II dedicated a major part of a new encyclical to the issue of private property and the universal destination of material goods (HY, 30–43). He scrutinized current developments and drew attention to some critical aspects regarding property issues, especially the emergence of new forms of ownership such as "the possession of know-how, technology, and skill" (HY, 32). In this letter, John Paul II once again interpreted the global monetary system as unjust and biased against poor nations and said cancellation of international debts was justified in certain cases: "It cannot be expected that the debts which have been contracted should be paid at the price of unbearable sacrifices" (HY, 35).

This statement certainly supports the view that having money does not generate automatically higher social status among Catholics, and it is by no means a reward for or confirmation of virtue. Instead, excessive wealth raises several potentially uncomfortable moral questions.

Catholic social teachings emphasize that the goal of life is not to accumulate wealth but to be more human in a God-like image. Therefore, voluntary poverty has always been highly respected in Catholic culture. It gains new relevance in today's global situation, when popes have called on the peoples of the rich continents to move toward an attitude of universal solidarity and "create lifestyles in which the quest for truth, beauty, goodness, and communion with others" (HY, 36) becomes more important than satisfying consumer urges.

Overall, Catholic social encyclicals have considered money an instrument of organizing human society: as a means, not an end. The prime goal of private property is to assist the integral growth of individuals and the creation of human communities and to ensure justice in the production and distribution of goods. Money is necessary for a decent living, but in the mathematics of Catholic values an excess of money can do more harm than good.

The Role of Public Authority

A key element of Catholic social doctrine deals with the role of public authorities, framed within the antagonistic dynamics between liberal capitalism and collective communism. The social encyclicals of the past century have critiqued both ideologies and have never unconditionally endorsed capitalism. The earliest letters in this series, especially "On the Conditions of Workers" and "The Reconstruction of the Social Order," are written in defense against communism. They reflect a Church that is worried about the spread of communism but has started to identify "sinful" structures within capitalist societies. Today we can see how accurate the analysis of communism and predictions about further developments were.

In 1931, Pius XI distinguished between hard-liners in communism and moderate socialists and suggested that "it may well come about that gradually the tenets of mitigated socialism will no longer be different from the program of those who seek to reform human society according to Christian principles" (RSO, 114). History has proven him right; long periods of coalition governments of socialist/democratic and Christian/democratic parties in many European countries have improved the standards of living, especially of poor working classes. Subsequent social encyclicals continued to warn Catholics, however, of the dangers of accepting political ideologies that diminish God's role.

In 1991, John Paul II interpreted the breakdown of communism in Eastern Europe. He wrote that the "true cause of the new developments (the downfall of communist governments) was the spiritual void brought about" (HY, 24) by the Marxist promise "to uproot the need for God from the human heart" (HY, 24).

Over the past century, warnings about the dangers of capitalism in the social encyclicals gradually have become systemic criticisms of capitalism. In the most recent letters, the Catholic Church's social doctrines have examined liberal capitalism and collective communism on the same level of analysis and claimed "both concepts being imperfect [are] in need of radical correction" (SC, 21) and that each of them "harbors in its own way a tendency toward imperialism" (SC, 22). In light of failing communist political systems, John Paul II wrote of a "risk that a radical capitalistic ideology could spread" (HY, 42) and further increase imbalances between rich and poor.

Social encyclicals also are a direct expression of the Vatican's efforts to define boundaries between church and state. As modern societies have undergone fundamental changes, public authorities have assumed more and more of the political, economic, and social responsibilities that previously were assigned to the church. At the same time, the Catholic Church has carefully guarded certain private realms of Church interest.

In 1981, John Paul II illuminated this interplay of public and private realms from many angles. For instance, when he analyzed working conditions, dangers of unemployment, and the need for comprehensive economic planning, he concluded:

> In the final analysis this overall concern weighs on the shoulders of the State, but it cannot mean one-sided centralization by the public authorities. Instead, what is in question is a just and rational coordination, within the framework of which the initiative of individuals, free groups and local work centers and complexes must be safeguarded (HW, 18).

Regarding the realm of ownership, Paul VI and the Second Vatican Council declared:

> The right of private control, however, is not opposed to the right inherent in various forms of public ownership. Still, goods can be transferred to the public domain only by the competent authority,

according to the demands and within the limits of the common good (PC, 71).

For our purpose, the role of state in the social welfare field is most interesting. As early as 1891, Leo XIII posted road signs leading toward emerging welfare states. He does not use the term "welfare state," but he comes close: "[T]he protection of public welfare is not only the supreme law, but is the entire cause and reason" (CW, 52) for the state. In addition, he emphasizes that the state is bound to serve each citizen and to "include . . . the great masses of the needy . . . under its special care and foresight" (CW, 54). Subsequent social encyclicals have reaffirmed this claim and the rights of people to a fair share of the common wealth of a nation. In 1961, John XXIII reformulated the original notion, demanding that the state "should safeguard the rights of all citizens, but especially the weaker, such as workers, women, and children" (CSP, 20).

As societies become more complex, so does charity: Traditional and individual forms of helping poor people are no longer adequate, and new forms of organized charities have to be developed. This changing situation leads to more and more genres of social interventions coming under the authority of various levels of governments. In his 1991 social encyclical, John Paul II summarized these developments:

> The range of such [state] interventions has vastly expanded to the point of creating a new type of state, the so-called "welfare-state." This has happened in some countries in order to respond better to many needs and demands, by remedying forms of poverty and deprivation unworthy of the human person. However, excesses and abuses, especially in recent years, have provoked very harsh criticism of the welfare state, dubbed the "social assistance state." Malfunctions and defects in the social assistance state are the result of an inadequate understanding of the tasks proper to the state. Here again the principle of subsidiarity must be respected: A community of a higher order should not interfere in the internal life of a community of a lower order, depriving the latter of its function, but rather should support it in case of need and help to coordinate its activity with activities of the rest of society, always with a view to the common good (HY, 48).

Catholic social doctrine opposes forms of states in which government suffocates initiative and freedom of individuals and intermediary groups (collective communism), as well as governments in which individuals and free groups of citizens are unprotected against the structural injustices of free markets (liberal capitalism). Social encyclicals of the past century have viewed states as mechanisms that ought to create opportunities for integral human growth and safeguard basic human rights; public authorities of the state are expected to play an active part in the process of facilitating and coordinating the socioeconomic well-being of its citizens. According to Catholic social doctrine, states have special obligations toward weak, poor, and disadvantaged people. Public welfare and private charities are needed and ought to complement each other.

Family

Matters of marriage and family have a central place in Catholic social teaching. Numerous Church documents, including particular encyclicals on the family, have considered the nature and principles of the family. "Authentic married love is caught up into divine love" (CP, 48) and thus a human expression of God's love, according to John XXIII. As a result of this attention paid to family issues elsewhere, the social encyclicals have not addressed internal family matters in great detail; they view the family in its functions within society.

Leo XIII emphasized the boundaries between family and state. He argued that a family "must have certain rights and duties of its own" (CW, 19) because the institution of the family is "older than any polity" (CW, 19). Only if there "is a grave violation of mutual rights within the family . . . and [the family] is entirely unable to help itself, is it right that the distress be remedied by public aid" (CW, 21). This sense of the independent role of the family as "society of the household" (CW, 19) has generated a sense of family rights in regard to ownership issues. For example, Leo XIII pointed out that wages should enable the worker "to provide comfortably for himself, his wife, and his children" (CW, 65). The notion of "family wages" has reemerged in each of the subsequent social encyclicals.

Catholic social doctrine declares "that human life is transmitted and propagated through the instrumentality of the family" (CSP, 193). This teaching applies not only to the biological transmission of life; it includes social, economic, and political aspects of the intergenerational continuity of human life. In 1967, Paul VI wrote that humans find identity only in a milieu "where the family plays a fundamental role" (DP, 36). "Thus the family is the foundation of society" (PC, 52).

Each recent social encyclical has added to the existing body of social doctrine emphasizing the need for structural and systemic support for families. In 1971, on the eightieth anniversary of "On the Condition of Workers," Paul VI outlined increasing difficulties for families and affirmed "that the family, without which no society can stand, has a right to the assistance which will assure it of the conditions for a healthy development" (CA, 18).

In 1991, John Paul II termed the family the "first and fundamental structure of 'human ecology'" (HY, 19) and continued to advocate family policies:

> It is urgent therefore to promote not only family policies, but also those social policies which have the family as their principal object, policies which assist the family by providing adequate resources and efficient means of support both for bringing up children and for looking after the elderly so as to avoid distancing the latter from the family unit and in order to strengthen relations between generations (HY, 49).

In Catholic social thought, "family is indeed sacred" (HY, 39) and constitutes the basis of human society—the key instrument that allows the experiences of generations to accrue in a collective human growth process. Therefore, it is the duty of the state to provide structures that allow families to function for the individual and common good.

Forgiveness and Otherworldly Orientation

Aspects of forgiveness and otherworldly orientation are elevated to sacramental value in the Catholic Church, although the forms of administrating issues of forgiveness and death have varied over the centuries. The Council of Trent (1551) institutionalized the process of forgiveness through the sacrament of confession and pastoral assistance in deathly illness in the sacrament of extreme unction. A broad body of theology accumulated around these matters and has been formulated in various council documents and canon laws. The social encyclicals of the past century have been grounded in these beliefs and reflect their interdependent nature.

"All of human life, whether individual or collective, shows itself to be a dramatic struggle between good and evil" (PC, 13). This core belief of Catholicism necessitates some arrangement to deal with "bad" individuals and collectives. "As man finds that by himself he is incapable of battling the assaults of evil successfully" (PC, 14), the Catholic Church makes the process of forgiveness an integral part of life. Catholics believe that they can be freed "from personal sin and from its consequences in social life" (JW, 5) through personal efforts and the grace of God. They are convinced that the world is emancipated by Christ "so that this world might be fashioned anew according to God's design" (PC, 2).

This focus on forgiveness and efforts to make this world a "kingdom of justice, of love and peace" (CSP, 261) is an indication of the Catholic Church's notions of eternity. However happy we are in this life, "yet it is not the ultimate goal for which we are born, but a road only and a means for perfecting, through knowledge of truth and love of good" (CW, 57). Working to become a better person helps each individual lift his or her "mind from the changing conditions of human existence to that heavenly country where he [or she] will one day enjoy unending happiness and peace" (CSP, 2). Thus, the ultimate goal of human life is "Heaven and eternity" (CW, 33). Throughout the past century, these social encyclicals have emphasized that the "reward of eternal happiness will follow upon virtue and merit alone" (CW, 37) and that "wealth is of no avail unto the happiness of eternal life but is rather a hindrance" (CW, 34).

The philosophy that held that individuals had two natures—"one directed to this world and this life, to which faith ought to remain extraneous; the other directed toward a purely otherworldly salvation, which neither enlightens nor directs existence on earth" (HY, 5)—has been supplanted by a view that synthesizes these two elements. For Catholics, eternity begins when the person "recognizes in himself a spiritual and immortal soul" (PC, 14).

This promise of eternal life is not only a private matter between God and a human being; it is of communal interest, even crossing the boundaries of the realms of death and life. Catholic doctrine teaches that faith gives humans "the power to be united in Christ with his loved ones who have already been snatched away by death" (PC, 18).

In summary, social encyclicals have explained forgiveness and otherworldly orientation as structures in the Catholic matrix of values, and interactions among individuals and collectives have been imprinted with these notions. The explanatory power of these two aspects on human conduct depends, however, on the social context and individual values.

The Catholic Ethic and the Spirit of Community

This very brief review of social encyclicals illustrates the uniquely Catholic view of the fabric of society. This body of knowledge is rooted in the collective experience of the Catholic community. It is still unfolding and developing within the dialectic of consensus and disagreements within the Catholic community. It envisions that Catholics will participate in the building of the Kingdom of God.

According to this Catholic body of knowledge, people are intrinsically good and social, and they can achieve their full humanity only within justly structured networks of human relations. Hence, the organizational and institutional structuring of these networks requires equally protection of human dignity and the rights of individuals and protection of the collective welfare and the common good.

Catholic Sites on the Internet

For a more detailed listing, see Fox (1997).

General Interest/Search Engines

alapadre.net/
www.catholic.web

Catholic Resources on the Internet

www.cs.cmu.edu/Web/People/spok/catholic.html/
Catholic Internet Directory: www.catholic-church.org/cid/
Catholic Online: www.catholic.org/
Peter's Net: www.petersnet.net
Roman Catholic Net: www.rc.net/

Vatican-Based Websites

Vatican Website: www.vatican.va
Vatican Observatory: clavius.as.arizona.edu/vo/
College of Cardinals:
   www.aquinas-multimedia.com/cards/alphabet.html

National Conference of Catholic Bishops

www.nccbuscc.org/

Social Services

Catholic Charities: www.catholiccharitiesusa.org/
Catholic Worker: www.catholicworker.org/roundtable
Covenant House: www.covenanthouse.org/en/standard/index.htm

Busy Christian's Guide to Catholic Social Teaching:
www.uscatholic.org/cstline/tline.html

Doctrinally Related Materials

New American Bible: www.nccbuscc.org/nab/bible/index.htm

Catechism of the Catholic Church

www.scborromeo.org/ccc.htm
Catholic Social Teaching: www.osjspm.org/cst/

Magazines/Publications/Media

America: www.americapress.org
St. Anthony Messenger: www.americancatholic.org
Catholic Digest: www.catholicdigest.org
Catholic New York: www.cny.org
Catholic Worker: www.catholicworker.org
National Catholic Reporter: www.natcath.com/
First Things: www.firstthings.com/
Our Sunday Visitor: www.osv.com
Commonweal: www.commonwealmagazine.org/
U.S. Catholic: www.uscatholic.org/

News Services

Catholic News Service: www.catholicnews.com
Catholic World News: www.cwnews.com/

Catholic Universities and Resources

Boston College: www.infoeagle.bc.edu
Catholic University of America: www.cua.edu/
College of the Holy Cross: www.holycross.edu
Fordham University: www.fordham.edu
Georgetown University: www.georgetown.edu
Notre Dame University: www.nd.edu
Saint Louis University: www.slu.edu
Santa Clara University: www.scu.edu

Scholarly Resources

Context Online (*U.S. Catholic*): www.contextonline.org
Humanities Internet Resources for Religion:
    www.wcsu.ctstateu.edu/library/h_religion.html
Journal for Religion and the Intellectual Life: www.crosscurrents.org
Woodstock Theological Center:
    www.georgetown.edu/centers/woodstock/

Christian Publications

Christian Century: www.christiancentury.org
Cross Currents: www.aril.org
Gospel Communications: www.gospelcom.net/
Sojourners: www.sojo.net

Sampling of Christian Denominations

Inter-faith: www.interfaithvoices.org/ifv/directory/orgs7a.cfm
Christian Theology Home Page:
    www.by.edu/people/bpstone/theology/theology.html
Christianity at About.com:
    http://christianity.about.com/religion.christianity/
Dietrich Bonhoeffer Home Page: www.dbonhoeffer.org/
North American Interfaith Network: www.nain.org/news/nainews.htm
Church of Jesus Christ of Latter Day Saints (Mormon): www.lds.org
Lutheran: www.iclnet.org/pub/resources/text/wittenberg-home.html
Methodist: www.umc-gbcs.org/
Presbyterian: www.pcusa.org/pcnews/briefs.htm

Sampling of World Religions

Buddhism: www.tricyvle.com/
Hinduism: www.hinduismtoday.org
Islam: www.islam-online.net/english/index.shtml
Judaism (social action): www.SocialAction.com/
Tikkun Magazine: www.tikkun.org/

Notes

Introduction

1. The 1956 imprint was a translation by the famous Harvard sociologist Talcott Parsons. He writes that Max Weber's essay, "*Die protestestische Ethik und der Geist des Kapitalismus,*" translated here, was first published in the *Archive for Sozialwissenschaft un Soziolpolitik,* volumes 20 and 21, for 1904–1905. Parsons, in Weber ([1906] 1956), ix.

2. My students routinely suggest that, in American society, an overall 70 percent weight for achievement and 30 percent weight for equality is about right. Surprisingly—or not—there is little variance around these numbers as students *inform* me about their view of society in which we live; they do, however, have substantial variation as they *report* on their own weightings.

Chapter 1

1. On a paradoxical level, the Reformation was in part a response to the "shopkeeper" model of salvation through works—good works, prayers, indulgences, and the like. It might not be unfair to say that the Reformation substituted the "celestial" shopkeeper with the "actual" shopkeeper.

2. It also has been used in the study of ethics. Gustafson (1978) uses the phrase in this sense in his book *Protestant and Roman Catholic Ethics,* as does Curran (1980) in "Is There a Catholic and/or Christian Ethic?" although Curran's usage really is different. Marciniac (1988) also refers to a Catholic work ethic, as does Mueller (1978) in "The Protestant and Catholic Ethic."

3. The notion that degrees matter also can be found in Catholicism's conception of sin (which isn't used much nowadays). There is venial with gradations up to mortal, and even these can be forgiven. Indeed, the Sin Against the Holy Spirit is the only sin from which you cannot be forgiven!

4. See my work on *American Values and Social Welfare* (Tropman 1986).

5. The extent to which such attitudes are contemporaneous is always open to question. Nevertheless, the use of moral categories to think about disadvantaged people is alive and well among us. A quote from the *Detroit Free Press* in October 1988 illustrates this point. The writer is a columnist for that paper named Nicki McWhirter. She is writing about a political conflict in the state concerning whether to pay for abortions for poor women through the Medicaid program. She is raising some questions about the anti-abortion forces and is speculating about the cause of the differing views. She comments, "This is a power struggle between haves and have-nots. The haves seek to teach the have-nots at the bottom of the power tower a lesson: people with jobs, money and influence are more powerful and, therefore, better beings than people without jobs, money and influence. To the superior beings go all rights and privileges. . . . To the inferior beings goes nothing."

6. It also may explain the affinity of American society, at least, for social Darwinism.

7. As Robert D. Vinter has indicated (personal communication), it is not completely clear where this idea that everyone is completely responsible for himself or herself came from. It is part of the "Protestant paradox" in that it stands in contradistinction to the complete lack of responsibility one has for one's own salvation. Indeed, this may be the exact point. Lack of "salvation control" may—"counterphobically," as my clinician friends would have it—cause a "reaction formation" and consequent overemphasis on control in "this world."

8. Let me say a word about my own values here. I classify myself as pro–community welfare. I also recognize, however, the presence and vitality of other approaches. I mention this point in order to invite readers to share an analytical rather than an ideological journey with me. My interest here is in explaining (or in trying to explain) why a certain development occurred. I happen to feel that the development was positive. Others, I suppose, may not. Those feelings, however, do not invalidate the utility of the effort. One may seek to explain the rise of Nazism and the presence of the Holocaust without being in favor of them. Therefore, I am not suggesting in general that society has been moving in the right or wrong direction (though, as I have indicated, I personally feel it is the right direction). It is a social event or series of social events that invite analysis and dissection. That is the purpose of this volume. I hope, therefore, that the exploration is guided by, not determined by, this hypothesis and that I am as fair to contrary evidence as I would like to think.

9. I have a personal experience that suggests to me how much this help is sought. When I was on sabbatical in Cambridge, Massachusetts, some years ago, at the (then) Joint Center for Urban Studies, my family and I rented a house that had a phone number that was different from that of the local parish house by one digit. The phone range constantly with parishioners eagerly seeking advice on this or that subject and often seeking permission to do this or that. When I answered, their experience was of a male answering during the day—hence, I must be the priest. "Father," they would say eagerly, often without pausing, "can I, . . . Is it alright to . . . what about. . . ." At first I explained that I was not the priest, that they had called the wrong number, and so forth. More often than not, they refused to believe me. Finally it struck me that I had the opportunity to perform what my Jewish colleagues call a *mitzvah*. I began giving permissions on a regular basis. I think the word got around (or at least the number did) because the phone began ringing even more incessantly.

10. The Catholic ethic did not always support the welfare state, however. For example, it had no doctrine of "rights" on which a "citizen" (recall the

French Revolution) might "claim" entitlements from the government. In time, however, accommodations were reached.

11. The campaign rhetoric of John F. Kennedy was filled with proposals for progress for delinquent youth, poor people, disadvantaged people, and so forth.

Chapter 2

1. In an earlier paper (Tropman, 1989), I suggested that Catholicism might be one of the elements that could lead to European commonality. That paper was written before the "communalizing" developments that surprised many people had occurred.

2. This prejudice is detailed in R. A. Billington's book, *The Protestant Crusade* (1964).

3. A similar pattern emerged within the Jewish community. German Jews arrived first, along with Catholics, in the mid-nineteenth century. (See *Our Crowd* [1967], by Stephan Birmingham.) They were followed, around the turn of the twentieth century, by their "poor cousins" (see *Poor Cousins* [1972], by Ande Manners).

4. Of course, drinking among Protestants was a problem before the immigration of Catholics. See Tropman (1986).

5. The piece is called "Sociology and Salvation: Do We Need a Catholic Sociology?"

6. This concern is not limited to Catholics. Japanese Americans—indeed, all hyphenated Americans—can be "suspect."

Chapter 3

1. It is only in the producer community context that the question "should women work?" has any meaning at all.

2. For a good history of attitudes toward paid work, see Williams (1983).

3. In some Jewish traditions, bathing is ritualized.

4. Activities involving preparation of a martini are one example of a ceremonialization of drinking.

5. Of course, the Protestant Reformation may have been both cause and result of these reconceptualizations.

6. Dialogue concerning provision of aid to needy people—who frequently are not working—has been marked by questions of whether jobs are available or poorhouses are full. Of course, it often is said—and must be said here—that "not working" is relative. There are "working poor," people with health limitations, and others.

7. The difference between a ceremony and a ritual is as follows: A ceremony recognizes; a ritual transforms. Whereas we speak of the "marriage ceremony," in this usage it would be a ritual.

Chapter 4

1. See Ellin (2000).

2. Money and weight are in about the same category here. One would hesitate to ask someone else how much he or she weighs. As someone said, "You can't be too rich or too thin."

3. Of course, there is the possibility that this view was making lemonade from lemons. If one is poor, then it is great if this is God's will! This view also would take some pressure off rich people. (Unless some of the worldly goods that Jesus' followers give up were debts to the rich—a sort of chapter 11. Thanks to Eileen Wiser for emphasizing this point.)

4. Some of this orientation also may reflect "familism/communitarianism," which I discuss later. This concept deals with the notion of the availability of property to others. For example, if a father has a tie that a son wants to wear, and the father fears that the son may spoil it, the father may say, "No, it's mine." That is the personal property orientation—namely, that property is yours, and others have no claim on it even if it is not being used. The son may say, however, "Hey, you're not using it." This counter statement reflects a *different norm:* that family property, to some extent, is community property, and *whoever needs something should, more or less, get to use it unless there is some overwhelming, overriding objection.*

5. Attitudes toward money are one of the important areas to consider in studying other religion-based ethics. As most survey researchers know, in the United States at least, the "income question" is always asked at the end of a survey instrument because of its great sensitivity. Other matters of a sensitive nature, such as previous sexual and criminal activity, appear to be easier. Hence, the degree to which money has become a symbol, and in what ways, becomes a crucial variable everywhere.

6. An academic example might be useful here. A professor or teacher wouldn't just give people points because they "needed" them. Yet, in one sense, why not? There has been a "gentleman's C" historically in colleges. Partly because grades are supposed to indicate how smart you are, it is unfair to provide that designation without evidence. The same kind of concern surrounds money and makes it always a difficult and touching subject. Within the Catholic ethic tradition, money is good, of course: It helps you do things. Yet there also is some suspicion about it. Perhaps its origins are questionable. The old phrase "it's easier for a camel to get through the eye of a needle than for a rich man to get into the kingdom of heaven" suggests this quasi-negative view.

7. Schervish, Coutsoukis, and Lewis (1994) construct a picture of very wealthy people through interviews with 130 multimillionaires, half of whom inherited the wealth and the other half of whom were entrepreneurs.

Chapter 5

1. This is true at least at one level. There is an important counterargument that these views actually are antifamily, in the sense that they allow family size to expand beyond the level that it can be supported in a local context. This is one of the reasons that Catholics support family allowances.

2. Perhaps the better phrase might be "have become traditional." The original impetus might have been protection of women through defining their function in the family.

3. From "The Death of the Hired Man."

4. The actress Maureen O'Hara, now living in Ireland, exemplifies this connection. In a biography, Goodman and Matsumoto (1961) report, "O'Hara has immersed herself in her extended family. Daughter Bronwyn, 46, a musician and actress lives in Dublin; grandson Beau attends school in Santa Monica. She remains close to her four stepchildren by Blair. . . . Then of course, there are her brothers and sisters and a pack of nieces and nephews. 'A small portion of my family went to see my new movie the other night,' she says proudly, 'and that was 20 people'" (Goodman and Matsumoto 1991, 72).

5. Ryan (1981) identifies "individual versus collective" and "different versus similar" as manifestations of this kind of difference.

6. Baum has pointed out, in conversation, that the Catholic conception of community as organic means that it includes a place for everyone—high and low, rich and poor—and that all members of the community are "God's children."

7. Mormans take a similar traditional view.

Chapter 6

1. An indulgence was—is—a sort of salvation "credit." Certain acts and certain prayers provide the faithful with "time off" in purgatory.

2. Catholicism makes the distinction between the individual and the act: "Love the sinner but hate the sin."

3. Indeed, in *this world of the soul,* the battle rages even after death. There is limbo (though that state is in low profile at the moment) and purgatory. One may have to wait a bit after death, while those still living offer prayers that increase one's celestial credit balance enough to enter the Kingdom of Heaven.

4. In the Protestant ethic tradition, it is possible to be "born again," but this process is largely intrapersonal, rather than institutional.

5. In Ireland today, one can still hear the word "sinner" used as a synonym for "human."

6. A priest is more central in the old "penance" where "confession" was involved.

7. This emphasis on remorse is an important element of the penance/reconciliation system that is not found, for example, in the American criminal justice system. There, the accused's remorse is more or less beside the point, although the judge may take it into account in sentencing. In Japan, on the other hand, repentance is among the more important concerns of the criminal justice system.

8. Baum has pointed out (personal communication, June 1991) that there is no text of which he is aware in Catholic theology that distinguishes between worthy and unworthy.

9. Compensating victims is becoming more important in the American criminal justice system. Two versions are being employed in several jurisdictions. One involves sentences of community service; another requires direct compensation to the victim.

10. More discussion of the effects of this mechanism appears in chapter 10.

11. Greeley (1990 [and elsewhere]) reflects on this counseling aspect when he looks at the happiness of women who have friends who are priests compared with those who do not.

12. The exact phrase is "I firmly resolve, with the help of thy grace, to sin no more and to avoid the near occasion of sin."

13. "Social" is in apologetic quotes in this context to differentiate it from the more contemporary usage of "social sin" as "sin" of a panpersonal nature, such as acts of communities, organizations, and societies. For an early and interesting discussion of this issue, see Niebuhr (1932).

14. That phrase comes from *The Pilgrim's Progress* (1678).

15. Pope John XXIII said this on a Christmas visit to the local jail.

16. Recall that in the bishops' letter there was a strong caution against negative judgmental thinking about poor people.

17. Of course Protestants use them as well, although the lived approach may be different.

18. Again, Murray (1990) makes this point in his discussion of the naturalness of the hospitable relationship.

Chapter 7

1. In other words, the steps to high social status become the same as the steps to high sacred status. Social and sacred status become synonymous

2. One should not conclude, however, that all is peaceful. Helping poor people is as fraught with conflict as any other human enterprise. A helping orientation does not necessarily imply a lack of ego, either. Murray (1990) documents the fights and staff breakups and bitterness that accompanied his sojourn with the Catholic Workers.

Chapter 8

1. For a fictional excursion into the organizational church, including its politics and global reach, see Case (1997).

Part III Introduction

1. Catholicism was born among the poor and suffered oppression. These two points might explain, in part, the attitude of altruism. Stinchcombe (1965), in his *Handbook of Organizations*, writes about the importance of the founding ethos of an organization (see chapter 3). An extension of this point in contemporary times and in contemporary America in particular is that individual Catholics typically have not been well-to-do. This point may be changing; Greeley argues that it is. However, if one can conceive of a refounding of Catholicism—for example, its refounding in the American crucible—then the immigrant church is a key factor that builds upon, extends, validates, and reifies the early tradition of poverty. Another point might be worth further consideration: Consider that Catholicism is a rural religion and Protestantism an urban one, especially with respect to the founding conditions. "Rurality," then, involves a tradition of helping, "bounty your hardship for all," and so on. "Urbanicity" involves greater individuality, greater mobility, and overall lack of sharing and involvement with others (Vidich and Bensman 1968).

2. "Chose" is in apologetic quotes because it really is semichoice. Society can take many views toward poor people. Sympathy, compassion, and identification are one alternative. Rejection, hostility, suspicion, and fault-finding are another. Causes of poverty or conditions of poverty may be stressed. Religions can reflect (dependent variable status) and engender (independent variable status) these ideas. These ideas also may exist, of course, without any religious association whatever. Achievement may be linked to the Protestant ethic, but it can also exist without it. Concern for poor people may be supported by the Catholic ethic, but it can also exist alone or be supported by other ethics (e.g., Islamic ethic).

3. Notice in this formulation that success is almost defined as "nonpoverty status." *Success* has synonyms such as *station, status, prosperity,* and so forth.

4. Wolf Wolfensberger (1972) deals with this very point. As a concentration camp survivor, he wanted to know how people can do things to people that you don't do to people. The answer was obvious: Transform them into nonpeople. The principle of "animalization" accomplishes this transformation nicely. *Rats, dogs, pigs, worms,* and *birdbrains* are all such transformative words. They permit great violence against those so named. After all, who *was* killing the Jews during the Holocaust? It was German Catholics and Protestants.

5. In the original, Fitzgerald wrote, "The rich are different"; Hemingway later commented, "Yes, they have more money!"

6. This distinction, which focuses on the causes of poverty, is so much with us that it may be hard to understand that at one time it may have been odd or now, in another context, would sound strange. Consider a condition to which this distinction is not applied (as yet, anyway, although the day may be coming): medical illness. Would it not sound a bit strained to talk about the "worthy ill" and the "unworthy ill"?

7. The Bishops' Letter is available from the National Conference of Catholic Bishops, 1312 Massachusetts Ave. N.W., Washington, D.C. 20005; the Simon/Novak article is available from the Lay Commission, P. O. Box 364, North Tarrytown, N.Y. 10591.

Chapter 9

1. Hamel's (1990, chapter 5) discussion of "the vocabulary of poverty" is most enlightening.

2. The amazing thing about this view is that at this point, *high status* is regarded as a potential for the occasion of sin. As I discuss shortly, the transformation of thought about poor people would create exactly the opposite perspective—that poverty, as an occasion for criminality, was an occasion of sin. Soon, the rich would be closer to God!

3. An encyclical is a policy statement made by the Catholic Church; a papal encyclical is such a statement made by the pope.

4. The dual themes of Christ as the suffering pauper and Christ as the religious entrepreneur seem to exist side by side, with the former dominant but the latter always present and vigorous.

5. The "dangerous class" is a phrase from a popular book by Brace (1872). See also Stephen O'Connor's *Orphan Trains* (2001).

6. In the language of the time, the Royal Commission Report was considered a "reform" of previous excesses, much like "welfare reform" in the United States in 1996.

7. In the early 1940s, England again had a Royal Commission look at issues of poverty relief. This time, the chair was Sir William Beveridge, and the report came to be known by his name. The actual title is "Social Insurance and Allied Services." Its message—considering that England was at war—essentially was the same as the old British Overseas Airways Company (BOAC) ad: "We'll take good care of you." The English government recognized that the war would entail extraordinary sacrifices from the citizenry. The Beveridge Report promised, in effect, that if they were victorious, the country would look after the widows, orphans, injured, and others.

8. The "house of correction" was one place where the connection between "poverty" and "crime" developed.

9. Scientific charity reflects "tacit assumption that human ills—sickness, insanity, crime, poverty—could be subjected to study, methods of treatment and that a theory of prevention could be formulated as well; they were not the results of "sin" or fate. . . . This attitude raised these problems out of the realm of mysticism into that of science" (Bruno 1948, 26).

10. These proceedings have been analyzed by Frank Bruno through 1948 (Bruno 1948). I am undertaking a reanalysis of the volumes with special emphasis on the period between 1948 and the 1980s, when the conference ceased to exist.

11. Concern about the possible inverse results of social helping have been a constant feature of critiques of social aid from the time of the English Poor Law Reform of 1834 until today. Hirshman call this posture the "perversity thesis" and phrases it thusly: "[T]he attempt to push society in a certain direction will result in its moving alright, but in the opposite direction" (Hirschman 1991, 11).

12. See also Curran's material in the frontmatter of this book.

Chapter 10

1. A hospice, then, was like a hospital—not a place for dying as we use the term today.

2. Pauperism later came to refer to people who were receiving alms.

3. In *Do Americans Hate the Poor?* (Tropman 1998), I develop the notion of social exploitation. I argue that in human societies, wants and needs always exceed available resources. Thus, there is always a need to balance social accounts, and one important way of accomplishing this balance is through the process of social exploitation—getting labor free or cheap. Exploitation of this kind—of women, slaves, children, and others—has been always a part of the human scene.

4. I do not want to overstate the uniqueness of each ethic. As I indicate in the early chapters, it is a question of dominance and subdominance. This struggle is clear in the development of English poverty relief policies. Nonetheless, there are differences, and it is useful to put them in perspective.

5. England is an interesting example of the development of poverty policy. Welfare statism was the logical development of hundreds of years of state interest and activity in poverty, some positive (The Poor Law of 1602–1603; Speenhamland) and some negative (the "reform" of 1832). Nevertheless, the point Wilensky (1981) makes about Sweden obtains here as well: There was a tradition of concern for the poor of historic—and Catholic—origins.

6. Further detail on the condition of poor people appears in *London Labor and London Poor* (Mayhew [1861–1862] 1968).

7. The doctrines of Malthus, the application of "social Darwinist" ideas to the development of poor relief, the idea—now called pauperism—that receiving aid was even worse than being poor because aid harmed rather than helped the recipient are all part of this picture.

8. The relentlessly moralistic conception of poverty naturally would lead some people to adopt a contrary explanation; hence the systemic, rather then the individualistic, explanation. It had its traditions too, but now they were subdominant, rather than dominant. Withdrawal of the state from an active helping role would lead one (or could lead one) to think that state action, if handled properly, could bring about a good life and, in any case, was the only reasonable force to counter the power of capitalists.

9. Marx's approach to poverty explanation can be described as a combination of the Protestant ethic and Catholic ethic backgrounds. On one hand, I consider him an "occupational" theorist as much as an "economic" one. He bases much of his thinking on alienation—the theft of meaning as well as money from the working class. This emphasis on the meaning of work sounds like a secularized calling. The Catholic ethic does not ascribe as much meaning to work, so theft of meaning is not as much of a problem. Theft of livelihood is a problem, however, because a principal element of the value of work in the Catholic ethic is to provide "the daily bread." One aspect of Marx's genius, then, was a combination of ethics in his central variable. He went further, however. His concern for material well-being also combined Catholic and Protestant elements. On one hand, the Protestant emphasis on worldly success was addressed through the idea that lack of success can't indicate damnation if it is not your fault. System-level causation, then, was a functionally neat escape for people trapped in the Protestant ethic. On the other hand, the Catholic ethic interest in spreading wealth and the social trusteeship of property also was captured. From a Catholic ethic perspective, the role of large institutions always had been important. Big government was not that different from Big Church. So Marx captured elements of the Catholic ethic structurally and ideologically.

10. This point is not entirely wrong. One example is construction of the aqueduct to bring water to Los Angles at the turn of the twentieth century. William Mulholland, the chief engineer of that project, "is said to have declared that whisky built the aqueduct, because no man would have kept to it unless whisky had kept him broke" (Heppenheimer 1991, 16).

11. That hospital still exists in Buffalo, New York.

12. For a discussion of the early years, see the outstanding, if little-known, history by John O'Grady (1930), *Catholic Charities in the United States: History and Problems.*

13. This concern is not limited to hospitals. Several years ago I assisted Catholic Social Services of Ann Arbor, Michigan, in a review of its program. One of the concerns shared by board and staff members was that the agency had drifted away from service to poor people. We sought to look at agency activities to see if this drift had occurred. (Some had, but not much.) A result of the review was that the agency rededicated itself to service to poor people.

14. These communities are located within the locales of poor and oppressed people.

15. Papal helping is regarded as connected to secular, governmental welfare statism because, in these early centuries, the Papacy and the Church as a whole occupied the role of governmental institution.

Chapter 11

1. An actor can be a person but also can be an organization, a church, a parish, the Vatican, and so forth. Attitudes may or may not be manifest in behaviors; behaviors may or may not reflect attitudes, beliefs, and values. This "gap" is called the "attitude/behavior problem"; it is of general concern in social science. See Schuman and Johnson (1976).

2. Recall that the phrase "the Catholic ethic" was used in a 1956 article— but not as a concept to be explored. Mack, Murphy, and Yellin (1956, 295) wrote, "The Catholic ethic propounded a culturally established emphasis on other-worldliness, the rational for the performance of tasks was other worldly." The phrase was used there as a literary device to aid the flow of the paragraph. The same could be said for Greeley's use of the term in his article "Protestant and Catholic: Is the Analogical Imagination Extinct?" (1989).

3. See Smith (1986), Sombart (1913), Sachar (1990).

4. The DAS is an annual study of sociological issues conducted by the sociology department of the University of Michigan in cooperation with the Institute for Social Research.

5. It should be noted that Lenski's suggestions were drawn from data of the Detroit Area Study, which used data of the Detroit region only.

6. Work commitment, as discussed in chapter 3, may be in the process of change.

7. These differences also emerge in my own analyses with a national database; see Table 11.10.

8. "Not large" means—for the dependent variables of spending time with relatives, friends, or neighbors or being a member of a voluntary association— values of r = 0.042, 0.052, 0.021, and −0.027 (McIntosh and Alston 1982, 863, table 1).

9. A "beta" is a standardized number, usually of two decimal places (e.g., .18; or −.13), that shows the power of one variable among others on some specific dependent variable. The metric used to assess them is the same as any .00–.99 array: .00 is low, and .99 is high; analysts also usually assess the probability that a particular result occurred by chance. Hence, a .03 beta may be "significant" statistically but not "important" as a practical matter.

10. What all this means is that Greeley's ideas were supported statistically.

11. Numerous studies use measures of the Protestant ethic: Albee (1977); Feather (1984); Fine (1983); Ganster (1981); Heaven (1980); Merrens and Garrett (1975); Mirels and Darland (1990); Mirels and Garrett (1971); Philbrick (1976); Ray (1982); Segalman (1968); Stephens, Metz, and Craig (1975); Waters, Batlis, and Waters (1975).

12. Greeley (1988) cites his paper in *Sociology and Social Research*.

13. True at least for the white Protestants. African American Protestants (called black Protestants in the survey) were different from white Protestants in many areas.

14. Alwin (1985) found a similar lack of difference in parental values.

15. Ralph Pyle, of the department of sociology, Purdue University, secured these data and performed these analyses. I owe him a deep debt of thanks for this work.

16. In the dialectical case, God is absent, and one approaches "Him" through dialogue with that "other." I consider this view to be essentially Platonic—that is, the world "reflects" reality, much as the shadow of a tree on the wall of a cave is not the actual tree or the "real tree." One must reach out toward the real tree. The analogical approach derives more from Aristotle. Reality is understood "by analogy," in the same way that one understands the reality of chairs by looking at many chairs and extracting the essence of *chair* (or generalizing, the social scientist might say) from those many examples. Interestingly enough, Greeley uses this approach. He seeks, through social science, to see what the thousands of bits of data (chair-analogues) tell us (reveal) about the whole, the "real."

17. Ralph Pyle again gets praise for this work.

18. *Natfarey* (it is not clear why this code name was chosen) = spending on assistance to help the poor: 1 = too little; 2 = about right; 3 = too much.

19. *Helppoor+* = Should the government improve the standard of living? 1 = government action; 2 = agree with both; 3 = people should help themselves.

20. *Eqwlth* = Should government reduce income differences? 1 = government should reduce differences; 2 = uncertain; 3 = no government action.

21. *Govless* = Government should spend less on the poor: 1 = disagree; 2 = neither; 3 = agree.

22. An index is useful because different measures of a concept—in this case, different kinds of attitudes toward poor—sometimes are somewhat independent each from the other, representing different "sectors" of the concept. An index can bring them all together and hence should have stronger relationships to the other variables than the components.

23. The full code is as follows: New England = 1; Middle Atlantic = 2; E. North Central = 3; W. North Central = 4; South Atlantic = 5; E. South Central = 6; W. South Central = 7; Mountain = 8; Pacific = 9.

24. One might ask why collectivities move in "community conscious" or "class conscious" directions. I ask the same question and suggest an answer in chapter 12.

25. "Specifically, this paper explores the relative strength of Catholic and left party dominance in explaining variations among nineteen rich democracies in welfare effort measured by social security expenditures as a fraction of GNP in 1966 and 1971; welfare output, here measured only by social security spending per capita, degree of reliance on painfully visible taxes, and the political response to spending and taxing, measured by tax-welfare backlash from 1965 to 1975" (Wilensky 1981, 348).

26. Here Wilensky makes an error, in my judgment. The quote continues, "... *which had its roots in the early modern era*" (Wilensky 1981, 364). I believe this phenomenon goes back much farther than that! Wilensky does, however, give an excellent historical example, from the history of Lyon, France. "We find Catholic humanists of the sixteenth century had considerable influence on the approach of urban businessmen and lawyers to their urban crises, and their poor, both 'deserving' and 'undeserving.' In 1532 the French cleric and humanist Jean de Vauzells urged the notables of Lyon to introduce sweeping new welfare measures ... " (Wilensky 1981, 364).

27. This answer is not complete, of course. There are helping traditions within Protestantism too, and these traditions found political and governmental or private and voluntary expression. Nevertheless, the idea of functional substitution and functional equivalency is important to consider, and a powerful, though certainly not complete, answer to the question of the emergence of welfare state policies in Protestant countries.

Chapter 12

1. As I have suggested, these differences may have been sharper at one point in history—just prior to the Reformation, when tensions between different attitudes about poverty may have been most serious. In a more recent example, tensions between the Catholic Ethic and the Protestant Ethic perspectives may be one cause for the social turmoil in Northern Ireland. These severe tensions may occur when a religious cleavage becomes linked with other social differences—for example, in status, wealth, or power.

2. This value is especially characteristic of American lotteries. Big prizes are what attracts, when one could argue, say, in terms of a recent $197 million prize, that 197 $1 million prizes would spread the goodies a bit.

3. The process of attachment and disattachment of affect to/from ideas is an important, and largely unexplored, question. A mundane example of the result of the process (see chapter 4) is the difference between income (in the Protestant ethic tradition, anyway) and bowling score. Both are ideas, or perhaps a step below ideas: information bits, as it were; ideas are interconnected information bits. As I suggest in chapter 4, "sacredization" is the process of adding "religious affect" to a secular idea. "Love[ization]," then, might be the process of adding affect to an otherwise ordinary set of interpersonal exchanges. "Patriotism[ization]" is the process of adding affect to identification with one's country. It is easy to point to the process and the result. What is more difficult is understanding the process and how the selection of effectual targets is made. The process of cathecting (here used in the broad sense of imbuing with feeling, not just libidinal energy) has an interesting inversion, too: decathexis. During World War II, Americans were prompted to hate Germans and Japanese, but most of that ill will has dissipated. There still is tension between "Yankees" and "good ol' boys" within American society, however—perhaps more than was felt between Americans and Germans and Japanese. Why? At this time, we don't know.

4. A tax expenditure is calculated as the amount of money the government would have collected had an item been taxed. Thus, if we were to add all of the "tax forgone" through the second-home deductions on federal taxes, we would have the amount of tax expenditure.

5. Social agencies in the first part of the twentieth century had the Social Service Exchange (SSX) in which every "client" was listed. This list usually was maintained by some central agency (such as a Council of Social Agencies); the helping organizations could call in to check whether a client asking for help had gotten/was getting help from another organization.

6. The important countercyclical emphases are the exception, of course.

7. The question of providing aid to children has always been difficult. On one hand, children are "innocent" and thus deserve help. On the other hand, aid to children (some of them illegitimate) aids the parents as well. The issue of how to help children without reinforcing parental behavior has not been resolved.

8. Regardless of the reason for loss of work, the process of applying for unemployment is very shaming.

9. I thank Faith Pratt for suggesting this quote.

Chapter 13

1. John E. Tropman, "Riding the Tiger: Religion and the Resurgence of Capitalism" (1991, unpublished). A key point to understand is that the "ethics" themselves—and perhaps the religions themselves—are shaped in an evolutionary way to meet needs of the human condition that have been unmet by previous belief systems. Basically, the argument suggests that the tensions argued to be present in the Protestant and Catholic ethics were not created by those religions but that the religions reflected and augmented wishes, tendencies, desires, and needs that were present in the society and culture but were unaddressed by then-current ethics. The Protestant Reformation came about, in this view, because the Catholicism of the time did not meet some needs for individualism, achievement, risk, and responsibility. The welfare state developed in part because of a resurgence of the emphasis on community, caring, families, and so forth embodied in Catholicism. The welfare state is now undergoing eclipse because of a resurgence of needs to express individualism, achievement, risk, and so forth. These needs are present within us, not external to us. Depending on the characteristics and competencies of any individual and the conditions and contexts of the times, one or another ethic will be preferred by some people, or many, in a particular society or culture.

2. In one case dialectical: God is absent, and one approaches "Him" through dialogue with that "other." I take this view to be essentially "Platonic"—that is, the world "reflects" reality, which is out there, much as the shadow of a tree on the wall of a cave is not the actual "tree itself" or the "real tree." One must reach out toward the real tree. The analogical approach derives more from Aristotle. Reality is understood by analogy, in the same way that one understands the "reality" of chairs by looking at many chairs and extracting the essence of *chair* (or generalizing, the social scientist might say) from those many examples. Interestingly enough, this latter approach is what Greeley himself uses. He seeks, through social science, to see what the thousands of bits of data (chair-analogues) tell us (reveal) about the whole—the "real."

3. See, for example, Sharlet (1999).

4. Kanter (1972).

5. These are the ones in the survey.

6. I have the views of experts as well. There are theological considerations (see Appendix A); practical issues involved in helping (see Appendix B); and, to a certain extent, ecclesiastical considerations (see Appendix D).

Appendix B

1. Catholic Charities USA is one of the largest "charities" in America—and one of the most efficient, with an extremely lage proportion (more than 90 percent) of its resources going into helping services. It is in many ways an operationalization of the Catholic Ethic and the spirit of community.

2. Mr. Harvey is the former chief executive officer of Catholic Charities USA. He currently works at the Alliance for Children and Families in Milwaukee, Wisconsin.

3. Consider, for example, Exodus 22:20–24; Isaiah 41:17; Amos 8:4–8, and Psalms 10 and 68.

4. Luke 10:25–37.

5. Matthew 25:31–46.

6. Matthew 11:2–6; Luke 7:18–23.

7. "The Call for a Prophetic Catholic Health System" in *Labor-Management Dialogue,* edited by Adam J. Maida (St. Louis: Catholic Health Association, 1982), 190–91.

8. June Axinn and Hermann Levin, *Social Welfare: A History of the American Response to Need*, 4th ed. (White Plains, N.Y.: Longman, 1997), 29.

9. Ibid., 30.

10. *Cadre Study, Toward a Renewed Catholic Charities Movement*, revised and annotated, (Alexandria, Va.: Catholic Charities USA, 1992), 21.

11. For a more extensive treatment of the conflictual attitudes in the history of the United States, see Thomas Harvey, *Government Promotion of Faith-Based Solutions to Social Problems: Partisan or Prophetic*, Practitioner Viewpoint Series (Washington, D.C.: Aspen Institute, 1997). The full document, *Cadre Study, Toward A Renewed Catholic Charities Movement*, is reprinted as Appendix C.

12. Cadre Study, 36.

13. Luke 7:18–23. All scriptural quotes are from *The Holy Bible, New Revised Standard Version, Catholic Edition* (Nashville; Tenn.: Thomas Nelson, Inc., 1993).

Appendix D

1. English names of encyclicals are not literal translations from the original Latin text; they refer to the main theme of the encyclical.

2. References to social encyclicals are abbreviations of their English names and the paragraph numbers, which are used across publishers and languages. These numbers sometimes hold just a few lines and sometimes up to several pages. "On the Conditions of Workers" = CW; "The Reconstruction of the Social Order" = RSO; "Christianity and Social Progress" = CSP; "A Call to Action" = CA; "On Human Work" = HW; "The 100th Year" = HY; "Pastoral Constitution of the Church in the Modern World" = PC; "On the Development of Peoples" = DP; "Justice in the World" = JW; "On Social Concerns" = SC.

3. Cardinal Roger Etchegaray, keynote address to "A Century of Social Teaching," Washington, D.C., Febuary 24, 1991

4. *De Nabuthe*, c. 12, n. 53; (P.L. 14, 747). *Cf.* J.-R. Palanque, *Saint Ambrose et l'empire romain* (Paris: de Boccard, 1933), 336*ff.*

Bibliography

Abell, A. I. 1960. *American Catholicism and social action: A search for social justice*, 1865–1950. Garden City, N.J.: Hanover House.

Albee, G. W. 1977. The Protestant ethic, sex and psychotherapy. *American Psychologist* 32 (February): 150–61.

Ashford, D. E. 1986. *The emergence of the welfare states*. New York: Blackwell.

Auchincloss, L. 1976. *The Winthrop covenant*. New York: Ballantine Books.

Baltzell, E. D. 1964. *The Protestant establishment: Aristocracy and caste in America*. New York: Random House.

Bane, M. J. 2000. Bowling alone, praying together. *America* 183, no. 14: 60.

Banfield, E., and J. Q. Wilson. 1963. *City politics*. New York: Vintage.

Baum, G. 1989. *Religion, economics, and social thought*. Vancouver, British Columbia: Fraser Institute.

Bellah, R. 1957. *Tokugawa religion: The cultural roots of modern Japan*. New York: Free Press.

———, ed. 1986. *Habits of the heart: Individualism and commitment in American life*. New York: Perennial Library.

Bellah, R., and P. Hammond. 1980. *Varieties of civil religion*. San Francisco: Harper and Row.

Bellamy, E. 1900. *Looking Backward (2000–1887): Or, Life in the year A.D. 2000*. London, Ontario: Socialist Publishing Co.

Benedict, R. 1934. *Patterns of culture*. Boston: Houghton Mifflin.

Berger, P. L. 1985. Can the bishops help the poor? *Commentary* 79: 31–35.

Berkovitch, S. 1975. *The Puritan origin of the American self*. New Haven, Conn.: Yale University Press.

Beveridge, W. 1942. *Social insurance and allied services*. New York: Macmillan.

Billington, R. A. 1964. *The Protestant crusade*. Chicago: Quadrangle Books.

Birmingham, S. 1967. *Our crowd*. New York: Harper and Row.

Bishop, K. 1991. Vouchers place money in the hands of the needy, instead of the greedy. *New York Times*, 26 July, 2.

Blantz, T. 1982. *A priest in public service*: Notre Dame, Ind.: University of Notre Dame Press.

Boorstin, D. 1958. *America, the colonial experience*. New York: Random House.

Brace, C. L. 1872. *The dangerous classes of New York and twenty years' work among them*. New York: Wyn Koop and Hallenbeck.

Brown, D., and E. McKeown. 1997. *The poor belong to us*. Cambridge, Mass.: Harvard University Press.

Bruno, F. 1948. *Trends in social work.* New York: Columbia University Press.

Bunyan, J. 1678. *The pilgrim's progress from this world to that which is to come: Delivered under the similitude of a dream, wherein is discovered the manner of his setting out, his dangerous journey, and safe arrival at the desired country.* London: Ponder.

Calvez, J. Y., S.J. 1987. Economic policy issues in Roman Catholic teaching. In *The Catholic challenge to the American economy,* ed. J. Gannon. New York: Macmillan.

Case, J. 1997. *The Genesis code.* New York: Ballantine.

Catholic Charities USA. 1997. *Vision 2000.* Alexandria, Va.: Catholic Charities USA.

Catholic Health Association. 1991. *Social accountability budget.* St. Louis: Catholic Health Association.

Charity Organization Society. 1927. *Fifty years of social work, 1877–1927.* Buffalo, N.Y.: Charity Organization Society.

Coleman, J. A. 1991. *One hundred years of Catholic social thought: A celebration and challenge.* Maryknoll, N.Y.: Orbis Books.

Connelly, M. 2000. The election; Who voted: A portrait of American politics, 1976–2000. *New York Times,* 12 November, 4.

Conwell, R. 1915. *Acres of diamonds.* New York: Harper.

Cort, J. C. 1988. *Christian socialism: An informal history.* Maryknoll, N.Y.: Orbis Books.

Cross, R. D. 1958. *The emergence of liberal Catholicism in America.* Cambridge, Mass.: Harvard University Press.

Crossen, C. 2000. Last 100 years show growth of luxury, greed. *Wall Street Journal.* 27 November, B1.

Curran, C. E. 1988. Ethical principles of Catholic social teaching behind the United States bishops' letter. *Journal of Business Ethics* 7: 413–16.

Curran, C. E., and R. A. McCormick, eds. 1988. *Dissent in the church.* New York: Paulist Press.

———. 1980. *The distinctiveness of Christian ethics.* New York: Paulist Press.

Dearman, M. 1974. Christ and conformity: A study of Pentecostal values. *Journal of the Scientific Study of Religion* 13 (December): 437–53.

Desan, P. 1993. Thinking in market terms. *University of Chicago Magazine* (October), 8–9.

De Smet, K. 1991. The private penance of Tom Monaghan. *Detroit Free Press,* 17 November.

De Schweinitz, I. [1943] 1961. *England's road to social security from the Statute of Laborers in 1349 to the Beveridge Report of 1942.* New York: Barnes.

De Vries B. 1998. *Champions of the poor: The economic consequences of Judeo-Christian values.* Washington, D.C.: Georgetown University Press.

Deveny, K. 1994. Immigrants: Still believers after all these years. *Wall Street Journal,* 12 July, B1.

Dudar, H. 1993. Art that can "make people laugh and frighten them, too." *Smithsonian* 24, no. 3: 70–86.

Duncan, G., and M. Hill. 1975. Attitudes, behaviors, and economic outcomes. In *Five thousand American families*, vol. 3, ed. G. Duncan and J. Morgan. Ann Arbor, Mich.: Institute of Social Research.

Durkheim, E. [1897] 1951. *Suicide*, trans. J. A. Spaulding and G. Simpson. New York: Free Press.

———. 1960a. The dualism of human nature and its social conditions, trans. C. Blend. In *Emile Durkheim, 1858–1917: A collection of essays,* ed. K. H. Wolff. Columbus: Ohio State University Press.

———. 1960b. *The division of labor in society,* trans. K. Lang. New York: Free Press.

Eisenstadt, S. 1985. *Macro-sociological theory: Perspectives on sociological theory.* Beverly Hills, Calif.: Sage Publications.

Ellin, A. 2000. Money money money. Guilt guilt guilt. *New York Times,* 19 July, BU14.

Ellis, J. T. 1969. *American Catholicism.* Chicago: University of Chicago Press.

Fanfani, A. 1936. *Catholicism, Protestantism, and capitalism.* New York: Sheed and Ward.

———. 1959. Catholicism, Protestantism, and capitalism. In *Protestantism and capitalism: The Weber theses and its critics,* ed. R. Green. Boston: Heath.

———. 1984. *Catholicism, Protestantism, and capitalism,* reappraisal and introductions by M. Novak and C. K. Wilbur. Notre Dame, Ind.: University of Notre Dame Press.

Feather, N. T. 1984. The Protestant ethic, consecration, and values. *Journal of Personality and Social Psychology* 46, no. 5 (March): 1132–41.

Fine, R. 1983. The Protestant ethic and the analytical idea. *Political Psychology* 4, no. 2 (June): 245–64.

Finn, J., ed. 1990. *Private virtue and public policy.* New Brunswick, Conn.: Transaction Books.

Fox, T. C. 1997. *Catholicism on the web.* New York: Iris.

Frank, R. 1999. *Luxury fever.* New York: Free Press.

Frank, R., and P. Cook. 1995. *The winner take all society.* New York: Penguin.

Frost, R. 1971. *The road not taken.* New York: Holt, Rinehart, and Winston.

Furnham, A. 1984. The Protestant work ethic: A review of the psychological literature. *European Journal of Social Psychology* 14: 87–104.

Galbraith, J. K. 1984. The heartless society. *New York Times Magazine,* 2 September, 20.

Gallup, G., Jr., and J. Castelli. 1989. *The people's religion.* New York: Macmillan.

Gallup, G., Jr., and S. Jones. 1989. *100 questions and answers: Religion in America.* Princeton, N.J.: Hermitage Press.

Gannon, T. M., ed. 1987. *The Catholic challenge to the American economy.* New York: Macmillan.

Ganster, D. C. 1981. Protestant ethic and performance: A reexamination. *Psychological Reports* 48, no. 1: 335–38.

Garvin, C., and J. E. Tropman. 1998. *Social work: An introduction.* Englewood Cliffs, N.J.: Prentice Hall.

Gerber, D. A. 1984. Ambivalent anti-Catholicism: Buffalo's American Protestant elite faces the challenge of the Catholic Church, 1850–1860. *Civil War History* (June): 119–43.

Gilbert, N. 1983. *Capitalism and the welfare state: Dilemmas of benevolence.* New Haven, Conn.: Yale University Press.

Gilder, G. 1981. *Wealth and poverty.* New York: Basic Books.

Girvetz, H. 1968. Welfare state. In *International encyclopedia of the social sciences,* vol. 16, ed. D. L. Sills. New York: Macmillan and Free Press.

Ginzberg, L. 1990. *Women and the work of benevolence: Morality, politics and class in the 19th-century United States.* New Haven, Conn.: Yale University Press.

Glazer, N. 1972. *American Judaism,* 2d ed. Chicago: University of Chicago Press.

Glazer, N., and D. P. Moynihan. 1963. *Beyond the melting pot.* Cambridge, Mass.: MIT Press.

Glenn, N. D., and R. Hyland. 1967. Religious preference and worldly success: Some evidence from national surveys. *American Sociological Review* 31, no. 1: 73–85.

Glenn, N. D., and C. N. Weaver. 1982. Enjoyment of work by full-time workers in the U.S. 1955 and 1980. *Public Opinion Quarterly* 46: 459–70.

Glock, C. Y. and E. Siegelman, eds. 1969. *Prejudice, U.S.A.* New York: Praeger.

Glock, C. Y., and Stark, R. 1966. *Christian beliefs and anti-Semitism.* New York: Harper and Row.

Goldberg, A. S., and S. Shiflett. 1981. Goals of male and female college students: Do traditional sex differences still exist? *Sex Roles* 7, no. 12: 1213–22.

Goodman, M., and N. Matsumoto. 1991. Maureen O'Hara: The eternal Colleen. *People* 35, no. 22 (June 10): 69–72.

Gonsalves, S., and B. Godwin. 1984. The Protestant ethic and conservatism scales. *High School Journal* 68, no. 4: 247–53.

Gorrell, D. K. 1988. *The age of social responsibility: The social gospel in the progressive era, 1900–1920.* Macon, Ga.: Mercer University Press.

Greeley, A. M. 1964. The Protestant ethic: Time for a moratorium. *Sociological Analysis* 24 (spring): 20–33.

———. 1977. *The American Catholic.* New York: Basic Books.

———. 1981. *Quadragesimo Anno* after fifty years. *America* 1, no. 8: 46–49.

———. 1987. *Happy are those who search for justice.* New York: Warner.

———. 1988. Evidence that a maternal image of God correlates with liberal politics. *Sociology and Social Research* 72, no. 3: 150–54.

———. 1989a. Protestant and Catholic: Is the analogical imagination extinct? *American Sociological Review* 54, no. 4: 485–502.

———. 1989b. *Religious change in America.* Cambridge, Mass.: Harvard University Press.

———. 1990. *The Catholic myth: The behavior and beliefs of American Catholics.* New York: Scribners.

———. 1991a. *The cardinal virtues.* New York: Warner.

————. 1991b. Who are the Catholic conservatives? *America* 165 (September 21): 158–62.

————. 1991c. With God on their sides (review of *Culture Wars* by J. D. Hunter). *New York Times Book Review,* 24 November, 13–14.

Greenberg, J. 1977. The Protestant ethic and reactions to the negative performance evaluations on a laboratory task. *Journal of Applied Psychology* 62, no. 6: 682–90.

————. 1978. Protestant ethic endorsement and attitudes toward commuting to work among mass transit riders. *Journal of Applied Psychology* 63, no. 6: 755–58.

————. 1979. Protestant ethic endorsement and the fairness of equity inputs. *Journal of Research in Personality* 13, no. 1: 81–90.

Greenberger, R. S. 1992. Bush courts U.S. votes in U.N. speech. *Wall Street Journal,* 22 September, A12.

Gremillion, J. 1976. *The gospel of peace and justice.* Maryknoll, N.Y.: Orbis Books.

Gronbjerg, K. A. 1977. *Mass society and the extension of welfare, 1960–1970.* Chicago: University of Chicago Press.

Gusfield, J. R. 1963. *The symbolic crusade: Status politics and the American temperance movement.* Urbana: University of Illinois Press.

Gustafson, J. M. 1978. *Protestant and Roman Catholic ethics: Prospects for rapproachement.* Chicago: University of Chicago Press.

Hadden, J. 1969. *The gathering storm in the churches.* New York: Doubleday.

Handler, J., and Y. Hasenfeld. 1991. *The moral construction of poverty.* Newbury Park, Calif.: Sage.

Hamel, G. 1990. *Poverty and charity in Roman Palestine, first three centuries* C.E. Berkeley: University of California Press.

Hamilton, S. 1993. The rise of the Nazis (review of *Hitler's Wahler,* by Jurgen Falter). *Contemporary Sociology* 22: 4.

Hammond, P., and K. Williams. 1976. The Protestant ethic thesis: A social psychological assessment. *Social Forces* 54, no. 3: 579–89.

Hartz, L. 1955. *The liberal tradition in America: An interpretation of American political thought since the revolution.* New York: Harcourt Brace.

Hasenfeld, Y. 1993. Review of *The new politics of poverty,* by L. Mead. *Contemporary Sociology* 22, no. 3: 376–77.

Haughey, J. C., S.J. 1997. *Virtue and affluence: The challenge of wealth.* New York: Sheed and Ward.

Hawley, A. H. 1950. *Human ecology.* New York: Ronald Press.

Heaven, P. C. 1980. The Protestant ethic scale in South Africa. *Psychological Reports* 47, no. 2: 618.

Heilbroner, R. L. 1970. Benign neglect in the United States. *Trans-action* 7, no. 12: 15–22.

Hennesey, J. 1981. *American Catholics: The history of the Roman Catholic community in the United States.* New York: Oxford University Press.

Henriot, P. J., E. P. DeBerri, and M. J. Schultheis. 1990. *Catholic social teaching: Our best kept secret.* Maryknoll, N.Y.: Orbis Books.

Heppenheimer, T. A. 1991. The man who made Los Angeles possible. *Invention and Technology* 7, no. 1: 11–18.

Herberg, W. 1960. *Protestant Catholic Jew*. New York: Doubleday Anchor.

Himmelfarb, G. 1984. *The idea of poverty*. New York: Knopf.

———. 1991. *Poverty and compassion*. New York: Knopf.

Hirschman, A. O. 1970. *Exit, voice, and loyalty: Responses to decline in firms, organizations, and states*. Cambridge, Mass.: Harvard University Press.

———. 1982. *Shifting involvements: Private interests and public action*. Princeton, N.J.: Princeton University Press.

———. 1991. *The rhetoric of reaction*. Cambridge, Mass.: Harvard University Press.

Hobel, E. A. 1968. Henry Sumner Main. In *The international encyclopedia of the social sciences,* ed. D. Sills. New York: Free Press.

Hobgood, M. 1991. *Catholic social teaching and economic theory: Paradigms in conflict*. Philadelphia: Temple University Press.

Hochschild, A. R. 1983. *The managed heart*. Berkeley: University of California Press.

Hoff, M. 1989. Response to the Catholic Bishop's letter on the economy. *Social Thought* 89: 41–52.

Hofstader, R. 1955. *The age of reform*. New York: Vintage.

Hofstede, G. 1980. *Culture's consequences: International differences in work-related values*. Beverly Hills, Calif.: Sage Publications.

Holland, J., and P. Henriot, S. J. 1983. *Social analysis: Linking faith and social justice*. Washington, D.C.: Center of Concern.

Hollenbach, D., S.J. 1979. *Claims in conflict*. New York: Paulist Press.

Holt, A. E. 1922. *Social work in the churches: A study in the practice of fellowship*. Boston: Pilgrim Press.

Hoover, A. J. 1987. Religion and national stereotypes: A German Protestant example. *History of European Ideas* 8, no. 3: 297–308.

Hudson, W. S. 1961a. *American Protestantism*. Chicago: University of Chicago Press.

———. 1961b. The Weber thesis reexamined. *Church History* 30: 88–99.

Independent Sector. 1990. Detailed tables, vols. 1 and 2. Washington, D.C.: Independent Sector.

Inglehart, R. 1990. *Culture shift*. Princeton, N.J.: Princeton University Press.

Ingrassia, P., and B. A. Sterz. 1990. Mea culpa; With Chrysler ailing, Lee Iacocca concedes mistakes in managing: I'm confessing my sins here. *Wall Street Journal* 17 September, 1.

Janowitz, M. 1978. *The last half century: Societal change in politics in America*. Chicago: University of Chicago Press.

Jansson, B. 2001. *The reluctant welfare state*. Cambria, Calif.: Wadsworth Thomson Learning.

John Paul II. 1981. *On human work*. Washington, D.C.: United States Catholic Conference.

Johnson, B. 1961. Do holiness sects socialize dominant values? *Social Forces* 39: 309–16.

Kahn, A. J., ed. 1959. *Issues in American social work*. New York: Columbia University Press.

Kammer, F., S.J. 1991. *Doing faith justice: An introduction to Catholic social thought*. New York: Paulist Press.

Kanter, R. M. 1972. *Commitment and community: Communes and utopias in sociological perspective*. Cambridge, Mass.: Harvard University Press.

———. 1991. Transcending business boundaries: 12000 world managers view change. *Harvard Business Review* (May/June), 151–65.

Katz, M. 1989. *The undeserving poor: From the war on poverty to the war on welfare*. New York: Pantheon.

Kemmelman, H. 1964. *Friday the rabbi slept late*. New York: Crown.

Kennedy, R., Jr. 1944. Single or triple melting-pot intermarriage trends in New Haven, 1870–1940. *American Journal of Sociology* 49, no. 4: 331–39.

Kersbergen, K. 1995. *Social capitalism: A study of Christian democracy and the welfare state*. London, New York: Routledge.

Kersten, L. L. 1970. *The Lutheran ethic: The impact of religion on laymen and clergy*. Detroit: Wayne State University Press.

Kersten, L., and K. K. Kersten. 1981. *The love exchange*. New York: Fell.

Killinger, B. 1992. *Workaholics: The respectable addiction*. E. Roseville, New South Wales: Simon and Schuster.

Kirschner, D. S. 1986. *The paradox of professionalism: Reform and public service in urban America, 1900–1940*. Westport, Conn.: Greenwood Press.

Klebaner, B. 1964. Poverty and its relief in American thought, 1815–61. *Social Service Review* 38, no. 4: 382–99.

Klein, J. 1994a. The politics of promiscuity. *Newsweek*, 9 May, 16–20.

———. 1994b. Shepherds of the inner city. *Newsweek*, 18 April, 28.

Knadler, A. 1986. Help seeking as a cultural phenomenon: Differences between city and kibbutz dwellers. *Journal of Personality and Social Psychology* 51, no. 5: 976–82.

Knudsen. D., J. Earle, and D. Schriver, Jr. 1978. The conception of sectarian religion: An effort at clarification. *Review of Religious Research* 20: 44–60.

Kohn, A. 1986. *No contest*. Boston: Houghton Mifflin.

Kosmin, B., and S. P. Lachman. 1993. *One nation under God: Religion in contemporary American society*. New York: Harmony.

Kristol, I. 1994. The tragic error of affirmative action. *Wall Street Journal*, 1 August, A18.

Kushner, H. S. 1983. *When bad things happen to good people*. New York: Avon.

Ladd, E. C. 1981. Americans at work. *Public Opinion* 4: 21–40.

Lamont, M. 1992. *Money, morals and manners: The culture of the French and the American upper middle class*. Chicago: University of Chicago Press.

Lang, K. 1964. Alienation. In *A dictionary of the social sciences*, ed. J. Gould and W. Kolb. New York: Free Press.

Lawrence, W. 1948. The relation of wealth to morals. In *Democracy and the gospel of wealth*. ed. G. Kennedy. Lexington, Mass.: Heath.

Lay Commission on Catholic Social Teaching and the U.S. Economy. 1984. *Toward the future: Catholic social thought and the U.S. economy.* New York: American Catholic Committee.

Leege, D. 1986. *Parish organizations: People's needs, parish services, and leadership* (report no. 8). Notre Dame, Ind.: University of Notre Dame, Study of Catholic Parish Life.

————. 1987. *Parish as community* (report no. 10). Notre Dame, Ind.: University of Notre Dame, Study of Catholic Parish Life.

Leiby, J. 1985. Moral foundations of social welfare and social work: A historical view. *Social Work* 30, no. 4: 323–30.

Lenski, G. 1963. *The religious factor.* New York: Anchor.

————. 1971. The religious factor in Detroit: Revisited. *American Sociological Review* 36, no. 1: 48–50.

Lerner, R. L. 1986. A case of religious counter-culture: The German Waldensians. *American Scholar* 55, no. 2: 234–47.

Levi, W. 1989. *From alms to liberation: The Catholic church, the theologians, poverty, and politics.* New York: Praeger.

Lewis, M. 1978. *The culture of inequality.* Amherst: University of Massachusetts Press.

Liebman, R. C., and R. Wuthnow. 1983. *The new Christian right.* New York: Aldine Publishing.

Liebman, R., J. R. Sutton, and R. Wuthnow. 1988. Social sources of denominationalism. *American Journal of Sociology* 53, no. 3: 343–52.

Liebow, E. 1993. *Tell them who I am: The lives of homeless women.* New York: Free Press.

Liepman, K. 1944. *Journey to work: Its significance for industrial and community life.* New York: Oxford University Press.

Lindberg, C. 1994. *Through the eye of a needle: Judeo-Christian roots of social welfare.* Kirksville: Thomas Jefferson University Press at Northeast Missouri State University.

Linder, R. 1954. *The fifty-minute hour: A collection of psychoanalytic tales.* New York: Rinehart.

Lipset, S. M. 1963. *The first new nation.* New York: Basic Books.

Lipset, S. M., and R. Bendix. 1959. *Social mobility in industrial society.* Berkeley: University of California Press.

Little, K., and M. M. Love. 1994. *The life and legacy of a social work pioneer.* New York: Western New York Heritage Institute.

Lykes, M. B. 1985. Gender in individualistic versus collectivistic bases for notions about the self. *Journal of Personality* 53, no. 2: 356–83.

Mack, R., R. J. Murphy, and S. Yellin. 1956. The Protestant ethic, level of aspiration, and occupational mobility: An empirical test. *American Sociological Review* 21: 295–300.

MacIntyre, A. 1981. *After virtue.* Notre Dame, Ind.: University of Notre Dame Press.

Malinowsky, B. 1948. *Magic, science, and religion and other essays.* Boston: Beacon Press.

March, J. G., and H. Simon. 1958. *Organizations.* New York: Wiley.

Marciniac, E. 1988. Toward a Catholic work ethic. *Origins*: 631–37.

Manners, A. 1972. *Poor cousins.* New York: McCann and Geoghegan.

Marshall, G. 1980. *Presbyteries and profits: Calvinism and the development of capitalism in Scotland 1560 to 1707.* Oxford: Clarendon Press.

———. 1982. *In search of the spirit of capitalism: An essay on Max Weber's Protestant ethic thesis.* New York: Columbia University Press.

Martin, R. K. 1957. *Social theory and social structure.* Glencoe, Ill.: Free Press.

Martinson, O. B., and E. A. Wilkening. 1983. Religion, work specialization, and job satisfaction: Interactive effects. *Review of Religious Research* 24, no. 4: 347–56.

May, H. F. 1976. *The enlightenment in America.* New York: Oxford University Press.

Mayhew, H. [1861–1862] 1968. *London labor and the London poor,* vols. 1–4. New York: Dover.

McCarthy, E., and W. McGaughey. 1989. *Nonfinancial economics: The case for shorter hours of work.* New York: Prager.

McClelland, D. C. 1953. *The achievement motive.* New York: Appleton-Centrury-Crofts.

McGregor, D. 1960. *The human side of enterprise.* New York: McGraw Hill.

McIntosh, W. A., and J. P. Alston. 1982. Lenski revisited: The linkage role of religion in primary and secondary groups. *American Journal of Sociology* 87: 852–82.

McJimsey, G. 1987. *Harry Hopkins: Ally of the poor and defender of democracy.* Cambridge, Mass.: Harvard University Press.

McWhirter, N. 1988. Abortion foes play power games. *Detroit Free Press,* October 28, 1B.

Mead, L. 1992. The *new politics of poverty.* New York: Basic Books.

Meeks, W. A. 1986. *The moral world of the first Christians.* Philadelphia: Westminister Press.

Merrens, M., and J. B. Garrett. 1975. The Protestant ethic scale as a predictor of repetitive work performance. *Journal of Applied Psychology* 60, no. 1: 125–27.

Merton, R. 1957. *Social theory and social structure.* Rev. ed. Glencoe, Ill.: Free Press.

Miller, W. B. 1959. Implications of urban lower-class culture for social work. *Social Service Review* 33, no. 3: 219–36.

Miller, W. C. 1976. *A handbook of American minorities.* New York: New York University Press.

Miller, W. D. 1982. *Dorothy Day.* New York: Harper and Row.

Mills, C. W. 1956. *The power elite.* New York: Oxford University Press.

Mirels, H., and D. M. Darland. 1990. The Protestant ethic and self characterization. *Personality and Individual Differences* 11, no. 9: 895–98.

Mirels, H. I., and J. Garrett. 1971. The Protestant ethic as a personality variable. *Journal of Consulting and Clinical Psychology* 36, no. 1: 40–44.

Misner, P. 1991. *Social Catholicism in Europe from the onset of industrialization to the first world war.* New York: Crossroads.

Mollat, M. 1986. *The poor in the Middle Ages: An essay in social history,* trans. Arthur Golhammer. New Haven, Conn.: Yale University Press.

Montgomery, J. D. 1970. Programs and poverty: Federal aid in the domestic and international systems. *Public Policy* 18, no. 4: 517–37.

Mooney, C. F. 1986. *Public virtue: Law and the social character of religion.* Notre Dame, Ind.: University of Notre Dame Press.

Morgan, E. 1958. *The Puritan dilemma: The story of John Winthrop.* Boston: Little, Brown.

Morris, C. 1997. *American Catholic.* New York: Vintage.

Mosqueda, L. 1986. *Chicanos, Catholicisim, and political ideology.* Lanham, Md.: University Press of America.

Mueller, G.H. 1978. The Protestant and the Catholic ethic. *Annual Review of the Social Sciences of Religion* 2: 143–56.

Mullin, R. B. 1986. *Episcopal vision/American reality.* New Haven, Conn.: Yale University Press.

Murray, C. 1984. *Losing ground: American social policy,1950–1980.* New York: Basic Books.

Murray H. 1990. *Do not neglect hospitality: The Catholic worker and the homeless.* Philadelphia: Temple University Press.

Myrdal, G. 1962. *An American dilemma.* New York: Harper and Row.

Nadler, A. 1986. Help seeking as cultural phenomenon. *American Psychologist* 52, no. 5: 976–82.

Nash, R. H. 1986. *Poverty and wealth: The Christian debate over capitalism.* Westchester, Ill.: Good News/Crossway.

National Conference of Catholic Bishops. 1986. *Economic justice for all: Pastoral letter on Catholic social teaching and the U.S. economy.* Washington, D.C.: United States Catholic Conference.

National Conference of Catholic Charities. 1983. *A code of ethics.* Washington, D.C.: National Conference of Catholic Charities.

Newman, K. S. 1988. *Falling from grace: The experience of downward mobility in the American middle class.* New York: Free Press.

———. 1993. *Declining Fortunes: The Withering of the American Dream.* New York: Basic Books.

———. 1994. Review of *Tell Them Who I Am: The Lives of Homeless Women,* by E. Liebow. *Contemporary Sociology* 23, no. 1: 43–44.

Niebuhr, G. 1998. Vatican Settles A Historic Issue with Lutherans. *New York Times,* June 26, A1.

Niebuhr, H. R. 1959. *The social sources of denominationalism.* Cleveland: World Publishing Co./Meridian Books (originally published by Henry Holt and Co., 1929).

Niebuhr, R. 1932. *Moral man in immoral society.* New York: Scribners.

———. 1937. *Beyond tragedy: Essays on the Christian interpretation of history.* New York: Scribners.

Novak, M. 1993. *The Catholic ethic and the spirit of capitalism.* New York: Free Press.

Nussbaum, M. 1989. Recoiling from reason. *New York Review,* December 7, 36–41.

Oates, J. C. 1969. *Them.* New York: Vanguard Press.

O'Brien, D. 1987. The economic thought of the American hierarchy. In *The Catholic challenge to the American economy,* ed. J. Gannon. New York: Macmillan.

O'Connor, S. 2001. *Orphan trains.* New York: Houghton Mifflin.

Odendahl, T. 1990. *Charity begins at home: Generosity and self-interest among the philanthropic elite.* New York: Basic Books.

Offe, C. 1984. *Contradictions in the welfare state.* Cambridge, Mass.: MIT Press.

O'Grady, J. 1930. *Catholic charities in the United States: History and problems.* Washington, D.C.: National Conference of Catholic Charities.

Orloff, A. S., and T. Skocpol. 1984. Why not equal protection? Explaining the politics of public social spending. *American Sociological Review* 49, no. 6: 726–50.

Organization for Economic Cooperation and Development (OECD). 1981. *The welfare state in crisis.* Paris: OECD.

Ostling, R. N. 1991. The search for Mary: Handmaid or feminist. *Time,* 30 December, 62–66.

Ouchi, W. 1981. *Theory Z.* New York: Bantam.

Paglia, C. 1991. The joy of Presbyterian sex. *New Republic* 205: 23–27.

Palmer, P. J. 1990a. Scarcity, abundance, and the gift of community. *Community Renewal Press* 1, no. 3: 2–6.

———. 1990b. *The active life.* New York: Harper and Row.

———. 1983. *To know as we are known.* San Francisco: HarperCollins.

Parsons, T. 1968a. Christianity. In *International Encyclopedia of the Social Sciences,* vol. 2, ed. D. L. Sills. New York: MacMillan Co. and Free Press.

———. 1968b. Anglo American society. In *International Encyclopedia of the Social Sciences,* vol. 2, ed. D. L. Sills. New York: MacMillan Co. and Free Press.

Parsons, T., and R. F. Bales. 1955. *Family: Socialization and interaction process.* Glencoe, Ill.: Free Press.

Pascale, R. T., and A. G. Athos. 1981. *The art of Japanese management.* New York: Simon and Shuster.

Paz, O. 1985. *A labyrinth of soltitude.* New York: Garwood Press.

Peters, T., and R. Waterman. 1982. *In search of excellence.* New York: Harper and Row.

Philbrick, J. L. 1976. The Protestant ethic in East Africa. *Psychologica Africana* 16, no. 3: 173–75.

Pieper, J. 1963. *Belief and faith.* New York: Pantheon Books.

Pines, A., and Kafry, D. 1981. Tedium in the life and work of professional women as compared with men. *Sex Roles* 7, no. 10: 963–77.

Piven, F., and R. Cloward. 1971. *Regulating the poor: The function of public welfare.* New York: Pantheon.

Poggi, Gianfranco. 1993. *Money and the modern mind: George Simmel's philosophy of money.* Berkeley: University of California Press.

Popcorn, F. 1991. *The Popcorn report.* New York: Dell.

Pope, L. 1942. *Millhands and preachers.* New Haven, Conn.: Yale University Press.

Potok, C. 1967. *The chosen.* Greenwich, Conn.: Fawcett.

Pumphrey, R. E., and M. W. Pumphrey, eds. 1961. *The heritage of American social work.* New York: Columbia University Press.

Putnam, R. 2000. *Bowling Alone.* New York: Simon and Schuster.

Pyle, R. 1991. Faith and committment to the poor. Unpublished paper, Purdue University Department of Sociology.

Quadango, J. S. 1984. Welfare capitalism and the Social Security Act of 1935. *American Sociological Review* 49, no. 5: 445–46.

Quatrochocchi, S. 1984. Fringe benefits as private social policy. In *New strategic perspectives on social policy,* ed. J. E. Tropman, M. Dluhy, and R. Lind. Elmsford, N.Y.: Pergamon Press.

Quinn, R. 1989. *Beyond rational management.* San Francisco: Jossey Bass.

Rauschenbusch, W. 1907. *Christianity and the social crisis.* New York: Macmillan.

Ray, J. J. 1982. The Protestant ethic in Australia. *Journal of Social Psychology* 116, no. 1: 127–38.

Reich, R. 1983. *The next American frontier.* New York: Times Books.

Reid, P. N. 1995. Social welfare history. In *Encyclopedia of Social Work,* ed. R. L. Edwards. Washington, D.C.: National Association of Social Workers.

Reisman, D., N. Glazer, and R. Denny. 1961. *The lonely crowd.* New Haven, Conn.: Yale University Press.

Rischin, M. 1965. *The American gospel of success: Individualism and beyond.* Chicago: Quadrangle Books.

Roberts, J. D. 1983. *Black theology today.* New York: Mellen.

Roberts, K. 1990. *Religion in sociological perspective,* 2d ed. Belmont, Calif.: Wadsworth.

Rokeach, M. 1968. *Beliefs, attitudes and values.* San Francisco: Jossey Bass.

———. 1969a. Part 1: Value systems and religion. *Review of Religious Research* 11: 1–23.

———. 1969b. Part 2: Religious values and social compassion. *Review of Religious Research* 11: 24–39.

Rojak, D. C. 1973. The Protestant ethic and political preference. *Social Forces* 52, no. 2: 168–77.

Roof, W., and W. McKinney. 1987. *American mainline religion: Its changing shape and future.* New Brunswick, N.J.: Rutgers University Press.

Root, L. 1984. Employee benefits and income security: Private social policy and the public interest. In *New strategic perspectives on social policy,* ed. J. E. Tropman, M. Dluhy, and R. Lind. Elmsford, N.Y.: Pergamon Press.

Rose, R. L. 1991. Milwaukee prelate irks conservative Catholics with abortion stance. *Wall Street Journal,* 11 July, 1.

Rotenberg, M. 1975. The Protestant ethic against the spirit of psychiatry: The other side of Weber's thesis. *British Journal of Sociology* 26, no. 1: 52–65.

Rothman, D. J., and S. Wheeler, eds. 1981. *Social history and social policy.* New York: Academic Press.

Rotter, J. 1966. Generalized expectancies for internal versus external control of reinforcement. *Psychological Monographs* 80, no. 1.

Russell, J. R. 1977. *The devil: Perceptions of evil from antiquity to primitive Christianity.* Ithaca, N.Y.: Cornell University Press.

Ryan, W. 1971. *Blaming the victim.* New York: Vintage.

———. 1981. *Equality.* New York: Pantheon.

Ryle, E. J. 1983. Catholic social thought and the new federalism. *Center Journal* (summer): 9–36.

———. 1985. Attitudes toward the poor and public policy development. In *Justice and health care,* ed. M. J. Kelly. St. Louis: Catholic Health Care Association of the United States.

———. 1987. Option for the poor in Catholic Charities: Policy and the social teaching of John Paul II. *Social Thought* (spring/summer): 139–49.

Sachar, H. M. 1990. *The course of modern Jewish history,* rev. ed. New York: Vintage.

Sampson, E. E. 1985. The decentralization of identity: Toward a revised concept of personal and social order. *American Psychologist* 40, no. 11: 1203–11.

Sandeen, E. R. ed. 1982. *The Bible and social reform.* Philadelphia: Fortress Press.

Santayana, G. 1944. *Persons and places: The background of my life.* New York: Charles Scribner's Sons.

Saveth, E. 1980. Patrician philanthropy in America: The late nineteenth and early twentieth centuries. *Social Service Review* 54, no. 1: 76–91.

Schaeffer, F. 1981. *A Christian manifesto.* Westchester, Ill.: Crossway Books.

Schaeffer, P. 1991. Presbyterians disagree over new work ethic. Religious News Service (New York), 29 July.

Schelling, T. 1978. Egonomics, or the art of self-management. *Journal of the American Economic Association* 68, no. 2: 290–94.

Schervish, P. 1991. Just compensation: Application and implication of Catholic social teaching. *Social Thought* 17, no. 4: 4–15.

Schervish, P., P. E. Coutsoukis, and E. Lewis. 1994. *Gospels of wealth: How the rich portray their lives.* Westport, Conn.: Praeger.

Schlessinger, A. M., Jr. 1957. *The crisis of the old order.* Boston: Houghton Mifflin.

Schiller, B. R. 1977. Relative earnings mobility in the United States. *American Economic Review* 67, no. 5: 926–41.

Schor, J. 1993. *The overworked American: The unexpected decline of leisure.* New York: Basic Books.

Schrag, P. 1970. *The decline of the WASP.* New York: Simon and Schuster.

Schuman, H. 1971. The religious factor in Detroit: Review, replication and reanalysis. *American Sociological Review* 36, no. 1: 30–47.

Schuman, H., and M. Johnson. 1976. Attitudes and behavior. In *Annual Review of Sociology*, vol. 2. San Francisco: Annual Reviews.

Segalman, R. 1968. The Protestant ethic in social welfare. *Journal of Social Issues* 24, no. 1: 125–41.

Sen, A. 1990. Individual freedom as a social commitment. *New York Review* 14 (June): 49–54.

Shapiro, H. T. 1982. The Jewish tradition of charity. Remarks at closing celebration of 1982 Allied Jewish Campaign—Israel Emergency Fund.

———. 1987. Philanthropy: Tradition and change. In *Tradition and change*, ed. H. Shapiro. Ann Arbor: University of Michigan Press.

Sharlet, J. 1999. Red kettle and a radical agenda. *Chronicle of Higher Education*, 14 May, A12.

Shelton, C. M. 1897. *In his steps*. Springdale, Pa.: Whitaker House.

Sherrill, R. A., ed. 1990. *Religion in the life of the nation: American recoveries*. Urbana: University of Illinois Press.

Shils, E., and M. Young. 1972. The meaning of the coronation. In *Center and periphery: Essays in macro-sociology*, ed. E. Shils. Chicago: University of Chicago Press.

Simon, W., and M. Novak, eds. 1984. *Toward the future: Catholic social thought and the U.S. economy*, a lay letter. Lay Commission on Catholic Social Teaching and the U.S. Economy.

Sinclair, U. 1950. *The jungle*. New York: Viking.

Skinner, B. F. 1971. *Beyond freedom and dignity*. New York: Bantam.

Slater, P. E. 1970. *The pursuit of loneliness: American culture at the breaking point*. Boston: Beacon Press.

Smith, H. 1986. *The religions of man*. New York: Harper and Row/Perennial Library.

Smith, T. L. 1957. *Revivalism and social reform*. New York: Abington Press.

Sombart, W. 1913. *The Jews and modern capitalism*. London: Unwin.

Sonnenfeld, J. 1983. Commentary: Academic learning, worker learning, and the Hawthorne studies. *Commentary* 61, no. 3: 904–09.

Stark, R. 1970. Rokeach, religion, and reviewers: Keeping an open mind. *Review of Religious Research* 11: 151–54.

Stark, R., and C. Glock. 1964. Prejudice in the churches. In *If Christ came to Chicago*, ed. C. Glock and E. Stead. New York: Living Books.

———. 1968. *American piety: The nature of religious commitment*. Berkeley: University of California Press.

Steers, R., and L. Porter. 1991. *Motivation and work behavior*, 5th ed. New York: McGraw-Hill.

Stein, J. 1964. *Fiddler on the roof*. New York: Washington Square Press.

Steinfels, P. 1991. Against those "old male celibates." Review of *Eunuchs for the kingdom of heaven: Women, sexuality and the Catholic Church*, by Uta Ranke-Heinemann. *New York Times*, 11 January.

Steffans, L. 1905. *The shame of our cities*. New York: McClure, Phillips.

Stephens, R., L. Metz, and J. Craig. 1975. The Protestant ethic effect in a multichoice environment. *Bulletin of the Psychonomic Society* 6, no. 2: 137–39.

Stinchcombe, A. J. 1965. Social structure in organizations. In *Handbook of organizations*, ed. J. G. March. Chicago: Rand McNally.

Stokes, R. G. 1975. Afrikaner Calvinism and economic action: The Weberian thesis in South Africa. *American Journal of Sociology* 81, no. 1: 62–81.

Susman, W. 1984. *Culture as history: The transformation of American society in the twentieth century*. New York: Pantheon.

Swasy, A. 1993. Stay at home moms. *Wall Street Journal*, 23 July, B1.

Swatos, W. H., Jr., ed. 1987. *Religious sociology: Interfaces and boundaries*. Westport, Conn.: Greenwood Press.

Swedenborg, E. 1985. *Heavenly secrets*. New York: Swedenbourg Foundation.

Tamney, J., R. Burton, and S. Johnson. 1988. Christianity, social class, and the Catholic bishops' economic policy. *Sociological Analysis* 49: 78–96.

Tannen, D. 1990. *You just don't understand*. New York: Morrow.

Tawney, R. H. 1926. *Religion and the rise of capitalism*. London: Murray.

———. 1948. *The acquisitive society*. New York: Harcourt Brace.

Taylor, G. 1954. *Sex in history*. New York: Vanguard.

Thaler, R. H., and H. M. Shefrin. 1981. An economic theory of self control. *Journal of Political Economy* 89, no. 2: 392–410.

Thurow, L. 1992. *Head to head*. New York: Morrow.

Tichy, N., and M. A. Devanna. 1986. *The transformational leader*. New York: Wiley.

Tiryakian, E. A. 1982. Puritan America in the modern world: Mission impossible. *Sociological Analysis* 43, no. 4: 351–68.

Tönnies, F. [1887] 1957. *Community and society—Gemeinschaft und Gesellschaft*, 2d ed., trans. C. P. Loomis. East Lansing: Michigan State University Press.

———. 1971. *On sociology: Pure, applied and empirical*. Chicago: University of Chicago Press.

Tracy, D. 1989. *The analogical imagination*. New York: Crossroads.

Trevor-Roper, H. 1988. *Catholics, Anglicans, and Puritans*. Chicago: University of Chicago Press.

Trine, R. W. 1910. *In tune with the Infinite, or, Fullness of peace, power, and plenty*. New York: Dodge.

Troeltsch, E. 1960. *The social teachings of the Christian churches*, vols. 1 and 2. New York: Harper Torch Books.

Troester, R., ed. 1993. *Voices from the Catholic Worker*. Philadelphia: Temple University Press.

Tropman, E. J., and J. E. Tropman. 1987. Voluntary agencies. In *The encyclopedia of social work*, vol. 2, ed. A. Minihan. Silver Spring, Md.: National Association of Social Workers, 825–42.

Tropman, J. E. 1978. The constant crisis. *California Sociologist* 1, no. 1: 61–88.

———. 1981. Copping out or chipping in. *The Humanist* 41, no. 2: 43–46.

———. 1986. The "Catholic Ethic" versus the "Protestant Ethic": Catholic social service and the welfare state. *Social Thought* 12, no. 1: 13–22.

———. 1987. *Public policy opinion and the elderly*. Westport, Conn.: Greenwood Press.

————. 1989. American *values and social welfare: Cultural contradictions in the welfare state.* Englewood Cliffs, N.J.: Prentice-Hall.

————. 1996. *The Catholic ethic in American society.* San Francisco: Jossey-Bass

————. 1998. *Do Americans hate the poor?* Westport, Conn.: Praeger.

————. 2001. *The total compensation solution.* San Francisco: Jossey-Bass.

Tropman, J. E., and G. Morningstar. 1989. *Entrepreneurial systems for the 1990s.* Westport, Conn.: Quorum.

Tropman, J. E., M. Dluhy, and W. Vasey. *Strategic perspectives on social policy.* New York: Pergamon Press.

Tuchman, B. 1984. *The march of folly.* New York: Knopf.

Tuckerman, J. 1813. *Christian ethics and sermons.* Boston: Monroe and Francis (microfilm).

Underhill, E. 1936. *Worship.* New York: Harper Torch Books.

Vaill, P. 1982. The purposing of high performing systems. *Organizational Dynamics* (autumn): 4–9.

————. 1989. *Management as a performing art.* San Francisco: Jossey-Bass.

Vande Kemp, H. 1984. *Psychology and theology in Western thought, 1672–1965.* Millwood, N.Y.: Kraus.

Vandewiele, M., and J. Philbrick. 1986. The Protestant ethic in West Africa. *Psychological Reports* 58, no. 3: 946–50.

Varenne, H. 1993. Review of *Money, morals and manners: The culture of the French and the American upper middle class,* by M. Lamont. *Contemporary Sociology* 22: 4.

Vidich, A., and J. Bensman. 1968. *Small town in mass society,* rev. ed. Princeton, N.J.: Princeton University Press.

Wallace, R. 1973. The secular ethic and the spirit of patriotism. *Sociological Analysis* 34, no. 1: 3–11.

Watson, S. 1991. Feast and famine shade marriage. *Detroit Free Press,* 9 August.

Wald, K. 1987. *Religion and politics in the United States.* New York: St. Martin's.

Walsh, T. J. 1980. *Nano Nagle and the Presentation Sisters.* Co. Kildare, Ireland: Presentation Generalate, Monasterevan.

Waterman, A. S. 1981. Individualism and interdependence. *The American Psychologist* 36, no. 7: 762–73.

Waters, L. K., N. Batlis, and C. Waters. 1975. Protestant ethic attitudes among college students. *Educational and Psychological Measurement* 35, no. 2: 447–50.

Weber, M. 1946. *From Max Weber,* trans. H. Gearth and C.W. Mills. New York: Oxford University Press.

————. [1906] 1956. *The Protestant ethic and the spirit of capitalism,* trans. Talcott Parsons. New York: Charles Scribner and Sons.

————. 1963. *The sociology of religion,* trans. E. Fischoff. New York: Beacon.

Weigel, G. R., and R. Royal. 1991. *A century of Catholic social thought.* Washington, D.C.: Ethics and Policy Center.

Welch, C. 1972. *Protestant thought in the nineteenth century: 1799–1870,* vols. 1 and 2. New Haven, Conn.: Yale University Press.

————. 1993. States forging ahead on welfare reform. *USA Today*, 13 August.

White, R., and C. H. Hopkins. 1976. *The social gospel: Religion and reform in changing America.* Philadelphia: Temple University Press.

Wiesel, E. 1972. *Souls on fire: Portraits and legends of Hasidic masters.* New York: Random House.

Wilbur, K. 1983. *A sociable God.* New York: New Press/McGraw Hill.

Wilensky, C., and C. Lebeaux. 1956. *Industrial society and social welfare.* New York: Russell Sage.

Wilensky, H. L. 1981. Leftism, Catholicism, and democratic corporatism: The role of political parties in recent welfare state development. In *The development of welfare states in Europe and America,* ed. P. Flora and A. J. Heidenheimer. New Brunswick, N.J.: Transaction Books.

Wilkes, P. 1991a. The education of an archbishop—1. *The New Yorker,* July 15, 37–59.

————. 1991b. The education of an archbishop—2. *The New Yorker,* July 22, 46–65.

Will, G. 1992. A sterner kind of caring. *Newsweek,* 13 January, 68.

Williams, C. 1983. The work ethic: Non-work and leisure in an age of automation. *Australian and New Zealand Journal of Sociology* 19, no. 2: 216–37.

Williams, R. M., Jr. 1960. *American society,* 2d ed. New York: Knopf.

Wills, G. 1990. *Under God: Religion and politics in America.* New York: Simon and Schuster.

Wilson, J. 1993. Review of *Christianity in the twenty-first century,* by R. Wuthnow. *Contemporary Sociology* 23, no. 3: 439–41.

Winslow, O. E., ed. 1966. *Jonathan Edwards: Basic writings.* New York: New American Library.

Wolcott, R. T., and D. F. Bolger, compilers. 1990. *Church and social action: A critical assessment and bibliographical survey.* Westport, Conn.: Greenwood Press.

Wolf, K., ed. and trans. 1950. *The sociology of Georg Simmel.* New York: Free Press.

Wolfensberger, W. 1972. *The principles of normalization in the human services.* Toronto: Leonard/Crawford/National Institute of Mental Retardation.

Wollack, S. 1971. Development of the survey of work values. *Journal of Applied Psychology* 53, no. 4: 331–38.

Wood, J. R. 1981. *Leadership in voluntary organizations: The controversy over social action in Protestant churches.* New Brunswick, N.J.: Rutgers University Press.

Woodward, K. L. 1991. Encountering Mary. *New York Times Book Review,* 11 August, 1.

Wortman, C. 1976. Causal atttributions and personal control. In *New directions in attribution research,* vol. 1, ed. J. Harvey and W. J. Ickes. Hillsdale, N.J.: Erlbaum.

Wright, R. C., Jr., and C. H. Hopkins. 1976. *The social gospel: Religion in the form and changing America.* Philadelphia: Temple University Press.

Wuthnow, R. 1989. *Communities of discourse*. Cambridge, Mass.: Harvard University Press.

———. 1991. *Acts of compassion*. Princeton, N.J.: Princeton University Press.

Wuthnow, R., V. Hodgkinson, and associates. 1990. *Faith and philanthropy in America*. San Francisco: Jossey-Bass.

Yankelovich, D. 1981. *New rules*. New York: Random House.

Yankelovich, D., and J. Immerwahr. 1983. *Putting the work ethic to work*. New York: Public Agenda Foundation.

———. 1984. Putting the work ethic to work. *Society* 21: 58–76.

Zangwill, I. 1922. *The melting pot*. New York: Macmillan.

Zaret, D. 1985. *The heavenly contract*. Chicago: University of Chicago Press.

Index

Page references followed by the letter "t" indicate tables.